MASTERING EMPLOYMENT DISCRIMINATION LAW

CAROLINA ACADEMIC PRESS MASTERING SERIES

RUSSELL WEAVER, SERIES EDITOR

For other titles, please go to caplaw.com.

Mastering Administrative Law, Second Edition
Linda D. Jellum

Mastering Adoption Law and Policy
Cynthia Hawkins DeBose

Mastering Alternative Dispute Resolution
Kelly M. Feeley, James A. Sheehan

Mastering Appellate Advocacy and Process, Second Edition
Donna C. Looper, George W. Kuney

Mastering Art Law, Second Edition
Herbert Lazerow

Mastering Bankruptcy
George W. Kuney

Mastering Civil Procedure, Fourth Edition
David Charles Hricik

Mastering Constitutional Law, Second Edition
John C. Knechtle, Christopher J. Roederer

Mastering Contract Law
Irma S. Russell, Barbara K. Bucholtz

Mastering Corporate Tax, Second Edition
Gail Levin Richmond, Reginald Mombrun, Felicia Branch

Mastering Corporations and Other Business Entities, Second Edition
Lee Harris

Mastering Criminal Law, Third Edition
Ellen S. Podgor, Cynthia E. Jones, Peter J. Henning, Neil P. Cohen, Sanjay K. Chhablani

Mastering Criminal Procedure, Volume 1: The Investigative Stage, Third Edition
Peter J. Henning, Cynthia E. Jones, Ellen S. Podgor,
Karen McDonald Henning, Sanjay K. Chhablani

Mastering Criminal Procedure, Volume 2: The Adjudicatory Stage, Third Edition
Peter J. Henning, Cynthia E. Jones, Ellen S. Podgor,
Karen McDonald Henning, Sanjay K. Chhablani

Mastering Elder Law, Third Edition
Ralph C. Brashier

Mastering Employment Discrimination Law, Third Edition
Jeffrey M. Hirsch, Joseph A. Seiner, Sandra F. Sperino

Mastering Environmental Law
Joel A. Mintz, Tracy D. Hester

Mastering Evidence
Ronald W. Eades

Mastering Family Law, Second Edition
April Carroll Meldrum

Mastering First Amendment Law
John C. Knechtle

Mastering Income Tax, Second Edition
Gail Levin Richmond, Christopher M. Pietruszkiewicz

Mastering Intellectual Property
George W. Kuney, Donna C. Looper

Mastering International Sales Law
Herbert Lazerow

Mastering Interviewing and Counseling
Kelly M. Feeley, Rebecca C. Morgan

Mastering Labor Law, Second Edition
Anne Marie Lofaso, Joseph E. Slater, Jeffrey M. Hirsch

Mastering Legal Analysis and Communication
David T. Ritchie

Mastering Legal Analysis and Drafting, Second Edition
George W. Kuney, Donna C. Looper

Mastering Legislation, Regulation, and Statutory Interpretation, Third Edition
Linda D. Jellum

Mastering Native American Law, Third Edition
Angelique Wambdi EagleWoman, Stacy L. Leeds

Mastering Negotiable Instruments (UCC Articles 3 and 4) and Other Payment Systems, Second Edition
Michael D. Floyd

Mastering Negotiation
Michael R. Fowler

Mastering Partnership Taxation
Stuart Lazar

Mastering Products Liability, Second Edition
Tim Kaye

Mastering Professional Responsibility, Second Edition
Grace M. Giesel

Mastering Property Law, Second Edition
Darryl C. Wilson

Mastering Sales
Colin P. Marks, Jeremy Kidd

Mastering Secured Transactions: UCC Article 9, Third Edition
Grace M. Giesel

Mastering Tort Law, Third Edition
Russell L. Weaver, Edward C. Martin, Andrew R. Klein,
Paul J. Zwier, II, John H. Bauman

Mastering Trademark and Unfair Competition Law, Second Edition
Lars S. Smith, Llewellyn Joseph Gibbons

Mastering Trusts and Estates, Second Edition
Gail Levin Richmond

MASTERING EMPLOYMENT DISCRIMINATION LAW

THIRD EDITION

Jeffrey M. Hirsch

GENEVA YEARGAN RAND
DISTINGUISHED PROFESSOR OF LAW
UNIVERSITY OF NORTH CAROLINA SCHOOL OF LAW

Joseph A. Seiner

PROFESSOR OF LAW &
OLIVER ELLSWORTH PROFESSOR OF FEDERAL PRACTICE
UNIVERSITY OF SOUTH CAROLINA
JOSEPH F. RICE SCHOOL OF LAW

Sandra F. Sperino

ELWOOD L. THOMAS MISSOURI ENDOWED PROFESSOR
UNIVERSITY OF MISSOURI SCHOOL OF LAW

CAROLINA ACADEMIC PRESS
Durham, North Carolina

Library of Congress Cataloging in Publication Data

Names: Hirsch, Jeffrey M. author | Seiner, Joseph A. author | Sperino, Sandra F. author
Title: Mastering employment discrimination law / by Jeffrey M. Hirsch, Joseph A. Seiner, Sandra F. Sperino.
Description: Third edition. | Durham, North Carolina : Carolina Academic Press, LLC, 2025. | Series: Mastering series | Includes bibliographical references and index.
Identifiers: LCCN 2025032775 | ISBN 9781531032876 paperback | ISBN 9781531032883 ebook
Subjects: LCSH: Discrimination in employment — Law and legislation — United States
Classification: LCC KF3464 .S425 2025 | DDC 344.7301/133 — dc23/eng/20250728
LC record available at https://lccn.loc.gov/2025032775

Carolina Academic Press, LLC
700 Kent Street
Durham, NC 27701
Telephone (919) 489-7486
www.cap-press.com

Printed in the United States of America

Dedicated to—

Lynn, Noah & Naomi (jmh)

Mary Elizabeth and Joseph (jas)

John and Joe (sfs)

CONTENTS

TABLE OF CASES

SERIES EDITOR'S FOREWORD

The Carolina Academic Press Mastering Series is designed to provide you with a tool that will enable you to easily and efficiently "master" the substance and content of law school courses. Throughout the series, the focus is on quality writing that makes legal concepts understandable. As a result, the series is designed to be easy to read and is not unduly cluttered with footnotes or cites to secondary sources.

In order to facilitate student mastery of topics, the Mastering Series includes a number of pedagogical features designed to improve learning and retention. At the beginning of each chapter, you will find a "Roadmap" that tells you about the chapter and provides you with a sense of the material that you will cover. A "Checkpoint" at the end of each chapter encourages you to stop and review the key concepts, reiterating what you have learned. Throughout the book, key terms are explained and emphasized. Finally, a "Master Checklist" at the end of each book reinforces what you have learned and helps you identify any areas that need review or further study.

We hope that you will enjoy studying with, and learning from, the Mastering Series.

Russell L. Weaver
PROFESSOR OF LAW &
DISTINGUISHED UNIVERSITY SCHOLAR
UNIVERSITY OF LOUISVILLE,
LOUIS D. BRANDEIS SCHOOL OF LAW

PREFACE

The third edition of *Mastering Employment Discrimination Law* coincides with a moment when questions about what constitutes illegal discrimination are roiling American society. This book addresses the current state of discrimination law as it applies to the workplace. The book begins first with coverage and jurisdiction issues and then turns to complex federal and state procedural topics surrounding the filing of administrative charges of discrimination. The book comprehensively addresses the substantive aspects of Title VII, the ADEA, the ADA, and the Equal Pay Act, as well as related issues such as remedies, attorney's fees, and settlements. New topics include the Pregnant Workers Fairness Act, changes to what counts as an adverse action, possible alterations in affirmative action law, and the new standard for religious accommodation.

In the third edition of this book, we are happy to add Professor Sandra Sperino of the University of Missouri School of Law as a co-author. Professor Sperino is a nationally prominent expert on employment discrimination law, especially in the areas of employment discrimination frameworks and causation.

It is our hope that this book will provide an instructive overview of employment discrimination law and offer an effective method for mastering this often-complex area of labor and employment law.

There are many to thank, including Series Editor Russ Weaver, the University of North Carolina School of Law, the support of Dean William C. Hubbard and the entire University of South Carolina Joseph F. Rice School of Law, and the University of Missouri School of Law. Many thanks also go to research assistants who worked on prior editions, Julia Mader, Dena Welden, Veronica Barkley, and Hailey Klabo.

Jeffrey M. Hirsch
Joseph A. Seiner
Sandra F. Sperino
July 2025

MASTERING EMPLOYMENT DISCRIMINATION LAW

CHAPTER 1

Introduction to Employment Discrimination Law

ROADMAP

- Opening Story—the genesis of a typical employment discrimination case
- What is employment discrimination law (and what it is not)
- Recurring themes in employment discrimination law
- Employment at will in relation to employment discrimination law
- Classification of employment discrimination cases
- Sources of employment discrimination law
- Jurisdiction over employment discrimination claims

A. An Opening Employment Discrimination Story

One of your law firm's clients is ABC Pharmaceuticals. Your company contact, John Shaw, in-house senior legal counsel, calls you to tell you that a charge of discrimination has just been filed with the Equal Employment Opportunity Commission (EEOC) by a male, Muslim, Arab-American former sales trainer, Omar Salah, who grew up in Egypt. The charge alleges race, national origin, religion, and sex discrimination and retaliation against ABC and three individuals, two supervisors, and a human resources manager.

Here's the story: Omar has been a rising young star at ABC. He started with the company as a sales representative in Memphis in 2015 and has steadily worked his way through the company. In the fall of 2020, he was promoted to sales trainer, a role in which he would train other sales representatives. All of Omar's performance evaluations were almost perfect, placing him at the very top of the company's young talent.

Things started to go downhill for Omar in the fall of 2023. He neglected to turn in his expense reports for the past year. When his supervisor, Mary Alexander, an African-American female, discovered this fact, she decided to suspend Omar while the expense report issues were being investigated. She was supported in this decision by her supervisor Richard Kim, an Asian-American male, and the human resources partner, Chuck Rocker, a white male. After a thirty-day investigation, while Omar was out of work but still being paid, Richard, Mary, and Chuck decide to demote Omar back to the sales representative position. The reasoning: let's take into account his past good work while at the same time send him a stern message that he must comply with all company policies, including expense reporting.

When Omar gets the news of his demotion, he is furious. He immediately shoots off a letter to Mary, Richard, and Chuck stating that he believes that he has been demoted because he is Egyptian, because he is a Muslim, because he is Arab-American, because he is white, and because he is male, all in violation of Title VII of the Civil Rights Act of 1964, 42 U.S.C. §2000e *et seq.*

Omar receives no response to his letter. By May of 2024, it is clear that Omar is no longer performing his work as a sales representative at his previous high standards. Consequently, on May 24, 2024, Mary recommends Omar's termination for poor performance and both Richard and Chuck sign off on the decision. Omar sends one last letter claiming that he has been treated unfairly at ABC because of his race, sex, religion, and national origin. In July 2024, Omar files a charge of discrimination with the Equal Employment Opportunity Commission Office in Memphis. He alleges, not surprisingly, that he was demoted and terminated because of unlawful race, sex, religion, and national origin discrimination, and that he was retaliated against for filing his two internal complaint letters. You are asked by your law firm to assist in representing ABC and Mary, Richard, and Chuck. Where to begin?

B. The Scope of Employment Discrimination Law

Welcome to employment discrimination law practice. This story is gleaned from the facts of a real case from federal court in Philadelphia. Some of you reading this book will no doubt find yourself in the young attorney's position one day. For others, the only difference is that you will be representing Omar or will be handling the case as an employee of the EEOC.

The best place to start our discussion of employment discrimination law is with an overview of the entire field of labor and employment law. To properly contextualize the practice of employment discrimination law it is necessary to see where it fits in relation to other workplace law courses. Currently, there are four primary courses in the study of labor and employment law: labor law, employment law, employee benefits law, and employment discrimination law.

1. Distinguished from Labor Law

Labor Law is primarily concerned with the interaction between unions and management, including the organization of the union, collective bargaining, and maintenance of the collective bargaining relationship. Labor law is mostly administrative in nature with some exceptions. The major statute is the Wagner Act, now more familiarly called the National Labor Relations Act (NLRA). We will largely not be discussing these topics in this book.

2. Distinguished from Employment Law

Employment Law concerns many different topics common to both union and non-union employees including the doctrine of at-will employment, common-law tort, contract, and public policy claims, privacy claims, covenants not to compete and other restrictive covenants, family and medical leave laws, unemployment compensation, wage and hours legislation under the Fair Labor Standards Act (FLSA), and occupational safety and health under the Occupational Safety and Health Act (OSHA). Again, with one small exception (employment at will), these are not topics which we will discuss in this book.

3. Distinguished from Employee Benefits Law

Employee Benefits Law concerns the study of employer-provided benefits under the Employee Retirement Income Security Act (ERISA) and the Internal Revenue Code (IRC). This type of law primarily involves pension law, including defined benefit plans and defined contribution plans; welfare benefits law, including most prominently health insurance plans; and issues of executive and deferred compensation. Because such ERISA plans must be qualified to gain the advantage of preferred tax treatment, there is a substantial tax component to these types of employee benefit cases. Of course, employee benefits is not the primary focus of this book, though we will discuss discrimination claims involving different types of employee benefits under different employment discrimination statutes.

4. Issues Covered by Employment Discrimination Law

What is covered in this book? Employment discrimination law concerns statutory responses, both federal and state, to unfair employment practices in the workplace. Title VII is the federal statute that prohibits discrimination because of a person's race, color, religion, sex (including pregnancy, sexual orientation, and gender identity), or national origin. The Age Discrimination in Employment Act (ADEA) prohibits age discrimination against people 40 and older. The Pregnant Workers Fairness Act (PWFA) requires accommodation for pregnancy, childbirth or related conditions. The Americans with Disabilities Act prohibits discrimination based on disability and requires employers to accommodate disabilities. Section 1981 prohibits discrimination because of race. State or local law may prohibit discrimination based on other characteristics. Because of the complex manner in which federal and state antidiscrimination laws interact and because of the various statutory proof schemes that populate employment discrimination law, you will soon see why employment discrimination is now being taught as a separate course and why it also deserves its own treatment in this book.

C. Recurring Themes in Employment Discrimination Law

We will be revisiting certain fundamental issues throughout the study of employment discrimination law in this book, including: (1) What constitutes discrimination; (2) What kinds of discrimination should be addressed by law; (3) How is unlawful discrimination proven; (4) Who should have the burden of proof; and (5) Once a violation of substantive law is proven, what is the appropriate relief?

D. Employment at Will and Employment Discrimination Law

Normally, the default rule for most employees (the major exception being employees who are represented by a union; currently only about 13% of the American workforce, or who have some type of job-security employment agreement) is employment at will. "Employment at will" means that an employer can hire, fire, promote, or transfer an employee for good reason, bad reason, or no reason at all. The implicit trade off for the employee is that the employee can leave the employer when he or she wants for good reason, bad reason, or no reason whatsoever.

Nevertheless, the law of employment discrimination makes some statutory exceptions for employment decisions based on protected characteristics. Thus, although you can fire Chuck because you want to hire your nephew instead, you cannot fire Chuck because he is black. You can refuse to hire Marie because your company needs to downsize because of economic realities, but you cannot refuse to hire Marie because she is a woman or because she is Catholic. The key to understanding the relationship between employment-at-will and employment discrimination laws is that the discrimination laws are federal, state, or local statutorily-enacted exceptions to the basic presumption of employment at will.

E. Classification of Employment Discrimination Cases

Let's turn to the text of Title VII. As a general matter, Title VII prohibits certain employment-related organizations from making certain employment-related decisions on the basis of five specifically enumerated criteria or classifications: race, color, religion, sex, and national origin. Under Title VII, the word "sex" also includes discrimination because of pregnancy, sexual orientation, and gender identity. Other federal laws prohibit disability, pregnancy, age, and pay discrimination (see Chapters 12–15) and state and local laws cover a variety of other protected groups including veterans and marital status.

Yet there is no definition of discrimination in Title VII. Thus, the twinned question: (1) How does one define discrimination; and (2) How does one prove discrimination under Title VII?

1. The Three Axes of Employment Discrimination Law

These questions further help us set up a conceptual framework for classifying different types of employment discrimination cases. Three axes exist in this conceptual framework:

> **First.** Cases can involve situations where direct evidence of discrimination exists or, more likely, where there is only circumstantial, or inferential, evidence of discrimination.
>
> **Second.** Cases can involve individual employees alleging discrimination or groups of individuals alleging discrimination (i.e., class actions).
>
> **Third.** Cases can involve employment decisions where intentional discrimination is alleged (so-called disparate treatment cases) or neutral policies which have a differential effect on different protected groups (disparate impact cases).

Based on these three axes, the following classifications of employment discrimination cases exist:

(1) Circumstantial vs. Direct Evidence Cases

(2) Individual vs. Group Cases

(3) Disparate Treatment (Intentional Discrimination) vs. Disparate Impact Cases (Nonintentional Discrimination)

This book will separately consider the idea of accommodation based on religion, disability, and pregnancy. Accommodation law does not neatly fit within this overall structure.

2. Individual Disparate Treatment Claims

Across the three axes, the largest group of cases consists of individual disparate treatment claims based on circumstantial evidence. Not surprisingly, in this day and age, few cases have direct evidence (such as an internal memo admitting to discriminatory intent) of discriminatory treatment in the workplace. When such direct evidence of discriminatory treatment exists, employers sometimes defend on the basis of a bona fide occupational qualification (BFOQ) (see Chapter 6). Moreover, group claims, whether of the intentional discrimination variety (pattern or practice claims) (see Chapter 7) or of the nonintentional discrimination sort (disparate impact claims) (see Chapter 8) are expensive to bring, require lots of resources, and therefore, are not litigated nearly as frequently.

Under the individual disparate treatment framework, there are two major proof schemes for showing that unlawful discrimination can be inferred from circumstantial evidence: pretext cases under the *McDonnell Douglas* framework and mixed-motive cases under the *Price Waterhouse*/Civil Rights Act of 1991 framework (Chapter 6). Additionally, another group of employment discrimination claims involves harassment allegations (see Chapter 9), or allegations of retaliation for participating in official proceedings, or for opposing unlawful employment practices (see Chapter 10).

3. Procedural Issues for Employment Discrimination Claims

However, before considering the substance of employment discrimination claims, it is first necessary to consider issues of jurisdiction (see below), statutory coverage (see Chapter 2), administrative procedural requirements (Chapter 3), and procedural requirements surrounding civil litigation (Chapter 4).

We start in this Chapter with some basic jurisdictional guideposts and then in the subsequent chapters consider other coverage and procedural issues under employment discrimination law.

F. Sources of Employment Discrimination Law

1. Statutory Sources

Employment discrimination statutes and ordinances exist on the federal, state, and local levels. The focus of this book will be on federal antidiscrimination statutes, with special emphasis on Title VII of the Civil Rights Act of 1964. Students would do well to become familiar with the different coverage provided by state antidiscrimination laws.

2. Constitutional Sources

In addition to statutory law, issues of employment discrimination may be addressed by federal and state constitutions. Under the equal protection clause of the Fourteenth Amendment of the federal constitution, discriminatory actions by state actors may be challenged. These types of cases mostly take place in the public employment context where state action is involved. The most protection for employment discrimination in the public sector occurs in the area of race, color, and national origin discrimination because those classifications by the government are subject to strict scrutiny. Gender classifications are handled under intermediate constitutional scrutiny, while age and disability distinctions only face rational basis review. Additional constitutional issues will be covered in Chapter 14.

3. Common Law Sources

Finally, there is the potential that certain common law theories may help protect against some forms of employment discrimination. For instance, and especially in harassment cases (see Chapter 9), it is not unusual for a federal or state statutory claim to be accompanied by a state tort claim for intentional infliction of emotional distress. To a lesser extent, torts of assault, battery, and harassment can be part of employment discrimination claims. On the other hand, some courts tend to conclude that theories of wrongful discharge in violation of the public policy to prevent unequal treatment in the workplace are preempted by the Title VII or state antidiscrimination schemes.

G. Jurisdiction for Employment Discrimination Claims

1. Enforcement of Employment Discrimination Law

As will be discussed in more detail in Chapters 3 and 4, plaintiffs may seek enforcement of antidiscrimination laws through several means. The EEOC—or Department of Justice if the employer is a state entity—can, if they wish, pursue a claim against an employer, or seek a settlement between the parties. State antidiscrimination agencies can often do the same with regard to state actions. The employment discrimination statutes also provide, if certain procedural requirements are followed, a private right of action that permits lawsuits in state or federal court. Since 1991, Title VII also permits a plaintiff to demand a jury trial for intentional discrimination claims.

2. Sovereign Immunity Issues

One complication for plaintiffs occurs when they are attempting to sue a state employer. Because of constitutional protections for state sovereign immunity, an individual's ability to sue a state can be quite limited. Under current Supreme Court precedent, state employees cannot sue their employers for monetary damages under the Americans with Disabilities Act (ADA) and Age Discrimination in Employment Act (ADEA) unless the state consents. However, state employees can typically seek injunctive relief under the ADA and ADEA. In contrast, state employees have been permitted to sue their employers for both monetary and injunctive relief under Title VII, even when the state employer has not consented to being sued. Finally, the federal government, via the Department of Justice, can always sue a state employer on behalf of an employee for monetary and injunctive relief without raising state sovereign immunity concerns.

3. Concurrent Jurisdiction

Title VII and other federal antidiscrimination statutes invoke federal question jurisdiction and, after proper exhaustion of federal and/or state administrative remedies, may be brought in federal court. It is important to stress that federal and state courts have concurrent jurisdiction over Title VII claims.

Plaintiffs may therefore choose to bring their federal claims in federal or state court. The U.S. Supreme Court addressed Title VII concurrent jurisdiction in *Donnelly v. Yellow Freight Systems*, 494 U.S. 820 (1990). In *Donnelly*, the Court held that federal courts do not have exclusive jurisdiction over Title VII claims because Title VII does not divest state courts of their concurrent authority to adjudicate federal claims.

CHECKPOINTS

- There are four primary courses in the study of labor and employment law: labor law, employment law, employee benefits, and employment discrimination law.
- Employment discrimination law concerns statutory responses, both federal and state, to unfair employment practices in the workplace.
- Employment at will, the rule for most American employees, means that an employer can hire, fire, promote, or transfer an employee for good reason, bad reason, or no reason at all and that an employee can leave work for good reason, bad reason, or no reason at all.
- The law of employment discrimination establishes statutory exceptions to employment at will for unlawful decisions based on protected characteristics.
- Title VII prohibits employment-related organizations from making employment-related decisions on the basis of five specifically enumerated criteria or classifications: race, color, religion, sex (including pregnancy, sexual orientation, and gender identity), and national origin.
- Other federal laws prohibit disability (ADA), age (ADEA), and pay discrimination (Equal Pay Act), and state laws cover a variety of other protected characteristics including: veteran status and marital status. The Pregnant Workers Fairness Act (PWFA) requires covered entities to accommodate pregnancy, childbirth, and related medical conditions.
- Because no definition of discrimination exists in Title VII, a large portion of this course is devoted to how one defines and proves discrimination.

- Three axes exist for classifying employment discrimination cases: (1) individual vs. group; (2) disparate treatment vs. disparate impact; and (3) direct evidence vs. circumstantial evidence cases. Most employment discrimination cases involve individual claims of disparate treatment based on circumstantial evidence.
- Employment discrimination law derives primarily from statutory sources, but such protections can also be found under constitutional and common law theories.
- Plaintiffs may seek enforcement of antidiscrimination laws through several means including through the EEOC or through private claims.
- State employees can sue their employers for monetary damages under Title VII, but not under disability or age discrimination laws without the state's consent.
- Title VII and other federal antidiscrimination claims invoke federal question jurisdiction and, after proper exhaustion of administrative remedies, may be brought in federal or state court.

CHAPTER 2

Coverage

ROADMAP

- Employers covered by employment discrimination laws
- Non-traditional employers and the small-employer exception
- The difference between joint and single employers
- Contingent employees and statutory exemptions
- Employees covered by employment discrimination laws
- Independent contractors vs. employers vs. employees
- Employment actions covered by employment discrimination laws

---

In the initial stages of an employment discrimination dispute, it is necessary to start with the essential threshold question: do any of the relevant statutes apply to my case? Numerous limitations to those statutes may mean that a given employment discrimination law does not apply to a given workplace dispute. Most of these limitations can be classified under three broad questions: (1) is the employer covered by the statute; (2) is the worker covered by the statute; and (3) is the employment decision covered by the statute?

A. Covered Employers

Most labor and employment statutes fail to cover all employers, and the employment discrimination laws are no exception. Just as the employment discrimination laws exclude certain types of workers, they also limit their applicability to certain employers. That coverage has expanded over the years, but there are still significant exclusions that apply to particular employers. Confusion may also arise over an entity's classification as an employer of a given employee. These issues are critical, as the majority of courts have held that the employment discrimination statutes do not permit actions against individuals. Accordingly, a plaintiff can seek redress only from their statutory employer.

Unlike the confusing definition of employee, which is discussed below, there is relatively little litigation addressing whether an employer meets the statutory definition. The definition of employer under Title VII, the ADA, and the ADEA all broadly cover "a person engaged in an industry affecting [interstate] commerce ... and any agent of such a person." Although it is not difficult to establish that an employer is engaged in an industry affecting interstate commerce, there are more complicated issues surrounding this definition, such as questions about the inclusion of labor unions, employment agencies, and small employers; liability among nominally separate employers that are affiliated with each other in some way; and coverage of businesses that use contingent or leased employees.

1. Nontraditional "Employers": Unions and Employment Agencies

Employment discrimination statutes apply to two types of entities that might not immediately fit under the traditional view of employer: labor organizations and employment agencies. In addition to their relationship with their own employees, which falls under the normal employer-employee rules, these entities are often intimately involved in hiring and maintaining terms and conditions of employment for employees of other businesses. Thus, Congress extended the employment discrimination statutes to certain actions of these entities to ensure that workplace discrimination did not go unremedied simply because a labor organization or employment agency was involved.

The definition of labor organization under employment discrimination statutes mostly tracks the definition under the National Labor Relations Act

(NLRA), 29 U.S.C. § 152(5), which broadly includes any organization that deals with employers over wages, hours, and other terms and conditions of employment. However, the employment discrimination statutes' reach is more limited. For instance, Title VII covers only labor organizations—generally more formal trade unions—that either operate a "hiring hall" that supplies workers to an employer or that represent a group of 15 or more employees at a Title VII-covered employer. The ADA uses the same definition as Title VII, and the ADEA uses a similar definition that differs slightly, such as requiring a non-hiring hall union to represent 25 or more employees. In contrast, the Pregnant Workers Fairness Act (PWFA) does not apply to labor organizations or employment agencies, except with regard to their own employees.

Covered unions may violate employment discrimination statutes by discriminatorily excluding or expelling an employee from union membership, discriminatorily segregating or classifying its membership, discriminatorily refusing to refer an employee for employment (the hiring hall situation), discriminatorily failing to investigate or pursue an employee's grievance, and by causing an employer to discriminate.

Similar to labor organizations, employment agencies are covered to account for their role in supplying workers and, at times, affecting workers' terms and conditions of employment. However, the employment discrimination statutes' application to employment agencies falls under a different analysis. The definition of employment agency under these statutes is a person who procures employees for an employer. Agencies of all sizes may be covered as long as their primary activity is to procure employees on a regular basis for at least one business that is a covered employer under the relevant employment discrimination statute. If this standard is met, an employment agency may be held liable for discriminatorily referring or failing to refer individuals for employment, discriminatorily classifying individuals, or otherwise discriminating against individuals.

2. Small-Employer Exception

All four of the employment discrimination statutes exempt small employers. Title VII, the PWFA, and the ADA apply only to employers with 15 or more employees; the ADEA applies only to employers with at least 20 employees. State antidiscrimination statutes—which exist in virtually all states—typically have small-employer exceptions as well, although they can be different from the federal thresholds. Moreover, if a dispute could be filed as a § 1981

Civil Rights Act claim, discussed in Chapter 14, no small-employer exception applies.

Counting the number of employees is not always as easy as it may seem. As a general baseline, most full- and part-time employees on the company's payroll in the relevant weeks are counted. *Walters v. Metropolitan Education Enterprises, Inc.*, 519 U.S. 202 (1997). However, other workers, such as unpaid interns, independent contractors, consultants, and worker-owners are not counted as employees. As described below, determining whether a worker is an employee or one of these other classifications can be quite difficult.

The theory for exempting small employers is that these businesses often lack the resources to comply with antidiscrimination regulations and that by allowing them to operate free from these possibly costly rules, the business will grow and ultimately become larger, covered employers. Countervailing interests exist—including the fact that a significant number of employees work for small employers and that those employers may well be able to thrive while still complying with antidiscrimination rules—but the small-employer exemption is a common feature of many employment laws and does not face serious challenge. Indeed, the size of the employer is of special import under Title VII, as the amount of compensatory and punitive damages available in a given case depends on the number of employees of the defendant. Moreover, under Supreme Court precedent, the small-employer exclusion is not jurisdictional; thus, an employer can waive the exclusion by not raising it in a timely manner. *Arbaugh v. Y & H Corp.*, 546 U.S. 500 (2006).

3. Joint or Single Employers

One issue that arises on occasion is how to treat two interrelated companies that influence the work of employees. For instance, a contractor and sub-contractor may be nominally separate businesses, but they both may play a significant role in establishing a given set of employees' terms and conditions of employment. This issue can be particularly relevant if the nominal employer does not meet the small-employer threshold or lacks the resources to remedy a claim. In certain circumstances, courts will treat the nominal employer and a related employer as joint employers, extending coverage to both entities and making them joint and severally liable for a claim. Courts use varying considerations to analyze a joint-employer issue, but the central focus generally is whether one business controls, or shares control of, the employment relations of the other—for example by controlling hiring, firing, discipline, work assignments, training, and pay.

A similar issue occurs when two business are classified as a single employer. This typically happens with parent and subsidiary companies. In making this determination, courts will generally look to factors such as interrelation between the businesses' general operations, the interrelation of their employment relations, and whether they have common ownership or management, although some courts focus more on the liability of the parent for the subsidiary, the parent's control over the challenged action, and whether an entity broke off into smaller units to avoid liability under anti-discrimination laws.

4. Businesses Using Contingent Employees

The use of contingent employees—workers whose tenure is short-term and who have no expectation of continued employment—has been growing and presents problems for determining the identity of a statutory employer. Contingent workers can be classified in many different ways, including as independent contractors who are not statutory employees. In this case, those workers are not counted towards the small-employer exception, which could preclude coverage of the hiring entity. However, contingent workers can be considered employees, such as those who are "leased" by one entity to another and part-time or job-sharing employees. Such situations often lead to questions whether both entities may be considered joint employers and whether the contingent employees count towards both entities' small-employer exception.

Leased employees, for instance, typically raise the most significant issues as to the identity of the employer's or employers' potential liability under the employment discrimination laws. When faced with a leased employee question, courts generally engage in a highly fact-specific analysis that looks to factors such as the details of the contract underlying the provision of the employee from one entity to the other, the type of work the employee is performing, and whether the putative employer is aware of the conduct of the other employer that underlies the discrimination claim.

A similar issue occurs when an employer discriminates against an individual who is not technically its employee. For instance, a nursing home may try to influence the work of private nurses who are employed by residents. Because the employment discrimination statutes prohibit discrimination by an employer "against an individual," some courts have permitted actions against a business—like the nursing home—that discriminatorily affect the work of an individual, even if there is no formal employer-employee relationship.

5. Statutory Exclusions

The antidiscrimination statutes also specifically exclude certain types of employers. Among these excluded entities are American Indian tribal employers; bona fide, tax-exempt membership clubs; some foreign employers that favor their own citizens under authority of a treaty; and some American employers operating in a different country whose laws preclude compliance with certain American laws. The federal government is covered by the employment discrimination statutes and the Civil Service Reform Act of 1978, but is subject to unique rules that are beyond the scope of this book.

B. Covered Employees

By their nature, employment discrimination laws are intended to regulate employment relationships (although § 1981 requires only a contractual relationship). Thus, even if an employer is covered by a given statute, an individual who performs work for that employer may not be. A frequent issue, therefore, is whether someone who is performing work for a business is truly an employee rather than, for instance, an independent contractor or an owner. Individuals may also be excluded from the statutory definition of employee if they perform work as volunteers, interns, students, or as part of a rehabilitative training program. Also, according to some courts, uniformed military workers are not covered. The question of who counts as a covered employee is frequently litigated because—save for some limited exceptions for union members and clients of employment agencies—only workers classified as "employees" of a given employer are covered by employment discrimination laws. This definition has been held to apply to former employees and individuals who have applied for a job.

Despite the importance of whether an individual is an employee, the employment discrimination statutes provide little guidance, as they all define "employee" solely as "an individual who is employed by an employer."

Faced with this circular definition, courts have relied on common-law agency principles, which rely on numerous factors to determine whether an employment relationship exists.

1. Employee or Independent Contractor?

The most frequently litigated issue regarding workers' status is whether to classify them as statutory employees or excluded independent contractors. For instance, if a person works through a ride-sharing platform, like Uber, is the person Uber's employee or is the person an independent contractor? This employee v. independent contractor question is not new, but advances in technology have resulted in more workers—like those at Uber and other "gig" companies—falling in the substantial gray area between these two classifications.

There is no firm definition for an independent contractor, but the concept is intended to represent a worker who is not in an employment relationship and is instead merely providing services for a business. Although the consequences of the distinction between employee and independent contractor are significant, the line between the two is often unclear.

Given the unhelpfulness of the statutory definition of employee, courts typically look to common law to classify workers. The common-law test arose out of the agency principle of "respondeat superior" or vicarious liability. Under this test, a principal—such as an employer—would generally be liable for the tort of one of its agents—such as an employee—only when the principal had a certain level of control over the agent's actions. This so-called "right-to-control" test has become the primary means by which courts distinguish employees from independent contractors who are not covered by the employment discrimination statutes, although courts often add factors to the common-law test. *Community for Creative Non-Violence v. Reid*, 490 U.S. 730 (1989). This right-to-control test is often referred to as the *Darden* test, after the case of *Nationwide Mutual Insurance Co. v. Darden*, 503 U.S. 318 (1992). In *Darden*, the Supreme Court interpreted an equally circular definition of employee under the Employee Retirement Income Security Act (ERISA), 29 U.S.C. § 1001 *et seq.*, to set forth several common-law based factors to distinguish employees from independent contractors. These non-exclusive factors include:

1. the hiring party's right to control the manner and means by which the product is accomplished;
2. the skill required;
3. the source of the instrumentalities and tools;
4. the location of the work;
5. the duration of the relationship between the parties;
6. whether the hiring party has the right to assign additional projects to the hired party;

7. the extent of the hired party's discretion over when and how long to work;
8. the method of payment;
9. the hired party's role in hiring and paying assistants;
10. whether the work is part of the regular business of the hiring party;
11. whether the hiring party is in business;
12. the provision of employee benefits; and
13. the tax treatment of the hired party.

Although no one factor is dispositive, the right to control is the most important consideration under the *Darden* test. There is some question regarding the extent of *Darden*'s applicability to employment discrimination laws. Traditionally, courts used a dual approach that took into account the *Darden*/right-to-control factors, while also considering the economic dependency of the worker on the business. This economic dependency consideration is the central focus of the "economic realities" test, which is used under the Fair Labor Standards Act (FLSA), 29 U.S.C. § 201 *et seq*. However, the Supreme Court in *Clackamas Gastroenterology Associates, P.C. v. Wells*, 538 U.S. 440 (2003), an ADA case, suggested that the right-to-control test is the appropriate approach under employment discrimination laws. The issue in *Clackamas* did not involve alleged independent contractors, but in its decision, the Court avoided using economic realities considerations and instead emphasized that the circular definition in the ADA was similar to that of ERISA; thus, both definitions should be analyzed under the right-to-control factors. The result of *Clackamas* is that most courts use the *Darden* right-to-control test for Title VII, ADA, and ADEA cases.

2. Employee or Owner?

The *Clackamas* case raised another issue: when will a partner or shareholder in a business be considered an employee as opposed to an excluded owner? In *Clackamas*, the Supreme Court addressed whether physicians who were the shareholders and owners of the business should be considered "employees" for purposes of the 15-employee small-employer exclusion under the ADA. The Court stressed that, like ERISA, the ADA's circular definition revealed Congress's intent that the definition of employee be determined under common-law principles. That is, the *Darden*/right-to-control factors generally apply. However, because the issue in *Clackamas* was different from the independent contractor issue in *Darden*, the Court relied on a modified list of right-to-control factors, borrowed from the EEOC:

1. whether the organization can hire or fire the individual or set the rules and regulations of the individual's work;
2. whether and, if so, to what extent the organization supervises the individual's work;
3. whether the individual reports to someone higher in the organization;
4. whether and, if so, to what extent the individual is able to influence the organization;
5. whether the parties intended that the individual be an employee, as expressed in written agreements or contracts;
6. whether the individual shares in the profits, losses, and liabilities of the organization.

The key to this test is distinguishing separate owners, who possess the ability to control and manage the business, from employees, who may have an ownership stake but who do not play a substantial role in business operations. *Mariotti v. Building Products, Inc.*, 714 F.3d 761, 768 (3d Cir. 2013). This modified *Darden* test is a good reminder that none of the right-to-control factors are necessary in every case and that there may be other, more unique, factors that warrant consideration in certain circumstances.

C. Covered Employment Actions

Title VII does not prevent all forms of discrimination. Rather, as an employment statute, it is focused on workplace decisions that have a negative impact on an employee or applicant.

Section 703(a)(1) of Title VII prohibits discrimination by failing or refusing to hire or discharging any individual, or by otherwise discriminating against any individual "with respect to his compensation, terms, conditions, or privileges of employment." Moreover, under § 703(a)(2), it is unlawful for an employer "to limit, segregate, or classify his or her employees or applicants for employment in any way which would deprive or tend to deprive any individual of employment opportunities or otherwise adversely affect his status as an employee because of such individual's" protected class.

Other sections include additional adverse employment actions, such as refusing to accommodate religious beliefs or practices and publishing discriminatory employment advertising. Generally, these adverse employment actions represent a negative effect on some economic aspect of employment.

Thus, a refusal to hire, termination, demotion, refusal to promote, reduction in pay, and reduction in work hours will usually qualify as adverse employment actions. Courts had held that minor changes in job duties (without a change in compensation or title) or negative reviews that do not impact any aspect of employment would not state a claim under the statutes because they were not what the courts called "adverse actions." The adverse action doctrine is in a state of flux following the Supreme Court opinion in *Muldrow v. St. Louis*, 601 U.S. 346 (2024). That case held that a change in a term or condition of employment does not need to be significant or substantial to lead to Title VII liability. In *Muldrow*, the Court examined whether a transfer would violate Title VII, if the employer made the transfer decision because of the plaintiff's race. The Court, rejecting the idea that a plaintiff must prove significant harm, held that a plaintiff can prevail on a Title VII claim if the transfer constituted a disadvantageous change in the "terms, conditions or privileges" of employment. In particular, the Court noted that these terms should not be understood in a narrow, contractual sense and do not require economic harm—contrary to what many courts had been requiring in Title VII cases. The Court issued *Muldrow* in April of 2024, and there are few cases applying the decision at the time of this book's publication.

The Supreme Court explored another aspect of this issue in *Hishon v. King & Spalding*, 457 U.S. 69 (1984). The question in *Hishon* was whether a failure to consider a female law firm associate for partner was a "term, condition, or privilege of employment." The Court held that consideration for a promotion may qualify if, as was the case in *Hishon*, the employer had represented to the employee that such consideration would occur. Under that circumstance, going up for partner had become a term, condition, or privilege of employment and discrimination associated with that consideration was an adverse employment action that could trigger Title VII liability. Had consideration for partnership not been among the terms of the employee's hiring, then the negative partnership decision would likely not be a covered employment decision under Title VII. A major reason for this is that the decision to make someone a law firm partner—who is often classified as an employer rather than an employee—is generally not considered a covered employment decision. However, where law firm (or other) partners have such limited authority that they act more like associates, they may be considered employees. *EEOC v. Sidley Austin Brown & Wood*, 315 F.3d 696 (7th Cir. 2002).

CHECKPOINTS

- An employer covered by the federal employment discrimination laws must be engaged in an industry affecting interstate commerce.
- Labor organizations and employment agencies may be considered statutory employers under certain circumstances.
- Employers with fewer than 15 employees are excluded from the ADA and Title VII; employers with fewer than 20 employees are excluded from the ADEA.
- Ostensibly separate employers may be considered joint employers or a single employer for purposes of an employment discrimination action if they are interrelated and share a substantial level of common influence over employees.
- The lack of a formal employer-employee relationship may not bar coverage of a business that leases employees to another or that has substantial influence over the work of an employee of another.
- American Indian tribal employers; bona fide, tax-exempt membership clubs; and American companies operating abroad in certain instances are excluded from the employment discrimination statutes.
- Workers must be considered statutory employees to be covered by the employment discrimination statutes.
- Independent contractors, which are not statutory employees, are generally classified pursuant to the common-law based *Darden*/right-to-control factors.
- An adverse action under Title VII is any disadvantageous change in terms, conditions, or privileges of employment, and need not constitute economic harm.
- Workers such as shareholders or partners may not be considered statutory employees under a modified *Darden*/right-to-control test.
- Covered employment actions must fall within the terms of each statute.

CHAPTER 3

Administrative Procedural Issues

ROADMAP

- The importance of procedure in employment discrimination law
- The charge of discrimination
- The overall EEOC process
- The different time limitations for charges
- The meaning of the date of discrimination
- The relationship between federal and state antidiscrimination agencies
- Time limitations for subsequent civil suits
- Issue and claim preclusion

A. The Centrality of Procedure to Employment Discrimination Claims

The procedural requirements of Title VII and the other employment discrimination laws are equally as important as the substantive requirements of these laws. Lawyers who ignore these procedural elements do so at their own peril. What otherwise might have been a meritorious employment discrimination claim can be lost if a proper charge of discrimination is not filed in a timely manner. Indeed, as a practicing attorney in this area of the law, much of your time will be spent determining whether the parties have met the procedural requirements of the different employment discrimination statutes. If such requirements are not met, plaintiffs' claims of employment discrimination may be easily dismissed for failure to state a claim before the case even gets under way.

Most of the procedural requirements of Title VII, as well as the workings of the Equal Employment Opportunity Commission (EEOC), are set out in Sections 705 and 706 of the Act. Under these sections, the EEOC must accept and investigate charges of discrimination filed by individuals or EEOC Commissioners. If the EEOC finds reasonable cause to believe that the charge is true (which occurs in only a small fraction of the actual charges files), it tries to eliminate such alleged unlawful practices through informal methods of conference, conciliation, and persuasion. If this proves unsuccessful, the EEOC can either file suit on behalf of the complainant or can allow the individual to bring a private action by issuing a right to sue letter.

Note the practical effect of this system. The incentive for parties is not to put many resources into the EEOC part of case. Why fight over difficult issues of what files to hand over or disclose potential litigation strategy when you are likely to have to litigate the same exact dispute in front of a court? Because most charges of discrimination end up with the complainant receiving a right to sue letter from the EEOC regardless of the claims' merit, the incentive is to defer real litigation and see if the case makes its way to court. This approach, however, is inconsistent with one of the reasons for establishing the EEOC: to act as a gatekeeper and to conciliate meritorious employment discrimination claims to avoid expensive and time-consuming litigation.

B. What Constitutes a Charge of Discrimination?

A prerequisite to any Title VII action is an EEOC charge. A charge is a formal complaint where the complainant (the party who is alleging discrimination) identifies the employment right that has been violated. The complaining party also provides information, through an intake questionnaire or through affidavits, so that the EEOC may investigate the charge of discrimination. In *Federal Express Corp. v. Holowecki*, 552 U.S. 389 (2007), the U.S. Supreme Court held that any filing that reasonably requests agency action and identifies the name of the charged party (usually the employer) may constitute a charge. In reaching its conclusion, the Court deferred to EEOC regulations on what constituted a charge. Moreover, if the charge is unverified by oath or affirmation within the statutory time period as required by Title VII, it may still be properly verified after the statutory period has expired. *Edelman v. Lynchburg College*, 535 U.S. 106 (2002).

C. The EEOC Administrative Process

After a charge is filed with the EEOC, the remaining steps can be divided into: (1) the investigation of the charge; (2) the determination of whether reasonable cause exists that unlawful discrimination occurred; and, if so, (3) an attempt by the agency to conciliate the charge of discrimination.

1. The Investigation of the Charge and Cause Determination

Even before the charge is processed, the EEOC must notify the employer of an EEOC charge within 10 days. If the EEOC fails to timely notify the respondent, the agency can be barred from bringing a later EEOC suit. That being said, a tardy notification does not affect the right of an individual to bring a private employment discrimination suit.

After the charge is processed, an investigator will determine whether there is sufficient cause to find discrimination. In the course of the investigation, the investigator may review the respondent's position statement (a response to the EEOC charge), make requests for information (an in-the-field form of discovery that can be enforced with a subpoena), and hold fact-finding conferences (meetings where the investigator asks both the charging party and the respondent questions on the record). If during an investigation a new form of discrimination is found, the EEOC may issue a Commissioner Charge to investigate that new basis for finding discrimination. *EEOC v. Shell Oil Co.*, 466 U.S. 54 (1984) (discussing the substantive and procedural requirements for Commissioner Charge). Where no reasonable cause is found (the large majority of charges filed), the individual will receive a right-to-see letter from the agency.

If the investigator finds evidence of discrimination, the investigator will prepare an investigation memorandum that includes a determination or dismissal recommendation. The office director will then decide if the case meets the reasonable-cause standard, and if it does, the EEOC will then try to conciliate the claim and come to a settlement between the parties.

Additionally, it is worth noting that in many instances, a full investigation may not occur as the employee (or the employee's attorney) may request that a right to sue letter be issued far earlier in the process. As detailed on the EEOC's website, "If you want to file a lawsuit before we have finished our investigation, you can request a Notice of Right to Sue." *See* https://www.eeoc.gov/filing-lawsuit#Filing%20A%20Lawsuit%20Before%20The%20Investigation%20Is%20Completed.

2. EEOC Attempts at Conciliation

An attempt at conciliation is a prerequisite for a lawsuit. Typically, after a reasonable-cause determination, the EEOC will try to promote a settlement between the charging party, the respondent, and the EEOC. In fact, the EEOC is obligated to attempt conciliation with the respondent throughout the administrative process; however, the respondent's rejection of an EEOC settlement proposal ends the EEOC's obligation until the respondent attempts to restart the negotiation.

While the EEOC need not reach an agreement, it must negotiate in good faith. Lastly, the interests of the EEOC and the private party may differ. Because interests can differ, the EEOC may not want to settle the claim even when the complainant is willing to settle. In such a case, the complainant and the respondent may enter into a private settlement, while the EEOC continues its investigation. Although private parties are generally concerned mostly with legal redress for the unlawful discrimination, the EEOC also has a public mandate to try to eradicate employment discrimination from workplaces in the United States.

If the EEOC fails to complete any part of the post-charge investigation on any claim of discrimination, it may be precluded from bringing civil litigation on that claim. In *Mach Mining v. EEOC*, 575 U.S. 480 (2015), the Supreme Court held that the courts can properly review the EEOC's conciliation efforts, but noted that this review is narrow. *See id.* at 483 ("We hold that a court may review whether the EEOC satisfied its statutory obligation to attempt conciliation before filing suit. But we find that the scope of that review is narrow, thus recognizing the EEOC's extensive discretion to determine the kind and amount of communication with an employer appropriate in any given case.").

D. Timeliness of Administrative Charges

The issue of timeliness has three distinct topics: (1) when a complainant must file a charge of discrimination; (2) with whom the charge must be filed; and (3) when the complainant must file an action with a state or federal court after an EEOC investigation has ended.

1. When the Charge Must Be Filed

Section 706(e) of Title VII provides that a complainant has either 180 days or 300 days to a file a charge of discrimination with the EEOC. The difference in time periods stems from the fact the EEOC usually does not act alone in employment discrimination matters. Numerous state and local fair employment practice agencies (FEPAs) handle thousands of charges annually.

For those states that have these parallel state agencies, so-called "deferral states," Title VII extends the time to file a charge of discrimination with the EEOC to 300 days from the date of discrimination. In those states where such a state agency does not exist, the statute of limitations remains at 180 days. The time period is expanded in cases involving a deferral state to give FEPAs time to complete their investigations of charges. Furthermore, under § 706(d), Title VII gives deferral states the first chance to remedy discrimination claims by precluding federal intervention for the first 60 days after a charge is filed, unless the state waives this requirement or completes its investigation before 60 days have passed (for more on waiver, see the discussion below on work sharing agreements).

Interestingly, employment discrimination claims can remain under investigation at the EEOC for quite some time. As already mentioned, however, in many instances, a full investigation may not occur as the employee (or the employee's attorney) may request that a right to sue letter be issued far earlier in the process.

Additionally, because the EEOC statute of limitations requirements are not considered a jurisdictional prerequisite, exceptions may exist to the normal 180- or 300-day statute of limitations. *Zipes v. Trans World Airlines, Inc.*, 455 U.S. 385 (1982). In *Zipes*, the Court held that "a timely charge of discrimination with the EEOC is not a jurisdictional prerequisite to suit in federal court, but a requirement that, like a statute of limitations, is subject to waiver, estoppel, and equitable tolling." Equitable tolling, specifically, may exist in instances involving: filing with the wrong agency, where misleading information is received from the agency, where misconduct of the defendant is involved, or where the mental illness of a plaintiff plays a role. Nevertheless, the statute of limitations is not tolled just because the employee is simultaneously pursuing their rights under a grievance provision in an applicable collective bargaining agreement.

a. When Is the Date of Discrimination?

Much time and litigation has been spent trying to figure out when the clock starts to run on an employment discrimination claim. While the substance of an EEOC charge is construed liberally, courts have not taken such a stance on the timeliness of an EEOC charge. A charge must be generally filed within a limited time from the discrete discriminatory act. A discrete discriminatory act would be the occurrence of a failure to hire, a termination, a failure to promote, or other tangible and adverse employment action. Such claims typically fall into either the 180-day or 300-day period, depending on whether the charge is filed in a deferral state. *National Railroad Passenger Corporation v. Morgan*, 536 U.S. 101 (2002). The time period starts when the employee has "notice of the decision" that creates an adverse employment action. *Delaware State College v. Ricks*, 449 U.S. 250 (1980). Also, the Supreme Court has held that the "continuing effects" of past discrimination into the present is generally not litigable as a continuing violation that satisfies the statute of limitations. *United Air Lines v. Evans*, 431 U.S. 553 (1979).

b. Exceptions: Harassment and Pay Discrimination Claims

There are two exceptions to the 180-day or 300-day time period for charges. The first exception to the timeliness rule is for claims of harassment, particular hostile work environment. Because a charge of harassment may involve the totality of the circumstances—involving many instances of discriminatory conduct over a period of time—the complainant need only file a charge within 180 or 300 days of an instance of harassment. *Morgan*, 536 U.S. 101 (2002). To require the filing of one of these claims within a 180- or 300-day period of a discrete discriminatory act would lead to the absurd result of requiring employees to bring a charge before their claim is actionable. It is sometimes not until many discriminatory acts have occurred that the injury becomes clear to the employee. Often, it takes many years for a recognizable pattern of sexual harassment to develop before the employee realizes that he or she might have a claim.

The second exception to the 180-day or 300-day period exists for claims of pay discrimination. As a result of the Ledbetter Fair Pay Act of 2009, pay discrimination claims now function somewhat analogously to harassment claims such that pay discrimination charges must only be filed within 180/300 days of at least one instance of pay discrimination—such as a paycheck—that makes up the claim. Like harassment claims, it is not until many discriminatory wage decisions have occurred that the harm may become clear to the employee. The Ledbetter Fair Pay Act overturned a contrary Supreme Court decision on the same issue. *Ledbetter v. Goodyear Tire & Rubber Co.*, 550 U.S. 618 (2007). As the statute provides, "an unlawful employment practice occurs, with respect to discrimination in compensation ... when a discriminatory compensation decision or other practice is adopted, when an individual becomes subject to a discriminatory compensation decision or other practice, or when an individual is affected by application of a discriminatory compensation decision or other practice, including each time wages, benefits, or other compensation is paid, resulting in whole or in part from such a decision or other practice." The Ledbetter Fair Pay Act is further clear as to potential damages, providing for "recovery of back pay for up to two years preceding the filing of the charge, where the unlawful employment practices that have occurred during the charge filing period are similar or related to unlawful employment practices with regard to discrimination in compensation that occurred outside the time for filing a charge."

c. Disparate Impact Claims

The Supreme Court has also decided when the statute of limitations begins to run in a disparate impact case involving an allegedly discriminatory job test given firefighter applicants in the City of Chicago. *Lewis v. City of Chicago*, 560 U.S. 205 (2010). In *Lewis*, the employer gave a test that produced a disparate impact, then over the next several years continued to hire firefighters off the list of applicants who received the highest range of scores on the test. A unanimous Court held that the plaintiffs' charge was timely because one of these applications of the test had occurred within the statute of limitations, even though the test itself had not. The Court pointed out that Title VII establishes a prima facie claim by showing that the employer "*uses* a particular employment practice that causes a disparate impact" on one of the prohibited bases. Section 703(k), 42 U.S.C. § 2000e-2(k) (emphasis added). The term "employment practice" clearly encompasses, the Court maintained, the conduct at issue in *Lewis*: exclusion of passing applicants who scored below 89 when selecting those who would advance. In fact, the City of Chicago "used" that practice each time it filled a new class of fire-fighters. So, despite the fact that § 703(k) does not address "accrual" of disparate impact claims, the plaintiffs timely filed a claim for disparate impact liability in *Lewis*. The upshot of *Lewis* is that the Court has adopted a version of the discovery rule in these types of cases.

2. With Whom the Charge Must Be Filed

In addition to questions arising over the nature of the relationship between the EEOC and state agencies in matters relating to when the charge must be filed, as discussed in the previous subsection, similar questions arise relating to the agency with whom the charge must be filed.

Generally speaking, those who potentially wish to pursue both state and federal antidiscrimination law claims must file a charge of discrimination with both the EEOC and the parallel state agency. In fact, under § 706(d) of Title VII, the EEOC must defer to the state agency for the first 60 days.

Many state antidiscrimination agencies have work sharing arrangements with the EEOC. These work-sharing agreements can supersede the 60-day deferral procedure under § 706(d), which means that the EEOC can start its investigation of the charge as soon as the complainant files it. Additionally, and significantly, charges received by the EEOC are deemed received by the state agency, and vice versa, for purposes of determining the timeliness of the charge. So, "if you file a charge with either EEOC or a FEPA [Fair Employment Practice Agency], the charge also will be automatically filed with the other agency. This process, which is defined as dual filing, helps to protect charging party rights under both federal and state or local law." *See How to File a Charge of Discrimination,* https://www.eeoc.gov/employees/howtofile.cfm.

Moreover, work sharing agreements can contain either self-executing or non-self-executing waivers. If a work sharing agreement waives the 60-day deferral period for all cases, then the waiver is self-executing, and the proceedings are *initiated* and *terminated* the same day that the EEOC receives the charge. If the agreement does not automatically waive the period, but requires the FEPA to decide whether to waive, then the waiver is not self-executing. One last wrinkle: If some action other than filing with the EEOC triggers an automatic waiver of the 60-day period under the agreement, like transmittal of the charge from the EEOC to the FEPA, then the waiver is still self-executing and timeliness is determined by looking to the specified action.

Finally, a number of these state agencies investigate and attempt to conciliate charges, much like the EEOC does. Some also adjudicate charges either as the sole remedy or as an alternative to litigation in court. Marcia L. McCormick, *The Truth is Out There: Revamping Federal Antidiscrimination Enforcement for the Twenty-First Century*, 30 Berkeley J. Emp. & Lab. L. 193 (2009).

3. Timing After Receiving Right to Sue Letter

After the EEOC has finished its investigation or after a request for a right to sue letter from a complainant, the EEOC can issue a right to sue notice to the complainant which allows them to file an action in federal or state court (recall that concurrent jurisdiction exists over Title VII claims). In fact, without this right to sue letter, the complaint will be dismissed for failure to exhaust administrative remedies. The complainant then has 90 days under the statute of limitations to file an action in state or federal court once a plaintiff has been issued a right to sue letter. The plaintiff satisfies this statute of limitations as long as he or she files within this 90-day period, no matter how long the charge was pending before the EEOC. This 90-day receipt requirement applies to Title VII, the ADA, and the PWFA. However, a right to sue letter is not necessary under the ADEA. *See* https://www.eeoc.gov/filing-lawsuit ("If you plan to file an age discrimination lawsuit, you must have filed a charge but you don't need a Notice of Right to Sue to file a lawsuit in court. You can file a lawsuit in court any time after 60 days have passed from the day you filed your charge (but no later than 90 days after you receive notice that our investigation is concluded))." It is also worth noting that claims brought under § 1981 do not follow this process, and bringing claims under this provision are discussed in more detail in Chapter 14 of this text.

Furthermore, just as it is important to file the proper information when one files a charge of discrimination with the EEOC, it is also important that one file an appropriate civil complaint in federal or state court after one receives a right to sue letter. For example, the Supreme Court has held that merely filing the right to sue letter itself with the federal court within the 90-day period does not satisfy the 90-day statute of limitation. *Baldwin County Welcome Center v. Brown*, 466 U.S. 147 (1984).

E. Issue and Claim Preclusion in Employment Discrimination Cases

1. Issue Preclusion (Collateral Estoppel)

Section 706 of Title VII makes resorting to state administrative remedies in deferral states a prerequisite to litigation under the Act. (Although, as discussed above, work sharing agreements have made it unlikely that an employee would file with the EEOC and not dual file with the state administrative agency.) The question sometimes arises as to when use of state administrative procedures precludes the claimant from also taking advantage of federal procedures.

An initial resort to state administrative procedures (that is, action leading to an unreviewed state administrative agency decision) does not deprive a plaintiff of federal remedies. *University of Tennessee v. Elliott*, 478 U.S. 788 (1986). On the other hand, resort to full judicial review in state court is equivalent to the state court considering the merits of the claim and precludes federal relief for the plaintiff. *Kremer v. Chemical Construction Corp.*, 456 U.S. 461 (1982). This is because Title VII does not supersede the full faith and credit statute, 28 U.S.C. § 1738, which requires that federal courts afford state-court judgments the same preclusive effect that the state's appellate courts would provide.

2. Claim Preclusion (Res Judicata)

Claim preclusion (also called res judicata) bars litigation of a claim which was litigated, or could have been litigated, in an earlier proceeding between the same parties. Under this theory, if two kinds of claims arise out of the same incident, a plaintiff may not split them between two proceedings when they could have been combined in one case.

For instance, in *Owen v. Kaiser Foundation Health Plan*, 244 F.3d 708 (9th Cir. 2001), the issue was whether the state court dismissal of a suit alleging breach of contract and other state law claims barred the later filing of a federal suit alleging unlawful Title VII discrimination arising out of the same nucleus of operative facts. The court held that the federal suit was barred, because "Title VII claims are not exempt from the doctrine of res judicata where plaintiffs have neither sought a stay from the district court for the purpose of pursuing Title VII administrative remedies nor attempted to amend their complaint to include their Title VII claims." Thus, if a state court plaintiff wants to preserve his or her Title VII claim while simultaneously maintaining a non-Title VII suit arising out of the same set of facts or occurrences, he or she must either apply for a stay in district court where the Title VII claim is pending or amend the state complaint to include the Title VII claim.

CHECKPOINTS

- Most of the procedural requirements of Title VII, as well as the workings of the EEOC, are set out in § 705 and § 706.
- A prerequisite to a Title VII action is an EEOC charge, a formal complaint where the complainant identifies the employment right that has been allegedly violated.
- Any filing can be considered a "charge" that reasonably requests agency action and identifies the name of the charged party.
- After a charge is filed with the EEOC, the remaining steps can be divided into:
  (1) the investigation of the charge; (2) the determination of whether reasonable cause exists that unlawful discrimination occurred; and, if so, (3) an attempt to conciliate the charge of discrimination.
- Timeliness issues actually address three separate issues: (1) when a complainant must file a charge of discrimination; (2) with whom the charge must be filed; and (3) after an EEOC investigation has ended, when the complainant must file an action with a state or federal court.
- Section 706(e) of Title VII provides that a complainant has either 180 days or 300 days to a file a charge of discrimination with the EEOC, depending on whether they are filing in a deferral state with a FEPA.
- A charge must generally be filed within a limited time from the discrete discriminatory act, and that time period starts running when the employee has "notice of the decision" that creates an adverse employment action.
- Exceptions to this general statute of limitations rule exist for harassment, pay discrimination, and disparate impact claims.
- Generally speaking, those who wish to pursue both state and federal antidiscrimination law claims must file a charge with both the EEOC

and FEPA, but this can be accomplished through work sharing agreements and dual filing.

- Once the EEOC has finished its investigation (or after a request for a right to sue letter), the complainant receives a right to sue letter and has 90 days to file an action in state or federal court.
- In many instances, a full investigation may not occur as the employee (or the employee's attorney) may request that a right to sue letter be issued far earlier in the process.
- A right to sue letter is not necessary to pursue litigation under the ADEA, though a charge with the EEOC must still be filed.

CHAPTER 4

Procedural Issues in Employment Discrimination Litigation

ROADMAP

- The relationship between the EEOC charge and the lawsuit
- Compulsory arbitration agreements
- Some characteristics of the employment discrimination litigation procedure
- The relationship between the EEOC and private parties in litigation
- Private and EEOC employment discrimination class actions

This chapter reviews the procedural requirements surrounding civil litigation of a federal antidiscrimination action (Title VII, ADA, ADEA, and PWFA). It is broken down into four subtopics: (1) the relationship between the EEOC charge and the lawsuit, (2) mandatory arbitration provisions, (3) employment discrimination litigation procedure, and (4) private and EEOC class actions. The EEOC does not play a formal role in § 1981 litigation, but the other topics in this chapter that do not relate to the EEOC are relevant in the § 1981 context.

A. The Relationship Between the EEOC Charge and Lawsuit

Simply put, the scope of the EEOC charge limits the scope of a Title VII lawsuit. The charge must identify any issue that will be litigated, and the charge must describe the basis for the discrimination allegation. The courts have held that a civil action is limited to the scope of investigation that would reasonably be expected to stem from the charge of discrimination (the scope of the investigation doctrine).

B. Mandatory Arbitration Clauses in Employment Discrimination Cases

Compulsory (sometimes called "mandatory" or "pre-dispute") arbitration clauses are a common feature in both union and non-union workplaces. By agreeing to arbitrate, parties waive their right to have their cases heard in a judicial forum. An arbitration agreement, under the Federal Arbitration Act, is just as enforceable as any other contract, and rises and falls on the same defenses applicable in contract law (lack of consideration, unconscionability, etc.).

So, cases exist where arbitration agreements are struck down on the basis of: (1) an employee's unilateral promise to arbitrate with no consideration; (2) an employer's retaining complete control over arbitration rules so consideration was deemed illusory; (3) one-sided arbitration agreements that would be either procedurally or substantively unconscionable to enforce because the neutrality of the proceedings would be undermined; and (4) an employer requiring the employee to pay all or some of the arbitration fee, making it more difficult for employees to have access to the process and vindicate their rights.

An employer can, as a condition of employment, make an employee agree to an arbitration agreement that requires the employee to arbitrate his Title VII claim rather than go to court. That being said, the Supreme Court has held that the EEOC's ability to bring a lawsuit on behalf of a private individual is not affected by the employee having an enforceable arbitration agreement with an employer. Indeed, in such circumstances, the employee is still able to file a charge of discrimination with the EEOC regardless of the arbitration provisions. The Court reasoned that the EEOC had independent statutory authority to pursue the matter based on the filed charge and needed to bring the case to vindicate the public interest of eradicating employment discrimination from society as a whole. *EEOC v. Waffle House*, 534 U.S. 279 (2002). However, *Waffle House* does not change the fact that a valid arbitration agreement will bar a private lawsuit.

In 2022, Congress amended the Federal Arbitration Act (FAA) through the Ending Forced Arbitration of Sexual Assault and Sexual Harassment Act. This Act amended the FAA to allow a person alleging "conduct constituting a sexual harassment dispute or a sexual assault dispute, or the named representative of a class or in a collective action alleging such conduct" to proceed with their claim even if it otherwise would be subject to a pre-dispute arbitration agreement.

The Act does not just apply to sexual assault and sexual harassment claims. Instead, it applies to any case that relates to a sexual assault or sexual harassment dispute. Importantly, the Act does not invalidate all arbitration agreements that fall within its parameters. Instead, it allows a person alleging a such a dispute (or a representative) to file suit despite the existence of a pre-dispute arbitration provision that otherwise would be enforced under the FAA. If a person bound by such an agreement wishes to proceed through arbitration, the Act allows this. The Act is not limited to overcoming arbitration agreements. The Act also allows class disputes to proceed even if they otherwise would be subject to a pre-dispute joint-action waiver.

Employment discrimination arbitration cases are generally divided between union cases and non-union cases.

1. Union Arbitration Cases

In the union context, most collective bargaining agreements contain grievance provisions whereby unions agree on their employees' behalf to grieve and eventually arbitrate claims under the collective bargaining agreement. In return for these grievance provisions, unions agree not to go out on strike during the duration of such an agreement. Ultimately, the union is the entity that decides whether to pursue a grievance on behalf of the employee.

The Supreme Court initially held that a discharged employee, whose grievance concerning his termination for discriminatory reasons was submitted to arbitration pursuant to a collective bargaining agreement, was not foreclosed from bringing his statutory claim for employment discrimination in a judicial forum. *Alexander v. Gardner-Denver Co.*, 415 U.S. 36 (1974). The salient points in *Gardner-Denver* were that the Court found that contractual and statutory rights are distinct, and that although arbitrators are well suited to resolve private disputes between union and management, they are not as qualified to decide issues of employment discrimination law.

In a later case, the Supreme Court further clarified the role of grievance provisions in collective bargaining agreements. Not only did the Court distinguish between these clauses in collective bargaining agreements from those contained in individual employment contracts (as discussed in the next subsection), but the Court required there to be a clear and unmistakable waiver if employees were to have their rights to pursue employment discrimination claims in a judicial forum waived. Although a permissible waiver was found lacking in *Wright v. Universal Marine Service Corp.*, 525 U.S. 70 (1998), the Court upheld the employer's right to mandatory arbitration for an employment discrimination claim where the waiver was clear and unmistakable. *14 Penn Plaza LLC v. Pyett*, 556 U.S. 247 (2009).

2. Non-Union Arbitration Cases

Arbitration issues are somewhat different in the individual employee setting. In these non-union cases, the primary issue is whether an individual, rather than the union, has waived the right to have his or her employment discrimination claims heard in a judicial forum. In one of the first Supreme Court cases in this area, the issue was whether a broker-dealer could be required by the National Association of Securities Dealers (NASD) to submit his claim under the Age Discrimination in Employment Act (ADEA) to binding arbitration and be forced to waive his right to a judicial forum as a condition of his employment.

The Court ruled that the NASD could force employees to mandatorily arbitrate their employment discrimination claims. *Gilmer v. Interstate/Johnson Lane Corp.*, 500 U.S. 20 (1991). Not only did the Court find nothing inconsistent with mandatory arbitration in the statutory language of the ADEA, but it also observed that the employee would not be foregoing his or her substantive rights under that statute. Moreover, the *Gilmer* Court distinguished its *Gardner-Denver* decision based on the fact that the *Gilmer* case involved a registration agreement rather than an employment contract; and because it was not a union waiving the statutory rights of an individual, but an individual agreeing to arbitrate his or her own statutory rights. Of course, whether such agreement on the employee's part is truly voluntarily is subject to debate.

In any event, the Court later determined that most employment relationships fall under the pro-arbitration Federal Arbitration Act (FAA), 9 U.S.C. §§ 1–14; 201–208. *Circuit City Stores v. Adams*, 532 U.S. 105 (2001). In *Circuit City*, the specific issue was whether a provision in § 1 of the FAA made it inapplicable to employment contracts. In a closely-divided opinion, the majority held that the provision—which concerned interstate commerce—should be construed narrowly and that § 1 of the FAA only excludes employment contracts of transportation workers.

Taken together, *Gilmer* and *Circuit City* mean that arbitration clauses in individual employment agreements are presumptively enforceable. This is true even of an arbitration clause that does not contain a clear and unmistakable waiver, as is required in collective bargaining agreements.

C. Employment Discrimination Litigation Procedure

There are two major topics regarding litigation procedure: the single filing rule (sometimes referred to as "piggybacking of a charge") and plaintiff intervention in EEOC-initiated cases.

1. The Single-Filing Rule

Under the single filing rule, plaintiffs who have not filed an EEOC charge within the requisite time period can join a suit without exhausting their administrative remedies. *Calloway v. Partners National Health Plans*, 986 F.2d 446 (11th Cir. 1993). The single filing rule is a judge-made exception to the requirement that plaintiffs exhaust their administrative remedies prior to filing suit. This situation comes up in two separate circumstances. First, in the class action context, it is applied to permit unnamed plaintiffs to rely on the EEOC charge filed by the named plaintiff. *Oatis v. Crown Zellerbach Corp.*, 398 F.2d 496 (5th Cir. 1968).

Second, it may apply when a plaintiff relies on an EEOC charge filed by another plaintiff in another lawsuit. In these cases, to qualify for the single filing rule, a plaintiff must meet two essential requirements: (1) the charge being relied upon must be timely and not otherwise defective; and (2) the individual claims of the filing and non-filing plaintiffs must have arisen out of similar discriminatory treatment in the same time frame. For those familiar with civil procedure rules, this last requirement is similar to the "same transaction" standard that is used for joinder and supplemental jurisdiction issues.

The courts have allowed these exceptions to the general rule that each plaintiff exhaust administrative remedies on each legal claim because in these limited circumstances the EEOC has already been given the opportunity of addressing the underlying legal claim. Because nothing would be gained by requiring additional plaintiffs with the same legal claims to go through the EEOC process, the courts do not require it.

2. Plaintiff Intervention in EEOC-Initiated Cases

Section 706(f)(1) of Title VII allows the EEOC, once conciliation has failed, to sue a private employer and also authorizes private parties to intervene as a matter of right in these EEOC suits. Plaintiffs may intervene in actions concerning their claims between the EEOC and the employer so they may participate in settlement negotiations and have their voices heard.

D. The Federal Complaint

Once in civil court, workers are subject to the Federal Rules of Civil Procedure just like any other civil litigant. This means, for instance, that an employee must file a satisfactory complaint—properly alleging the cause of action. In two controversial Supreme Court cases, *Bell Atlantic Corp. v. Twombly*, 550 U.S. 544 (2007), and *Ashcroft v. Iqbal*, 556 U.S. 662 (2009), the Court adopted a *plausibility* standard for all civil cases, including those brought under Title VII. While there is still debate as to whether this plausibility test has created a heightened pleading standard, workers must now make sure to plead enough facts in the complaint to give rise to a *plausible* claim. Workers must do more than simply parrot the statutory language, and they must include more than conclusory statements.

E. Employment Discrimination Class Actions

Because discrimination is often class-wide in scope, it naturally lends itself to class actions under Rule 23 of the Federal Rules of Civil Procedure. As an initial matter, for a plaintiff to bring a class action under Rule 23, the named plaintiff must have timely filed a charge of discrimination with the EEOC and must have completely exhausted the relevant administrative processes. The other members of the class do not need to have filed charges (remember the single filing or piggyback rule discussed above). Rule 23 is divided into two basic parts, requirements under 23(a) and requirements under 23(b).

1. Rule 23(a) Requirements

Under Rule 23(a), a plaintiff seeking to maintain a class action must satisfy four requirements:

- **Numerosity**—the members of the proposed class must be so numerous that joinder of these individuals as named plaintiffs would be impractical
- **Typicality**—the named plaintiff's claims or defenses are typical of the class
- **Commonality**—common questions of law and fact exist
- **Adequacy of Representation**—the named plaintiff can fairly and adequately represent the class, has no conflicts of interest with other members of the class, and will use qualified counsel

a. Traditional Rule 23(a) Practice

Initially, in Title VII cases from the 1960s and the 1970s, courts were extremely liberal in applying these requirements to class actions under Title VII. Under the so-called across-the-board actions, diversely situated members of the class were able to allege different forms and bases of discrimination, while still certifying the class. Certification was still possible under the across-the-board theory because the court found that common discriminatory policies formed the basis for all of the employer's actions.

In this regard, a typical across-the-board case was *Johnson v. Georgia Highway Express, Inc.*, 417 F.2d 1122 (5th Cir. 1969). In that case, a discharged black employee sought to represent a class composed of all other similarly situated black employees seeking equal employment opportunities. Even though such a class would not seem to meet typicality and commonality concerns under Rule 23(a), the 5th Circuit reversed the district court and permitted such a class under the across-the-board theory, reasoning that the alleged underlying policy of racial discrimination was sufficiently common to, and typical of, the claims of all members to permit joinder of all the claims. In a concurring opinion in that case, Judge Godbold wrote an influential opinion, expressing reservations that such a liberal construction of Rule 23(a) would lead to difficulty in protecting the interests of absent class members since they were so spread out among different facilities.

The reason that the needs of absent class members are so important in these situations is that members of the class are normally bound by the outcome of the class litigation. Therefore, if people are bound by a judgment which does not address their type of concern, they never will have a chance to litigate their claims.

b. Modern Day Rule 23(a) Practice

In any event, the Supreme Court now requires closer scrutiny of the Rule 23(a) requirements. In *General Telephone Co. of Southwest v. Falcon*, 457 U.S. 147 (1982), the plaintiff alleged that he had been denied a promotion because of his Mexican national origin. He sought to bring a class action on behalf of other Mexican Americans for discrimination on the basis of promotions and hiring (even though his individual claim did not concern hiring discrimination). The Court held that class action certification was not appropriate under these circumstances for two reasons.

First, the class action device is supposed to promote conservation of judicial resources by allowing litigation of many related claims in one place at one time. The action in *General Telephone Co. of Southwest* did not advance economy and efficiency because there were different theories of proof advanced for the promotion claim (disparate treatment) and the hiring class claims (disparate impact). Each claim was also proved by different kinds of evidence, so rather than conserving judicial resources, a class action would needlessly complicate the action and lead to the wasting of judicial resources.

Second, the named plaintiff did not meet the typicality and commonality requirements for the discriminatory hiring claim. As the court held, neither commonality nor typicality could be found based on the mere fact that the named plaintiff and the other members of the class were of the same national origin. In the end, the limited nature of Falcon's claim made him ineligible to be the class representative for those with hiring discrimination claims. In this manner, the majority opinion identified the inherent error in across-the-board cases as a failure to demand that a plaintiff's individual claim encompass the claims of the class. Indeed, if one allegation of specific discriminatory treatment were sufficient to support an across-the-board attack, every Title VII case could be a potential company-wide class action.

c. Size of the Class

As mentioned above, one of the prerequisites for certification under Rule 23(a) is that the class is so numerous that joinder of all members is impractical. However, there is no magical number of plaintiffs beyond which joinder is considered impractical. The determination is made by the court on a case-by-case basis. Some factors courts consider include: the size of the class, the ease of identifying its members and determining their addresses, the ease of making service on them if joined, and the geographic dispersion of the proposed class. *Garcia v. Gloor*, 618 F.2d 264 (5th Cir. 1980). The *Garcia* case involved a proposed class of 31 persons whose identity and addresses were readily ascertainable and who all lived in the same area. The court rejected class certification on the grounds that joinder was practical.

d. Commonality Redefined

In *Wal-Mart Stores, Inc. v. Dukes*, 564 U.S. 338 (2011), the Supreme Court raised the bar for "commonality" for class action employment discrimination cases. In that case, the Court rejected a purported class of over a million current and former workers brought under Title VII. The Court concluded that there was no "glue" holding the claims together. The Court emphasized the sheer size and geographical scope of the class and found insufficient commonality of those claims. More specifically, the Court held that, "Because [plaintiffs] provide no convincing proof of a companywide discriminatory pay and promotion policy, we have concluded that they have not established the existence of any common question." *Id.* at 359.

After *Wal-Mart*, plaintiffs must carefully assess whether there is a common thread in the case sufficient to satisfy the heightened commonality standard created by the Court. Plaintiffs must be particularly cautious in classes that appear massive both in size and geography.

2. Rule 23(b) Requirements

Not only must the four prerequisites of Rule 23(a) be satisfied, but the class must also be certified as one of the designated types of class actions allowed under Rule 23(b). Each type of class has different requirements and different associated rules.

Some Rule 23(b)(1) class actions are referred to as limited fund cases. In these classes, a limited fund, like an insurance policy, must be distributed ratably so that every class member gets a proportional piece of the recovery. This class action device is generally not used in employment discrimination class actions. Instead, most of the employment discrimination class claims are either certified under Rule 23(b)(2), dealing with a type of case where injunctive relief equally applies to all members of the class, and Rule 23(b)(3), which involve actions for monetary damages.

The primary distinction between Rule 23(b)(2) and Rule 23(b)(3) classes is that the former primarily seek equitable or declaratory relief, while the latter are monetary class actions seeking compensatory and punitive damages. Because money is involved, unlike in the other types of classes, Rule 23(b)(3) class members are entitled to notice and may opt out of the class if they so choose. This is based on constitutional considerations of due process and the right to a jury trial under the Seventh Amendment in damage actions.

In addition to the notice and opt-out requirements, Rule 23(b)(3) also requires that "questions of law and fact common to the members of the class *predominate* over any questions affecting only individual members." Furthermore, the Rule 23(b)(3) device must be *superior* to other ways of proceeding based on a set of listed factors. Not surprisingly, because it is expensive to give notice to a large class, to work around opting-out members, and meet the additional predominance and superiority requirements, plaintiffs tend to prefer 23(b)(2) certifications, while defendants prefer the stricter requirements of Rule 23(b)(3).

The ability of Title VII plaintiffs to receive compensatory and punitive damages as a result of the Civil Rights Act of 1991 has made it difficult to determine whether certification under Rule 23(b)(2) or Rule 23(b)(3) is more appropriate in employment discrimination class actions. Although looking like monetary-type relief, backpay (the lost income amount received from the time discriminated against to time of judgment) has been historically considered a type of equitable relief. As such, many courts view this type of backpay relief as merely incidental to the primary injunctive nature of the relief and therefore, these cases were allowed to proceed under Rule 23(b)(2). Although Rule 23(b)(2) classes used to be the most common certification class for Title VII suits when relief was primarily injunctive, such is not the case anymore with the ability to receive damages under the Civil Rights Act of 1991.

Consider for example the case of *Jefferson v. Ingersoll International, Inc.*, 195 F.3d 894 (7th Cir. 1999). In *Jefferson*, a class of black applicants who applied for jobs with Ingersoll, but were not hired, brought a class action claim. Plaintiffs sought both an injunction requiring Ingersoll to change its hiring practices and individual monetary relief of compensatory and punitive damages. Focusing on the damages that the plaintiffs sought, Judge Easterbrook for the Seventh Circuit concluded that the Rule 23(b)(3) class action device was the most appropriate when substantial damages are sought. Rule 23(b)(2) injunctive classes are, on the other hand, only appropriate when the monetary relief is incidental to the equitable remedy.

Jefferson is not the only approach courts have taken on the Rule 23(b) issue in employment discrimination cases. For instance, the court in *Robinson v. Metro North Commuter Railroad Co.*, 267 F.3d 147 (2d Cir. 2001), applied an ad hoc approach that determined the type of class by looking to the relative importance of the remedies sought. Yet another court has pointed out that the problem with monetary damages is that they tend to be individual in nature and thus individual issues may *predominate* over common class issues in violation of Rule 23(b)(3). *Allison v. Citgo Petroleum Corp.*, 151 F.3d 402 (5th Cir. 1998). The Seventh Circuit also pointed out that divided certification is permitted by Rule 23 and might be appropriate in a case like *Jefferson*. In this scenario, the damages part of the case is certified under Rule 23(b)(3), while the injunctive part of the case is certified under Rule 23(b)(2). Under Seventh Amendment right to jury principles, the damage part of the case is given precedence in order to preserve this constitutional right.

The issue also arose in *Wal-Mart Stores, Inc. v. Dukes*, 564 U.S. 338 (2011), and that case enhances our understanding of this provision. In *Wal-Mart*, the Court held that the plaintiffs' "claims for backpay were improperly certified under Federal Rule of Civil Procedure 23(b)(2). Our [previous] opinion ... expressed serious doubt about whether claims for monetary relief may be certified under that provision. We now hold that they may not, at least where (as here) the monetary relief is not incidental to the injunctive or declaratory relief." This further clarification of Federal Rule of Civil Procedure 23(b)(2) is therefore helpful in addressing class-action employment discrimination claims, and in clarifying the previous lower court decisions on this issue.

3. The EEOC and Class Actions

When the EEOC brings suit on behalf of a group of litigants, it is not required to meet Rule 23 requirements. This is because the EEOC is seen as having a broader public policy mandate and does not merely vindicate private interests. *General Telephone Co. of the Northwest, Inc. v. EEOC*, 446 U.S. 318 (1980).

4. Class Actions and Arbitration

It is also worth noting that in *Epic Systems Corp. v. Lewis*, 584 U.S. 497 (2018), and *AT&T Mobility LLC v. Concepcion*, 563 U.S. 333 (2011), the Supreme Court also made it more difficult to aggregate arbitration claims. Thus, workers pursuing relief in this forum may find it more difficult to bring their claims on a systemic level. The Supreme Court has continued to follow this approach in more recent years as well. *See, e.g., Lamps Plus, Inc. v. Varela*, 587 U.S. 176, 183 (2019) ("We therefore face the question whether, consistent with the FAA, an ambiguous agreement can provide the necessary 'contractual basis' for compelling class arbitration.... We hold that it cannot—a conclusion that follows directly from our [prior] decision.... The statute therefore requires more than ambiguity to ensure that the parties actually agreed to arbitrate on a classwide basis."); *Coinbase, Inc. v. Bielski*, 599 U.S. 736, 747 (2023) (holding that following the company's appeal "from the denial of its motion to compel arbitration, the District Court was required to stay its proceedings. On remand, we anticipate that the [appellate court] will proceed with appropriate expedition when considering [the company's] interlocutory appeal from the denial of the motion to compel arbitration."); *Smith v. Spizzirri*, 601 U.S. 472, 478 (2024) ("When a district court finds that a lawsuit involves an arbitrable dispute, and a party requests a stay pending arbitration, § 3 of the FAA compels the court to stay the proceeding."); *Coinbase, Inc. v. Suski*, 602 U.S. 143, 147–53 (2024) ("We granted certiorari to answer the question of who—a judge or an arbitrator—should decide whether a subsequent contract supersedes an earlier arbitration agreement that contains a delegation clause.... We conclude that a court, not an arbitrator, must decide whether the parties' first agreement was superseded by their second.").

The Ending Forced Arbitration of Sexual Assault and Sexual Harassment Act allows a plaintiff to nullify an otherwise enforceable class action waiver in a case that relates to a sexual harassment or sexual assault dispute.

CHECKPOINTS

- A civil action is limited to the scope of investigation which would reasonably be expected to stem from the charge of discrimination (the scope of the investigation doctrine).
- Compulsory arbitration clauses are a common feature in the union workplace and in the non-union workplace and are generally enforceable. For cases related to a sexual assault or sexual harassment dispute, a plaintiff has a choice to nullify an otherwise enforceable arbitration agreement.
- Under the single filing rule, a plaintiff who has not filed an EEOC charge within the requisite time period can join a suit without having exhausted his or her administrative remedies.
- Section 706(f)(1) of Title VII allows the EEOC, once conciliation has failed, to sue a private employer and authorizes private parties to intervene as a matter of right; it also permits a court to allow the EEOC to intervene in private litigation.
- A federal employment discrimination complaint must state a *plausible* claim.
- Because discrimination is inherently class-wide in scope, it naturally lends itself to class actions under Rule 23 of the Federal Rules of Civil Procedure; however, Rule 23 does not apply to EEOC class actions. After the Supreme Court's decision in *Wal-Mart Stores, Inc. v. Dukes,* it may be increasingly difficult to have employment discrimination claims certified.
- Under Rule 23(a), plaintiffs seeking class action status must satisfy four requirements: numerosity, typicality, commonality, and adequacy of representation.
- Under Rule 23(b), most employment discrimination class actions are brought as either primarily injunctive classes under Rule 23(b)(2) or as monetary classes under Rule 23(b)(3).

CHAPTER 5

Employment Discrimination Remedies, Settlement, and Tax Issues

---

ROADMAP

- Equitable and injunctive relief awarded under Title VII
- Determining backpay and frontpay awards
- Alternative theories for determining amount of relief
- Damages available under the Civil Rights Act of 1991
- Statutory damage caps under the Civil Rights Act of 1991
- Class action remedial approaches
- Prevailing parties and attorney's fees
- Rule 68 offers of judgment
- Tax considerations surrounding employment discrimination remedies

---

This chapter reviews the framework for awarding remedies under employment discrimination law (including attorney's fees), as well as issues to consider in deciding whether to settle an employment discrimination case (including tax considerations). As far as the statutes, this chapter focuses primarily on Title VII of the Civil Rights Act of 1964, 42 U.S.C. § 2000e *et seq.* Specific remedial issues under other employment discrimination statutes will be explored in later chapters dealing with those statutes. As a general guide, remedies under the ADA and PWFA are substantially similar to Title VII's remedies. Section 1981 provides broader remedies because it is not subject to damages caps. The ADEA provides a more limited set of remedies than Title VII. This chapter is broken down into five subtopics: (1) non-monetary equitable relief, (2) monetary equitable relief, (3) damage relief and the Civil Rights Act of 1991, (4) attorney's fees issues, and (5) settlement and tax issues.

A. Non-Monetary Equitable (Injunctive) Relief

1. Relief Available to Plaintiffs

Section 706(g)(1) of Title VII allows for reinstatement and equitable relief as the court deems appropriate. Importantly, affirmative or injunctive relief constitutes a form of equitable relief available under Title VII. For instance, the statute allows for reinstatement or restoration to positions the plaintiff would have held in absence of discrimination. Indeed, a presumption exists that if a plaintiff is unlawfully discriminated against, the plaintiff should generally receive reinstatement-type relief. *Franks v. Bowman Transportation Co.*, 424 U.S. 747 (1976).

Although frontpay also exists under Title VII (as discussed in more detail below), reinstatement is the preferred remedy unless it would produce a dysfunctional working environment or reinstatement is otherwise not possible under the circumstances. That being said, a general prohibition exists against bumping a current employee for a former employee that suffered discrimination. In either a "bumping" or "dysfunctional" situation, frontpay is preferred in lieu of reinstatement.

Title VII also permits so-called "rightful place relief." Rightful place relief is based on remedying unlawful conduct that caused a denial of a future employment opportunity. For instance, one type of rightful place relief is retroactive seniority. Under § 703(h) of Title VII, courts cannot modify an existing bona fide seniority system, as they are considered lawful even if they produce discriminatory results (except where an employer intends such results, as discussed in Chapter 6). That section does permit, however, an award that gives employees the same amount of seniority they would have had but for the discrimination. Indeed, such an award complies with § 706(g)'s make-whole requirement.

There are other limits on the extent of affirmative equitable relief. Although "a court can in appropriate circumstances order a promotion as make-whole relief for a victim of discrimination," it "cannot ... properly order the promotion of an employee to a position for which he or she is not qualified." *Locke v. Kansas City Power & Light Co.*, 660 F.2d 359 (8th Cir. 1981). Additionally, although affirmative action is not something that the EEOC can require (indeed quotas and other rigid goals are prohibited by § 703(j) of Title VII), judges can issue orders that mandate affirmative relief to eliminate the effects of past discrimination against plaintiffs.

2. Defenses Available to Defendants

Defenses to affirmative or injunctive relief also exist. Although courts will generally provide affirmative relief, an employer may still attempt to show that the unlawful discriminatory conduct stopped before judgment and that injunctive relief is unnecessary to prevent future noncompliance. Further, if there is a class of successful plaintiffs, not all of them are necessarily entitled to the same injunctive relief. For example, if an employer has been found liable for having an unlawful pattern or practice of discriminatory promotions, the employer can avoid an order to promote an individual plaintiff by showing that the plaintiff was not qualified for the higher position. *International Brotherhood of Teamsters v. United States*, 431 U.S. 324 (1977).

3. Third-Party Relief

Affirmative relief also exists for third parties. For instance, by ordering an employer to adopt a sexual harassment policy, this action benefits parties not before the court. Similarly, the issuance of an order that an employer adopt a race-conscious affirmative action plan may also benefit non-parties. *Firefighters Local 1784 v. Stotts*, 467 U.S. 561 (1984).

B. Equitable Monetary Relief

Equitable relief also includes various forms of monetary relief, including backpay and frontpay.

1. Entitlement to Backpay Relief

a. Plaintiff's Entitlement to Relief

Like with injunctive relief under *Franks*, a presumption exists in favor of a backpay award, as long as that award is consistent with the purpose of the Act. *Albemarle Paper Co. v. Moody*, 422 U.S. 405 (1975). In *Albemarle Paper*, the Court described the purposes of Title VII as remedying past discrimination and making a victim of past discrimination whole. Although lack of bad faith on the part of the employer is irrelevant, laches (defined as an undue delay by the plaintiff causing prejudice to the defendant) may still come into play. One instance where backpay will not be presumed is where its ordering would upset the legitimate expectations of non-parties. *Arizona Governing Committee v. Norris*, 463 U.S. 1073 (1983) (not awarding backpay in pension case because award would upset expectations of other pension plan participants).

Backpay is provided for under § 706(g) of Title VII. The employee has the burden of establishing the value of the lost compensation by providing evidence on lost pay, lost employee benefits, speculative future raises, prejudgment interest, and expenses incurred in mitigating damages (i.e., finding new work).

As far as calculating the period of recovery for backpay, one generally starts at the point where the discriminatory act caused the employee to suffer an economic injury. This period does not accrue unless the employee is ready, willing, and able to work but for the employer's discriminatory practice. Under § 706(g), the employee can get backpay for up to two years before the employee filed the charge with the EEOC. The period ends when the plaintiff no longer suffers the effects of the discrimination, which most commonly is the date that judgment is rendered for the plaintiff or when the plaintiff assumes a comparable position of employment. Thus, in a normal case, backpay liability begins up to two years before the charge was filed (depending on when the discriminatory event occurred) and generally ends on the date when the final judgment is entered or the plaintiff gets a new job.

b. Employer Defenses to Backpay Awards

Employers have several defenses to backpay awards. The defenses tend to fall into one of two categories: (1) defenses that decrease the amount of backpay owed by offsetting it with other income; and (2) defenses that reduce the amount of backpay owed by decreasing the duration of the backpay period.

The primary way to reduce the amount of backpay owed is to offset the backpay with other sources of earned income. Like any plaintiff, a Title VII plaintiff has a duty to mitigate his or her injury, and he or she must make a reasonable attempt to find suitable employment. To succeed on a failure to mitigate defense, the employer has the burden to prove that the employee did not undertake reasonable efforts to mitigate his or her losses.

There are a few ways a defendant can reduce the backpay period. One way is by arguing that the plaintiff acquired a comparable job during this period, and thus the employee has no need for equitable relief at that point. Thus, when an employee obtains comparable employment, the backpay period ends. However, if the employee is unable to find comparable employment, and the employee only obtains a lesser form of employment (e.g., lesser in pay), the employer can offset the backpay owed by the amount of income earned by the employee during the backpay period.

Another defense that reduces the duration of the backpay period is a demonstration by the employer that employee misconduct would have resulted in the employee's termination (e.g., like stealing from the cash register). Using "after-acquired evidence" of employee misconduct, the backpay period ends when the employee would have been terminated for the misconduct. *McKennon v. Nashville Banner Publishing Co.*, 513 U.S. 352 (1995). Not only does after-acquired evidence prematurely end the backpay period, but it also reverses the presumption of whether an employee is entitled to backpay or frontpay and allows courts to determine the amount of backpay payment owed depending on the circumstances of the employee's misconduct.

Defendants can also seek to limit the duration of backpay period by demonstrating that the plaintiff refused its unconditional offer of reinstatement. *Ford Motor Co. v. EEOC*, 458 U.S. 219 (1982). Under the *Ford Motor* rule, if the employer offers the employee the job back, it cuts off the accrual of backpay damages as of the day of the offer. However, under *Ford Motor*, the offer must be to a sufficiently comparable job and the employee cannot be forced to waive or compromise his or her legal claims as a condition of accepting the offer.

A final backpay defense allows the employer to reduce the backpay period if the employer can show that the employee's job would have been eliminated. In other words, an event that would have terminated employment even if there was not discrimination precludes the recovery of backpay from that point on. So, in the *Price Waterhouse*/mixed-motive context, a court can order backpay relief where the defendant was *motivated* by the employee's protected class status. 42 U.S.C. § 2000e-2(m) (§ 703(m)); *Desert Palace, Inc. v. Costa*, 539 U.S. 90 (2003). But if the employer succeeds in arguing an affirmative defense that it would have made the "same decision" with regard to the employee without reference to the employee's protected characteristics, then the court is limited to declaratory relief, injunctive relief (other than reinstatement, hiring, promotion or payment), and attorney's fees and costs. 42 U.S.C. § 2000e-5(g)(2)(B) (§ 706(g)(2)(B)).

2. Alternative Theories for Determining Amounts of Relief

One of the issues that arises frequently is how to calculate wages when uncertainty exists about what the plaintiff's wage would have been if the unlawful discrimination had not taken place. One approach is to consider the progression of the average worker in the plaintiff's position. *Griffin v. Michigan Department of Corrections*, 5 F.3d 186 (6th Cir. 1993). This approach makes the most sense in bureaucratic structures such as government employment where promotion data and pay is available and promotion takes place in a relatively lock-step manner. One of the challenges in this approach is to find a comparable employee who did not face unlawful discrimination from the employer. In *Griffin*, the appellate court rejected the district court's use of another employee to model what plaintiff would have earned because the employee did not provide a good representation of how others, including plaintiff, would have likely been promoted.

Another minority approach to determining the amount of relief a plaintiff receives is the lost chance theory approach (borrowed from tort law). *Doll v. Brown*, 75 F.3d 1200 (7th Cir. 1996). Especially in competitive hiring or promotion cases, the court may decide that the appropriate monetary award is not the value of the lost job, but the value of the lost chance of receiving that job. For instance, if four plaintiffs were unlawfully rejected for the same position, which paid $100,000 a year, because of their race, and each plaintiff had an equal chance in a nondiscriminatory environment to obtain the job, then lost chance theory would suggest that each plaintiff receive $25,000, even though each by themselves only had a 25% chance of getting the job without discrimination. For more examples of how this theory works, see Paul M. Secunda, *A Public Interest Model for Applying Lost Chance Theory to Probabilistic Injuries in Employment Discrimination Cases*, 2005 Wisc. L. Rev. 747.

3. The Availability of Frontpay under Title VII

Section 706(g) of Title VII also provides for the awarding of frontpay to successful plaintiffs under certain circumstances. Frontpay is meant to compensate plaintiffs for the future effects of the unlawful discrimination they suffered. It is a remedy for losses that have not yet occurred and is sometimes referred to as "catch-up pay" as it seeks to compensate plaintiffs for the amount of time it will take them to catch up to what they would have made in their old job if they had not been discriminated against in the first place.

Because of its necessarily speculative nature, the preferred remedy is to reinstate or instate the plaintiff to the job in question. Sometimes, however, this is not possible because extreme hostility exists in the workplace, the employer is no longer in business, the plaintiff has already acquired alternative employment, or there has been a change in the plaintiff's interests or career goals.

Whereas backpay concerns the amount of income lost from the time of the discrimination usually through judgment in the case, frontpay works prospectively. It is generally measured from the time of judgment to the time when the court believes the plaintiff will be in the same position in the future, as if the past discrimination never took place. Because of its speculative nature, frontpay awards are usually no more than two or three years. In addition, a court will make deductions and offsets from a frontpay award based on a plaintiff's interim earnings, amount of separation or severance payments, and sometimes where the plaintiff received social security payments or other payments during the time he or she is out of work.

C. Damages Available under the Civil Rights Act of 1991

Under the originally-enacted version of Title VII, monetary damages were not available. This approach was based on the National Labor Relations Act (NLRA) framework, which to this day still does not provide for damage remedies. Care should be taken here. Under Title VII, backpay has always been available, but it is characterized as equitable relief.

The Civil Rights Act of 1991 (CRA of 1991), 42 U.S.C. § 1981a, changed the type of recovery available to plaintiffs and also now allows for jury trials where compensatory and punitive damages are sought in cases of intentional discrimination (such damages are not available for non-intentional/disparate impact claims).

1. Compensatory Damages Available under Title VII

Although non-economic damages (like pain and suffering) are not automatically awarded under Title VII, plaintiffs may receive them if they can show actual harm that was caused by the employer's discriminatory conduct. *Carey v. Piphus*, 435 U.S. 247 (1978) (requiring specific evidence of harm for compensatory damages).

2. Punitive Damages Available under Title VII

To be eligible in a disparate treatment case for punitive damages after the enactment of the CRA of 1991, the plaintiff must show willfulness in the defendant's adverse employment actions. In other words, the defendant employer must have engaged in a discriminatory practice with malice or reckless indifference to the federally protected rights of the aggrieved individual.

The Supreme Court explored the punitive damage standard in *Kolstad v. American Dental Association*, 527 U.S. 526 (1999). There, the Court determined that a higher standard existed for punitive damages than for compensatory damages. The Court held that a plaintiff is not required to show outrageous or egregious behavior to obtain punitive damages. The Court indicated that the terms "malice" and "reckless indifference" pertain to the "employer's knowledge that it may be acting in violation of federal law, not its awareness that it is engaging in discrimination." The Court clarified that "an employer must at least discriminate in the face of a perceived risk that its actions will violate federal law to be liable in punitive damages."

Additionally, *Kolstad* establishes the standard for vicarious punitive liability in Title VII cases. In this regard, the Court held that liability for punitive damages does not extend to an employer when that employer makes good faith efforts to comply with Title VII (for example, by disseminating and training on a sexual harassment policy). Additionally, an employer may be liable for punitive damages related to actions of those employed in a *managerial capacity* and acting in the scope of their employment.

In addition to *Kolstad*, the Supreme Court has limited the amount of punitive damages available in all cases under the federal constitution's due process clause. Under the *Gore* standards, a court is supposed to review punitive damage awards based on: (1) the disparity between the harm or potential harm suffered by the plaintiff and the punitive damages awarded; (2) the differences between the punitive remedy and the civil penalties authorized or imposed in comparable cases; and (3) the degree of reprehensibility of the defendant's conduct. *BMW of North America, Inc. v. Gore*, 517 U.S. 559 (1996). Moreover, the wealth of the defendant cannot justify an otherwise unconstitutional punishment. As a general rule of thumb, few awards that exceed a single digit ratio between punitive and compensatory damages will satisfy due process. *State Farm Mutual Automobile Insurance Co. v. Campbell*, 538 U.S. 408 (2003).

3. Statutory Caps for Compensatory and Punitive Damages

The CRA of 1991 provides for statutory caps on the amount of compensatory and punitive damages a plaintiff can receive under Title VII. The caps are for the *combined* award for compensatory *and* punitive damages and are established based on the size of the employer (the caps run from $50,000 for employers with 15 to 100 employees, $100,000 for employers with 101 to 200 employees, $200,000 for employers with 201 to 500 employees, and $300,000 for employers with more than 500 employees). The caps do not limit equitable relief (backpay or frontpay) and do not apply to parallel state antidiscrimination claims or claims for race discrimination under § 1981.

D. Issues Surrounding Class Relief

Employment discrimination class actions are normally bifurcated into a liability phase (Stage I) and a damages phase (Stage II). Liability to the class, whether through disparate impact or disparate treatment theory, and the claims of individual class representatives, are generally tried in Stage I. Only if class-wide discrimination is found does the case proceed to Stage II for the purposes of determining the relief due to the named plaintiff and individual class members. A finding of group disparate treatment discrimination does not mean that every member of the class will gain a recovery. The burden of proof does not follow the *McDonnell Douglas* or other proof schemes (see Chapter 6–8) in Stage II because the employer has already been found to have unlawfully discriminated. Instead, the Supreme Court's decision in *International Brotherhood of Teamsters v. United States*, 431 U.S. 324 (1977), indicates that the burden is on the employer in Stage II to show that the individual class member was denied an employment opportunity for lawful reasons such as lack of qualification or the fact that more qualified applicants would have been chosen for a vacancy in the absence of discrimination.

E. Attorney Fees and Offers of Judgment

1. Prevailing Parties and Attorney's Fees

As a general matter, prevailing plaintiffs have a right to an award of their attorney's fees under § 706(k) of Title VII. The statute actually uses the language "prevailing party," but awards of fees to defendants are rather unusual. *Christianburg Garment Co. v. EEOC*, 434 U.S. 412 (1978) (only awarding attorney's fees to defendants where plaintiff's claim is frivolous, unreasonable, without foundation or brought in bad faith). This is because the fee-shifting mechanism in Title VII is meant to encourage individual plaintiffs to act like private attorneys general to vindicate the purposes of Title VII (this is true especially because the EEOC brings relatively few enforcement actions).

One of the trickier issues under Title VII remedial law is trying to figure out who qualifies as a prevailing plaintiff. Generally speaking, success on any issue of significance in litigation that achieved some of the benefit the plaintiff initially sought will qualify. *Hensley v. Eckerhart*, 461 U.S. 424 (1983). The Supreme Court later clarified that "[a] prevailing plaintiff must obtain relief on the merits of his claim by materially altering the legal relationship between the parties by modifying the defendant's behavior in a way that directly benefits the plaintiff." *Farrar v. Hooby*, 506 U.S. 103 (1992). So, although any amount the plaintiff obtains means the plaintiff has prevailed to some extent, the fee award may be limited by the *extent* of the plaintiff's success.

In *Buckhannon Board & Care Home, Inc. v. West Virginia Department of Health*, 532 U.S. 598 (2001), the Court rejected the "catalyst" theory that awarded fees to the plaintiff where the defendant voluntary changed its conduct to comport with the plaintiff's request. Under *Buckhannon*, to obtain attorney's fees, the change in relationship must be court ordered. So, whereas a private settlement between the parties favorable to the plaintiff will not lead to attorney's fees being awarded, a consent decree between the same parties, with the same terms of settlement, will lead to the award of attorney's fees. Note, however, that the parties may negotiate attorney's fees as part of a settlement.

The most common method for courts to calculate the amount of reasonable attorney's fees under Title VII is to multiply the number of hours reasonably expended on the litigation by a reasonable hourly rate (this method is referred to as the "lodestar" approach). The party seeking an award of fees usually submits evidence supporting the hours worked. Courts in their discretion can, and do, adjust for waste or excessive submissions. Provided that the plaintiff meets the *success* requirement described above in *Hensley*, the plaintiff may be able to recover the full cost of litigation even if he or she is not successful on every claim. If the claims on which the plaintiff prevailed overlap evidentiarily with the unsuccessful claims, the court should award full attorney's fees for the efforts that supported the overlapping claims.

2. Offers of Judgment under Rule 68

Federal Rule of Civil Procedure 68(a) provides: "More than 10 days before the trial begins, a party defending against a claim may serve on an opposing party an offer to allow judgment on specified terms, with the costs then accrued." Under Rule 68(d), "[i]f the judgment that the offeree finally obtains is not more favorable than the unaccepted offer, the offeree must pay the costs incurred after the offer was made."

In *Marek v. Chesney*, 473 U.S. 1 (1985), the Supreme Court set out the appropriate calculus to determine whether a plaintiff has received a more favorable judgment than what the defendant offered. There, the Court made clear that the proper comparison is the amount of the verdict and the plaintiff's pre-offer costs on the one side of the ledger, and the defendant's offer of judgment on the other. Significantly, this comparison omits post-offer costs borne by the defendant because those costs merely offset part of the expense of continuing the litigation. One of the difficulties in undertaking this calculation is figuring out the value of injunctive or non-monetary relief the plaintiff might have received.

Another issue that frequently arises in the Rule 68 context is whether the statute at issue defines "costs" to include attorney's fees, and whether those fees may be recovered as "costs" under Rule 68. Title VII, the ADEA, the PWFA, and the Americans with Disabilities Act have the same prevailing-party language that the Court addressed in *Marek* (Sections 1983 and 1988 of the civil rights statutes, as discussed in Chapter 14) to allow for the award of attorney's fees as part of the costs of litigation. 42 U.S.C. § 2000e-5(k); 42 U.S.C. § 12205; 29 U.S.C. § 626(b) (incorporating by reference the Fair Labor Standards Act, 29 U.S.C. § 216(b) (1994)). Nevertheless, most circuits have held that this prevailing party language does not mean that a plaintiff who loses under the Rule 68 calculus must pay a defendant's post-offer attorney's fees; rather, the plaintiff must only pay the defendant's other post-offer costs. *Crossman v. Marcoccio*, 806 F.2d 329 (1st Cir. 1986). In this regard, the *Marek* Court observes that, "[c]ivil rights plaintiffs ... who reject an offer more favorable than what is thereafter recovered at trial will not recover attorney's fees for services performed after the offer is rejected." Notice that this approach is consistent with the principle in *Christianburg Garment* that defendants do not generally receive attorney's fees as a prevailing party unless bad faith can be proven. This is because it is very hard to argue that a plaintiff who prevails in court (which is required for Rule 68 to be triggered) brought the suit in bad faith or that the suit was frivolous, vexatious or without foundation.

F. Settlement and Taxation Issues under Title VII

1. Tax Considerations for Court-Ordered Relief

When it comes to backpay or frontpay received as equitable relief, or when a party receives damages as a result of a verdict, tax considerations need to be taken into account both by the parties and their attorneys. Backpay and frontpay are both considered gross income and therefore, are taxed because the payment functions like wages. *United States v. Burke*, 504 U.S. 229 (1992).

As for monetary damages, when compensatory and punitive damages first became available under the CRA of 1991, Congress specified that these awards were generally to be taxed. However, the statute further provides that "emotional distress shall not be treated as a physical injury or a physical sickness," which means that awards for emotional distress are not taxable as gross income.

The Supreme Court has considered whether the portion of the jury verdict paid to a plaintiff's attorney under a contingent-fee contract is income to the taxpayer and, thus, may be taxed to the plaintiff. The Court concluded that such money is generally considered income and subject to tax. *Commissioner v. Banks*, 543 U.S. 426 (2005). However, employment discrimination awards now come under an exception to this general rule because of a provision in the American Jobs Creation Act of 2004. 26 U.S.C. § 62(a)(20).

2. Tax Considerations in Settlement of Employment Discrimination Claims

The same rules apply in the settlement context, but there is more flexibility in avoiding adverse tax consequences. As an initial matter, the parties can structure the settlement so that a smaller sum is includable in the plaintiff's income. Second, parties can agree on whether an employer needs to withhold payroll taxes or instead can just pay the sum to the employee as an independent contractor. Of course, such agreements are subject to IRS review to verify that the applicable independent contractor test is met. As a result, in many instances, a defendant will require a plaintiff to agree to indemnity language if the IRS should ever come after an employer for mischaracterizing the status of a worker as an independent contractor.

CHECKPOINTS

- Section 706(g)(1) of Title VII allows for reinstatement and equitable relief (which includes injunctive relief) as the court deems appropriate.
- A presumption exists that if a plaintiff is unlawfully discriminated against, he or she should generally receive reinstatement-type relief and retroactive seniority.
- Although frontpay exists under Title VII (to compensate plaintiffs for the time it will take to catch up to the position they would have been in absent discrimination), reinstatement is the preferred remedy.
- A presumption exists in favor of backpay, as long as that award is consistent with the purpose of Title VII.
- In a normal case, backpay liability begins up to two years before the charge was filed and runs until the date when the final judgment is entered.

- Employers have several defenses to backpay awards including an unconditional offer of reinstatement or after-acquired evidence of misconduct.
- Lost-chance theory and average-worker progression are two ways to calculate wages when uncertainty exists about what the plaintiff's wage would have been in the future.
- The Civil Rights Act 1991 now permits jury trials where compensatory and punitive damages are sought in cases of intentional discrimination; such damages are capped.
- Punitive damages may be awarded when the employer acted with reckless indifference to the federally-protected rights of aggrieved individuals.
- The burden is on the employer in the remedial stage of class action cases to show that individual class members were denied employment opportunities for lawful reasons.
- As a general matter, prevailing plaintiffs have a right to an award of their attorney's fees under § 706(k) of Title VII, while defendants do not.
- Under Rule 68, if the plaintiff prevails and the judgment is less that what the defendant offered, then the plaintiff must bear the "costs" (plaintiff's own attorney's fees and the defendant's non-attorney's fees costs).
- A number of tax and settlement issues (including adverse tax consequences) need to be considered by the parties.

CHAPTER 6

Title VII Individual Disparate Treatment Claims

ROADMAP

- Introducing Title VII's individual disparate treatment theory of discrimination
- Single-motive disparate treatment claims and the *McDonnell Douglas* analysis
- Mixed-motive disparate treatment claims and the Civil Rights Act of 1991
- Evidentiary issues in showing discriminatory motive
- Employer defenses to disparate treatment claims, such as BFOQ

The most basic—and most common—type of Title VII dispute is the "individual disparate treatment" claim. As the name suggests, these claims involve individual employees who were subject to disparate treatment in the workplace because of their protected status. The individual disparate treatment claim is not nearly as straightforward as it first appears, because there are numerous structural and evidentiary issues that have confounded courts for decades.

A. The Single-Motive Claim

The starting point for understanding Title VII's disparate treatment analysis is the single-motive claim. This claim involves a dispute in which there was a solitary motivation for an adverse employment action; the dispute centers on the parties' attempts to convince a factfinder that their version of that motive is the most believable. The employee's version is that the adverse employment action occurred because of their protected status, while the employer argues that the action was because of some nondiscriminatory factor. Courts tend to use the word motive when discussing intentional discrimination claims, but it is more accurate to use the concept of causation. Title VII prohibits employment discrimination that occurs because of a protected trait.

The single-motive individual disparate treatment claim arises under § 703(a)(1) of Title VII, which makes it unlawful for an employer "to fail or refuse to hire or to discharge any individual, or otherwise to discriminate against any individual with respect to his compensation, terms, conditions, or privileges of employment, because of such individual's race, color, religion, sex, or national origin." Section 703(a)(1) encompasses three broad requirements: (1) there must be a negative consequence, such as a termination, failure to hire, or other negative change in the terms and condition of employment; (2) the employee must be a member of a protected class or perceived to be a member; and (3) the negative action must be "because of" the employee's protected status.

One of the central questions in a single-motive claim is how to define "because of." That term could mean anything from the employee's protected status being the sole cause of the adverse employment action to being merely a partial cause. In 1991, Congress amended Title VII to clarify that discrimination claims only require plaintiffs to establish that a protected trait was a "motivating factor" in an outcome. In contrast, the Supreme Court later interpreted Title VII's retaliation provision and the ADEA to require a plaintiff to establish "but for" cause.

The difference between a "but for" cause standard and a motivating factor standard may be less important after the Supreme Court's opinion in *Bostock v. Clayton County*, 590 U.S. 644 (2020). *Bostock* described "but for" cause as a "sweeping" standard, noted that events can have multiple "but for" causes, and stated that a reason can still be a "but for" cause even if it is not the primary reason for the outcome. Pre-*Bostock*, some courts misapplied "but for" cause, requiring the plaintiff to establish that her protected activity was "the" cause of an outcome, rather than a "but for" cause.

1. The Traditional Civil Single-Motive Case

In "direct evidence" disputes, the plaintiff bears the burden of convincing the factfinder that unlawful discrimination was a cause of an adverse employment action, and the defendant's role is to present evidence to counter the plaintiff's evidence. The causal burden varies by statute, as mentioned in the prior section. These cases typically involve strong evidence for the plaintiff, such as comments or written statements that directly show the employer's improper motivation. Recent Supreme Court precedent also suggests that very strong circumstantial evidence could also be sufficient for this basic type of claim.

Although the norm in other civil areas, this straightforward analysis is relatively rare under Title VII. One reason is that strong evidence of the employer's motive is often lacking in employment discrimination cases. More often, plaintiffs must rely on various types of circumstantial evidence to show the employer's motivation. A related reason is that courts have become so accustomed to using the Supreme Court's circumstantial case analysis—the *McDonnell Douglas* test—that they often apply the test even in cases with strong direct evidence of discrimination. In the end, this is not a major issue, as strong cases of discrimination fit easily under the *McDonnell Douglas* analysis.

2. The *McDonnell Douglas* Single-Motive Case

The difficulties in establishing the employer's motive can lead to significant problems for employees. Without strong evidence of motive, the employee must generally present a set of circumstantial evidence pointing to unlawful discrimination. But because an employee bears the burden of proof to show a discriminatory motive, circumstantial evidence may be inadequate to convince the factfinder that some other reason was not the cause.

As a result of this conundrum the Supreme Court established a three-part analysis in *McDonnell Douglas v. Green*, 411 U.S. 792 (1973). The Court in *McDonnell Douglas* noted that the analysis is not required in all cases, but it has become the de facto analysis for individual disparate treatment claims under Title VII. However, as noted below, some courts have abandoned the *McDonnell Douglas* framework in favor of a new mixed-motive analysis under § 703(m) of

Title VII. Additionally, a few circuits use a *McDonnell Douglas* framework that accommodates both single-motive and mixed-motive scenarios.

a. The Employee's Prima Facie Case

In the first part of the *McDonnell Douglas* analysis, the employee must establish what the Court called a prima facie case. However, unlike the burden shifting that occurs after most prima facie cases are established, the employee bears the burden of persuasion throughout the entire three-part *McDonnell Douglas* analysis. The primary purpose of the prima facie case is to filter out common, nondiscriminatory reasons for adverse employment actions, thereby leaving discrimination as a likely motive.

The prima facie requirements can vary depending on the situation, but the refusal to hire issue in *McDonnell Douglas* provides a good example. In that situation, the employee can meet their prima facie case by showing that (1) they belong to a class protected by Title VII; (2) they applied for and were qualified for a job that the employer was seeking to fill; (3) they were rejected; and (4) the employer chose someone else for the position or continued to seek applicants to fill it. Other cases, such as those involving termination, discipline, or failure to promote will differ slightly from the exact *McDonnell Douglas* elements. For instance, in a termination case, an employee would show that they were a member of a protected class, they were qualified (usually easy to meet for a job the plaintiff held), they were terminated, and the employer hired someone to replace them. Despite these fact-specific differences, the general obligations for an employee in all of the various disparate treatment prima facie cases is to show that they were a member of a protected class and faced some sort of negative consequence despite their qualifications or in a manner inconsistent with similarly situated individuals.

If the employee establishes these elements by a preponderance of the evidence, they have satisfied the prima facie case. Once the plaintiff establishes a prima facie case, a rebuttable presumption of discrimination arises.

In a so-called "reverse discrimination" case, an employee alleges discrimination against a majority or normally favored class. These cases are permitted under Title VII, and litigants use the same frameworks for proving discrimination as they do for other discrimination cases. *McDonald v. Santa Fe Train Transportation Co.*, 427 U.S. 273 (1976); *Ames v. Ohio Dep't of Youth Servs.*, 145 S. Ct. 1540 (2025).

b. The Employer's Legitimate, Nondiscriminatory Reason

Once the employee has established an inference of discrimination through their prima facie evidence, the employer has the burden to articulate some legitimate, nondiscriminatory reason for the negative action. In contrast to the employee's burden of both production and persuasion in establishing the prima facie case, the employer only has a lesser burden of production. To meet this burden, the employer need only have admissible evidence and does not bear the burden of persuading the factfinder that its stated reason is more likely true than not. *Texas Department of Community Affairs v. Burdine*, 450 U.S. 248 (1981).

This burden is quite low. As long as the reason is not unlawful under Title VII, and somewhat specific, it is considered "legitimate" and "nondiscriminatory," even if it appears to violate another statute. *Hazen Paper Co. v. Biggins*, 507 U.S. 604 (1993). The legitimate, nondiscriminatory reason also need not be plausible. Essentially, this stage of the analysis is intended merely to narrow the dispute by making the employer present its alternative explanation for the negative action. The employer's failure to present such a reason is typically fatal. If both parties meet their respective burdens at this stage, the analysis then moves to the real question in the case: does the factfinder believe that the reason for the negative employment action was discrimination or not?

c. Employee Ultimately Establishes Discrimination as Employer's Motive

Once the employer produces a legitimate, nondiscriminatory reason, the employee then must establish that discrimination caused the adverse employment action. That question is the focus of the third and final stage of the *McDonnell Douglas* analysis and is often the deciding factor in whether an employee can survive summary judgment.

Although there are many confusing aspects to this stage, the central focus is the employee's "ultimate burden of persuading the court [or jury] that [the employee] has been the victim of intentional discrimination." *Texas Department of Community Affairs v. Burdine*, 450 U.S. 248 (1981). The employee can meet this burden in several ways, including a traditional civil litigation strategy of producing enough evidence to convince the factfinder that the employee's explanation—discrimination—was the most likely cause of the adverse employment action. Another option is to show "pretext" by convincing the factfinder that the employer's stated legitimate, nondiscriminatory reason was not the real cause of the adverse employment action. That is, the employer's stated reason was mere "pretext" for a discriminatory motive.

Pretext is but one means for the employee to meet her ultimate burden, but it is so common that this part of the test is often referred to as the "pretext stage." Its popularity stems from the difficulty in producing enough non-pretext evidence to show discrimination. It is often easier to challenge the veracity of the employer's legitimate, nondiscriminatory reason; if done successfully, this showing of pretext can "merge" into the ultimate burden of showing discrimination. *Texas Department of Community Affairs v. Burdine*, 450 U.S. 248 (1981).

An employee has several options for establishing pretext. They can point to similarly situated employees—save for their membership in the employee's protected class—who were not treated in the same fashion. As discussed below, this "comparator" evidence has become increasingly important in litigation, although adequate comparators are not always readily available. The employee could also provide evidence of the employer's past practices, the employee's qualifications in relation to more favorably treated individuals, comments that suggest discrimination, changing explanations by the employer, the time between the adverse employment action and some type of protected activity, and statistics on the employer's workforce.

Successfully showing that the employer's stated reason was pretext can be enough for an employee to win his or her case or survive summary judgment, but is not necessarily enough. In a pair of decisions, the Supreme Court explored how pretext evidence alone affects the employee's ability to meet his or her ultimate burden.

On the one hand, showing pretext does not guarantee a win. Because there may be unstated, yet nondiscriminatory, reasons for an adverse employment action, establishing pretext alone does not mean that the employee should always win. *St. Mary's Honor Center v. Hicks*, 509 U.S. 502 (1993). For instance, an employer could cite poor job performance as a reason for terminating an employee. The employee may be able to show that this reason is pretext by establishing that their performance was equal to, or better than, other employees who were not terminated. The employee still does not deserve to win, however, if the factfinder believes that there was another nondiscriminatory reason for the termination—for instance, a personality conflict unrelated to the employee's protected status. Similarly, as the Supreme Court noted in *Reeves v. Sanderson Plumbing Products, Inc.*, 530 U.S. 133 (2000), the employee may not win when they barely establish pretext through weak evidence, but there also exists "abundant and uncontroverted independent evidence that no discrimination had occurred."

On the other hand, the Court in *Reeves* held that an employee whose evidence in the third stage focuses solely on establishing pretext can win on that evidence alone. Take the previous example, in which the employee has convinced the factfinder that job performance was a pretextual explanation for the termination. If there is no reason for the factfinder to believe that another motive was in play, the only remaining inference is that which was established by the employee's prima facie case—discrimination. A factfinder can use that inference of discrimination, in combination with the employer presenting only a pretextual explanation for the negative action, to conclude that discrimination was the true cause. The Supreme Court has held that several factors should be considered in determining whether an employee should win or survive summary judgment when pretext only was established, such as the strength of the employee's prima facie case, whether the evidence of pretext suggested a discriminatory motive or mendacity on the part of the employer, and any other evidence that might point to a nondiscriminatory motive.

B. The Mixed-Motive Theory

The single-motive theory of discrimination provides a straightforward view of the dispute: the adverse action was the result of discrimination or some legitimate factor. That view, however, is overly simplistic in most cases. Employment decisions are usually the result of numerous factors, some of which may be discriminatory and some of which may be legitimate. When one of the employer's motivations is unlawful under Title VII and another is lawful, a "mixed-motive" case exists.

The basic structure for a Title VII mixed-motive theory is relatively straightforward, although many complications exist below the surface. In the 1991 Civil Rights Act Amendments (CRA of 1991), Congress added § 703(m) to Title VII, which states that "an unlawful employment practice is established when the complaining party demonstrates that race, color, religion, sex, or national origin was a motivating factor for any employment practice, even though other factors also motivated the practice." Moreover, the CRA of 1991 added § 706(g)(2)(B), which provided a partial defense to § 703(m) liability. Under this defense, if the employer demonstrates that it "would have taken the same action in the absence of the impermissible motivating factor," only limited injunctive relief, attorney's fees, and litigation costs may be awarded—no damages, reinstatement, instatement, or promotions are permitted. A full understanding of those sections, however, requires knowledge of their development.

In *Price Waterhouse v. Hopkins*, 490 U.S. 228 (1989), a majority of Justices recognized that a plaintiff could prevail on a Title VII claim if legitimate and discriminatory reasons both caused a negative outcome. Yet, the Court's approach to that claim was fractured. A plurality of Justices, in an opinion written by Justice Brennan, concluded that an employee could establish a presumption of liability under Title VII by showing that discrimination was a "motivating factor" in the challenged adverse employment action. To make that showing, an employee could use either circumstantial or direct evidence. Moreover, if an employee proved that discrimination was a motivating factor, the employer would have an opportunity to establish an affirmative defense by showing that it would have made the same action absent the discrimination. If successful, the employer would escape all liability.

Justice O'Connor wrote a concurring opinion in *Price Waterhouse* and, because it was narrower than the plurality opinion, the concurrence became the standard mixed-motive analysis in the vast majority of district and appellate courts. Under Justice O'Connor's analysis, an employee could establish a mixed-motive Title VII case with less than but-for causation, but only in limited circumstances. She concluded that an employee could establish a presumption of liability by showing—with direct evidence—that discrimination played a "substantial role" in the adverse employment action. If successful, Justice O'Connor would permit the employer to escape liability by proving the same affirmative defense as the plurality. In short, the plurality's standard for an employee's case required proof by circumstantial or direct evidence that discrimination was a motivating factor, while Justice O'Connor required direct evidence showing that discrimination was a substantial factor. Both analyses recognized the "would have done the same thing" affirmative defense for the employer.

Two years after *Price Waterhouse*, Congress amended Title VII in multiple areas, including the mixed-motive analysis, through the CRA of 1991. Congress added § 703(m), which followed Justice Brennan's plurality decision by mandating that an employee can prove discrimination under Title VII by showing that discrimination was a "motivating factor" for an employment action, even if other factors contributed. Yet, the CRA of 1991 was silent on another disagreement between Justice Brennan and Justice O'Connor's decisions: whether the employee needed direct evidence to establish their mixed-motive burden. Subsequently, in *Desert Palace, Inc. v. Costa*, 539 U.S. 90 (2003), the Supreme Court resolved that issue by holding that congressional silence on that question meant that the default evidentiary standard, which allows for both direct and circumstantial evidence, applied. Thus, under Title VII—there are questions about *Desert Palace*'s application to the ADA and ADEA (see Chapters 13 and 14)—an employee can use direct or circumstantial evidence to show that discrimination was a motivating factor.

In the CRA of 1991, Congress also addressed the employer's affirmative defense, taking a different approach than the Court. Rather than providing a true affirmative defense—a defense to all liability—§ 706(g)(2)(B) created only a quasi-defense for employers. Under that section, if an employer can prove that it would have taken the same action absent the discriminatory motive, it is still liable for violating Title VII. However, the available damages are curtailed. In particular, an employer who satisfies its affirmative defense is not liable for any monetary damages and is instead subject only to certain types of injunctions, attorney's fees, and litigation costs.

Although clarifying the disparity in the Court's opinions, § 703(m) has spawned a new wave of confusion. Because § 703(m) does not explicitly limit itself to mixed-motive cases, courts have struggled to determine whether the motivating factor analysis should also apply to single-motive claims or whether the *McDonnell Douglas* analysis should have any application to mixed-motive claims. Some courts have interpreted that ambiguity as meaning that the standard in all disparate treatment claims is the mixed-motive analysis. Other courts, however, have pointed to the fact that Congress did not eliminate § 703(a)(1) and have held that § 703(m) applies only to mixed-motive cases. Still other courts have sought some sort of middle ground, often using a modified *McDonnell Douglas*/motivating-factor analysis. The Supreme Court in *Desert Palace* expressly refused to answer this split. A practitioner, therefore, must be aware of a given jurisdiction's approach to this issue.

C. Evidentiary Issues in Individual Disparate Treatment Cases

Underlying all individual disparate treatment cases is the need to establish whether the protected trait caused the negative outcome. Proving causation is often difficult and can draw on a wide range of evidence. Some of the most common types of evidence include how other employees or applicants were treated, comments or documents indicating discrimination, timing of comments to the employment action, the employer's general policies or practices, the employer's changing explanations, and statistics on the workplace demographics. Many other types of evidence—both direct and circumstantial—may be relevant, as this list is not exclusive. Evidence is also highly contextual, and certain facts may appear more discriminatory in certain situations than others, such as whether the term "boy" is evidence of racial animus. *Ash v. Tyson Foods*, 546 U.S. 454 (2006). Other types of evidence, however, have posed special concern in employment discrimination cases. Discussion of those evidentiary issues follows.

1. Comparator Evidence

One of the most popular types of evidence is the comparison of the plaintiff to other employees or applicants who are similar in most respects, except for membership in a protected class. This "comparator" evidence has become increasingly important in Title VII cases and is often expected by many courts, as it can provide strong inferential evidence of a discriminatory motive or lack of one. *McDonald v. Santa Fe Train Transportation Co.*, 427 U.S. 273 (1976). Comparator evidence can be used by either the employee or employer, depending on the situation.

The strength of comparator evidence is driven by context, particularly the degree of similarity between the plaintiff and comparator individuals. In *Ash v. Tyson Foods*, 546 U.S. 454 (2006), the 11th Circuit rejected the plaintiffs' introduction of pretext evidence allegedly showing that they were equally if not more qualified for a promotion than the two employees of a different race who got the jobs. The 11th Circuit, citing earlier circuit precedent, held that "[p]retext can be established through comparing qualifications only when 'the disparity in qualifications is so apparent as virtually to jump off the page and slap you in the face.'" The Supreme Court rejected the "slap you in the face" rule, finding it "unhelpful and imprecise." Although the Court declined to set a standard for this type of comparator evidence, it seemed to approve the approaches of other courts, which would accept qualification comparisons when the disparities are so weighty and significant that no reasonable person could have selected the chosen candidate over the plaintiff. If the plaintiff's qualifications were "clearly superior" to the chosen candidate, a reasonable factfinder would have found the plaintiff to be "significantly better qualified," especially when superior qualifications are combined with other evidence.

2. "Me Too" Evidence

One type of evidence that could be considered a subset of the comparator situation is "me too" evidence. This refers to evidence of employees other than the plaintiff that allege similar discriminatory treatment. Such evidence is generally uncontroversial if these other employees were subjected to an employment action by the same decisionmaker as the plaintiff. More controversial is evidence from employees who were subject to actions of a different decisionmaker.

The federal appellate and district courts had been split on the proper approach to this situation, with some never allowing such evidence and others permitting it in many circumstances. In 2008, the Supreme Court appeared to resolve the issue in *Sprint/United Management Co. v. Mendelsohn*, 552 U.S. 379 (2008). Although it was technically dicta, the Court suggested that "me too" evidence involving different decisionmakers is not per se inadmissible or admissible. Instead, admissibility of such evidence should be based on the trial court's determination of the evidence's relevance and prejudice against the employer.

3. Cat's Paw Evidence

The unhelpfully termed "cat's paw" theory—named after an Aesop's fable in which a monkey manipulates a cat to sacrifice its paws to collect roasting chestnuts from a fire—refers to a situation in which the employee with a discriminatory motive was not the ultimate decisionmaker. Usually, evidence of motive must focus on the ultimate decisionmaker; however, when another individual influenced the decision to engage in an employment action, evidence of that individual's motive may also be relevant.

In a case involving a different statute, the Court formally recognized cat's paw liability. In *Staub v. Proctor Hospital*, 562 U.S. 411, 423 (2011), the Court held that under the Uniformed Services Employment and Reemployment Rights Act (USERRA)—an employment law that protects against military-based discrimination—cat's paw liability exists if a "supervisor performs an act motivated by antimilitary animus that is *intended* by the supervisor to cause an adverse employment action, and ... that act is a proximate cause of the ultimate employment action...." Given that both USERRA and Title VII have explicit "motivating factor" causation, courts have applied *Staub* analysis to cat's paw liability claims in Title VII disparate treatment cases. *See, e.g.*, *Zamora v. City of Houston*, 798 F.3d 326 (5th Cir. 2015).

4. Same Decisionmaker Evidence

Employers often cite the identity of the decisionmaker to defend against an allegation of discriminatory conduct. Typically, they do so with a "same decisionmaker" defense—meaning that the decisionmaker accused of making the adverse employment action was the same decisionmaker who hired, promoted, or otherwise assisted the employee in some manner. Such evidence is not sufficient on its own to reject a discrimination claim, as earlier positive treatment does not mean that the decisionmaker did not act in a discriminatory fashion at a later date. Indeed, the decisionmaker may have harbored bias during the initial decision, for instance by hiring an individual with a heightened expectation of performance because of the employee's protected characteristic. That the employee failed to meet that expectation and faced an adverse employment action as a result should not shield the employer from liability simply because the same decisionmaker was involved. However, same decisionmaker evidence can be relevant, as it may undermine claims that a decisionmaker harbors certain types of animus.

A related evidentiary defense by employers is to note that the decisionmaker was a member of the same protected class as the employee. This evidence, although not completely irrelevant, generally receives even less credence than the previous situation. Courts have consistently noted that members of a certain class can still discriminate against other members of that class. For example, a senior woman in a male-dominated workforce may expect more from junior women and hold them to a higher standard. The facts of a given case will determine how much, if any weight, this evidence deserves, but it will never serve as an absolute defense for the employer.

5. After-Acquired Evidence

Another type of evidence raised by employers on occasion involves a situation in which, following a Title VII challenge to an adverse employment action, an employer discovers misconduct by the employee (this topic is also covered as a remedial issue in Chapter 5). This situation raises two major issues. First, even if the misconduct might normally have justified the adverse employment action, the employer was unaware of the misconduct at the time it made the decision, thereby suggesting that this so-called "after-acquired evidence" should not play a role in the case. Second, if the employee engaged in misconduct that warrants termination or some other form of discipline, it might be viewed as unfair to the employer to force it to reinstate the employee or otherwise ignore that misconduct.

The Supreme Court ultimately settled this issue, essentially charting a middle course. In *McKennon v. Nashville Banner Publishing Co.*, 513 U.S. 352 (1995), an employee—correctly anticipating that she would be terminated because of her age—improperly copied confidential records as protection. This copying, which the employer argued justified termination under its policies, came to light only during litigation of the employee's age discrimination claim. The Supreme Court held that this after-acquired evidence could not absolve the employer of liability for violating the ADEA. However, the Court also held that the employer should not have to reinstate an employee who committed terminable misconduct or pay that employee frontpay. The Court's approach to backpay was more complex. Under *McKennon*, an employer will have to pay backpay from the time of the adverse employment action, but that backpay obligation ends once the employer becomes aware of the after-acquired evidence.

To take advantage of the after-acquired evidence rule, the employer must establish that the misconduct actually justified termination under either its previously established policies or because the misconduct was serious enough that any reasonable employer would terminate an employee in that situation. If the employer can meet this burden, it may take advantage of the after-acquired evidence rule, no matter when it was discovered—including during litigation, as was the case in *McKennon*. This rule gives employers an incentive to scour records of employees who have filed employment discrimination suits or who might do so. Discrepancies in resumes are a particularly fruitful ground of investigation, as they provide information that can be objectively confirmed and are viewed as serious by most courts.

D. Employer Defenses in Individual Disparate Treatment Cases

As noted, an employer can limit its liability though the mixed-motive affirmative defense and through the use of after-acquired evidence of misconduct. However, neither of these is a true affirmative defense—that is, a defense that eliminates liability under Title VII. Other defenses, however, do provide full immunity, such as the less common defense that applies when an American employee works for an American employer in a foreign country and compliance with Title VII would violate the foreign country's laws. Two more commonly used defenses are the bona fide occupational qualification defense (BFOQ) and the affirmative action defense, both of which permit the employer to discriminate without violating Title VII.

1. Bona Fide Occupational Qualification Defense

Under § 703(e) of Title VII, an employer can discriminate on the basis of religion, sex, or national origin where those characteristics are "a bona fide occupational qualification reasonably necessary to the normal operation of that particular business or enterprise." The "BFOQ" defense does not extend to race or color discrimination.

The Supreme Court has repeatedly emphasized that the BFOQ defense should be interpreted narrowly. For instance, in *UAW v. Johnson Controls, Inc.*, 499 U.S. 487 (1991), the Court held that an employer could not forbid women capable of becoming pregnant from working in a job that presented the risk of birth defects; the Court reasoned that concern for the health of a fetus was not related to "the normal operation of that particular business or enterprise" because such women could perform the job as well as men.

Johnson Controls also stressed that a BFOQ defense must focus on the essence or core mission of the employer. An earlier example of this test was the district court decision in *Wilson v. Southwest Airlines Co.*, 517 F. Supp. 292 (N.D. Tex. 1981), in which a male challenged the airline employer's policy of hiring only women for jobs with customer contact. Despite evidence that this policy helped the employer's business, the court rejected the BFOQ defense because being a woman was not necessary to the employer's core business: safely transporting passengers.

The BFOQ defense can be successful in some instances. One such set of circumstances is an employer in the sex entertainment business, where the sex of employees is central. The privacy concerns of customers—for instance, a female nursing home resident who wants only a female nurse—might also justify certain types of discrimination. Moreover, safety issues can also provide a defense, such as a ban against female prison guards in particularly dangerous parts of an all-male prison. *Dothard v. Rawlinson*, 433 U.S. 321 (1977).

The BFOQ defense can also conflict with the typical rule that discrimination claims are to focus on each individual plaintiff, rather than the characteristics of their class. This is particularly true when an employer wants to use a protected characteristic as a proxy for a valid safety concern. For instance, in *Western Airlines v. Criswell*, 472 U.S. 400 (1985) (also discussed in Chapter 13 on ADEA issues), the Supreme Court addressed an airline employer's rule that required flight engineers to retire once they turned 60 years old. The rule was justified as being needed for the safety of passengers, as the flight engineer would be responsible for flying the plane if the pilots were incapacitated. The problem was that some individuals over 60 are perfectly healthy, even though others may be more at risk for a health emergency.

In *Criswell*, the Supreme Court recognized the possibility of a BFOQ proxy defense if serious safety issues are at stake. Relying on the standard set by two 5th Circuit cases—*Usery v. Tamiami Trail Tours, Inc.*, 531 F.2d 224 (5th Cir. 1976), and *Weeks v. Southern Bell Telephone & Telegraph Co.*, 408 F.2d 228 (5th Cir. 1969)—the Court held that an employer could use age (or religion, sex, and national origin under Title VII) as a proxy for a safety-related business need under two conditions: (1) the employer can show that it had reasonable cause to believe, and that there is a factual basis for believing, that all or substantially all members of a class would be unable to perform safely and efficiently the necessary job duties; or (2) the employer can show that it is "impossible or highly impractical" to make individual assessments of employees in a protected class. The employer bears the burden of proving one of these conditions and, as the failure of the employer's evidence in *Criswell* demonstrates, it is not an easy burden to meet.

2. Voluntary Affirmative Action Plan Defense

Another important defense against a charge of intentional discrimination is to argue that the adverse employment action occurred as part of a valid affirmative action plan. Affirmative action plans can be used as a defense in both Title VII cases and constitutional equal protection cases. It should be noted that this area is in flux after the Supreme Court's opinion in *Students for Fair*

Admissions, Inc. v. President & Fellows of Harvard College, 600 U.S. 181 (2023). There, the Supreme Court indicated that race-based decisions were allowable under the Equal Protection Clause of the Constitution, but only "within the confines of narrow restrictions." The Court held the admissions plans of Harvard and the University of North Carolina did not meet the requirements of strict scrutiny. It is unclear what impact this case will have in the Title VII context. The constitutional law cases are described in more detail in Chapter 14. Moreover, unlike with a true affirmative defense, the employer only has the burden of production to put an affirmative action plan in play. That said, courts typically engage in searching reviews of affirmative action plans.

The term "affirmative action" comes from § 706(g) of Title VII, which provides district courts with the power to order certain remedies, including "such affirmative action as may be appropriate." Although this provision refers to judicial remedies, the term has expanded in general usage to include even voluntary actions taken by employers to address problems of discrimination and inequity in the workplace. Affirmative action plans have generated much controversy, but the Supreme Court has approved certain types of plans since the early days of Title VII. That said, the current Justices have exhibited increasing hostility to affirmative action goals. This fact, in addition to a dearth of recent Supreme Court affirmative action cases in the employment context, means that the analysis could change in the near future. Until that happens, however, the Court's current jurisprudence provides some guidance for employers seeking to implement affirmative action measures.

The basic affirmative analysis under Title VII was explained in *Johnson v. Transportation Agency, Santa Clara County*, 480 U.S. 616 (1987), and consists of two main prongs. Much like—although not identical to—the "compelling government interest" and "narrowly tailored" prongs of the constitutional equal protection analysis (discussed in Chapter 14), a valid affirmative action plan in a Title VII action must (1) intend to eliminate a "manifest imbalance" in the workplace, and (2) not "unnecessarily trammel" the interests of non-minority employees. Congress appeared to approve of this test in the CRA of 1991 by stating that the amendments should not be construed to affect affirmative action plans that were legal at the time.

The manifest imbalance prong essentially asks "why" the employer is trying to implement affirmative action measures. A valid answer to "why?" is that there is an underrepresentation of a certain protected class in traditionally segregated jobs. This imbalance is established by comparing the numbers of a class in the workforce to the numbers in the relevant labor pool or general population for lower-skilled jobs. *United Steelworkers of America v. Weber*, 433 U.S. 193 (1979). This prong focuses primarily on statistical disparities and need not have as much evidence as would be required for a prima facie pattern or practice case, as will be discussed in Chapter 7.

Even if there is a manifest imbalance, an affirmative action plan must not unnecessarily trammel the interests of nonminority employees. In other words, even if the employer can successfully argue "why" it needs an affirmative action plan, it must still justify "what" the plan does. This question is crucial, because the Court has strongly emphasized that affirmative action plans must be narrowly targeted to their justification and must be as limited as possible to minimize the burden on majority employees.

Important factors in determining whether the plan itself is valid include the need for a plan to be temporary, to attempt to achieve a balance rather than maintain one, to avoid strict quotas, to avoid laying off current employees, and to have flexibility in case conditions change or the goals become unachievable.

The Supreme Court has become increasingly skeptical of affirmative action in the higher education context. In *Students for Fair Admissions, Inc. v. President & Fellows of Harvard College*, 600 U.S. 181 (2023), the Court invalidated college admissions plans that took race into account as one factor in a multi-factor admissions process. The Court found that the reasons articulated by the universities were not "sufficiently coherent" for strict scrutiny because courts could not measure the goals, determine when they had been met, or establish a logical end point. It is unclear how this case applies in the employment discrimination context. That context traditionally has not relied on a diversity rationale as the basis for affirmative action.

CHECKPOINTS

- Title VII prohibits negative employment actions that occur "because of" an employee's protected status.
- Most single-motive cases are analyzed under the *McDonnell Douglas* analysis: (1) employee's prima facie case; (2) employer's articulated legitimate nondiscriminatory reason; and (3) employee's proof that discrimination caused a negative employment action, often through evidence of pretext.

- Section 703(m), added by the CRA of 1991, establishes a Title VII claim when an employee's protected status is a "motivating factor" in an employment action.
- If an employee proves that discrimination was a motivating factor, the employer violates § 703(m), but can eliminate monetary relief by proving that it would have made the same decision absent the discriminatory motive.
- All Title VII disparate treatment cases permit circumstantial and direct evidence.
- Comparator evidence—comparing treatment of a similarly situated employee to the plaintiff—is commonly used by both employees and employers.
- "Me too" evidence of other employees who faced similar discrimination is admissible, even where different decisionmakers are involved, if a court determines that its probative value outweighs possible prejudice to the employer.
- Plaintiffs may also use cat's paw evidence, which is evidence of discriminatory intent by an employee who lacked official authority to make the employment action at issue, but influenced that action.
- Evidence that the decisionmaker hired the plaintiff or is a member of the same protected class is admissible, but is not necessarily fatal to the plaintiff's case.
- After-acquired evidence of employee misconduct cannot eliminate the employer's liability for disparate treatment discrimination, but bars reinstatement and stops backpay on the date that the employer learned of the misconduct.
- Employers avoid all Title VII liability if they can prove that their discrimination based on sex, religion, or national origin was a "bona fide occupational qualification" that was essential to their core business operations.
- Under existing case law, employers avoid liability in all classes of disparate treatment cases if they act pursuant to affirmative action plans that addressed a manifest imbalance in the workplace and did not unnecessarily trammel the interests of non-minorities. However, this area of law is in a state of flux given recent Supreme Court opinions in the education context.

CHAPTER 7

Title VII Systemic Disparate Treatment Claims

ROADMAP

- Introducing systemic disparate treatment cases
- Establishing systemic, or "pattern or practice," disparate treatment
- Determining remedies for pattern or practice cases

Although the majority of Title VII cases deal with individual plaintiffs, at times an employer's discriminatory policies are so pervasive that they can result in what is called a pattern or practice of discrimination. These pattern or practice cases can be filed by employees or by the EEOC.

Pattern or practice cases involve some of the most serious forms of discrimination, as they involve employers in which discrimination is a regular part of the business operations. These cases are not easy to win, however; plaintiffs must often provide both evidence of discriminatory motive and statistical proof confirming widespread discrimination.

A. Systemic Disparate Treatment Analysis

1. Establishing a Pattern or Practice of Discrimination

The Supreme Court set forth the pattern or practice analysis in *International Brotherhood of Teamsters v. United States*, 431 U.S. 324 (1977). That case involved an employer that prevented Black and Spanish surname truck drivers from attaining higher-paying, long-distance hauling jobs. The Court stressed that to make out a pattern or practice case, plaintiffs must show more than isolated acts of discrimination. Instead, there must be proof that discrimination was a repeated and routine practice.

a. Statistical Evidence

To make out such a pattern or practice case, plaintiffs typically begin with statistical evidence of a disparity in the workforce. The aim is to demonstrate that the employer's workforce has a disproportionately low number of a certain class of workers. Theoretically, the plaintiffs can rely solely on statistics to establish a pattern or practice of discrimination if the disparity is particularly severe, but in reality, other proof of discrimination is required. Indeed, in *Wal-Mart Stores, Inc. v. Dukes*, 564 U.S. 338 (2011)—which was a pattern or practice case in which the Supreme Court denied class certification—the Court emphasized the need to supplement statistics with strong non-statistical evidence of discrimination.

The key issue is often determining the comparison group. The Supreme Court has focused on what it calls the "relevant labor market," which is the group that is closest in geography, skill-level, and interest to the employer's workforce. In some circumstances, especially when the employees at issue are low-skilled, general population numbers may be used as the relevant labor market. In contrast, higher-skilled jobs typically require a pool of workers with the necessary level of training or a group likely to achieve such training. Many employers argue that their applicant pool should serve as the comparator, as it represents a group that is interested in working for the employer and presumably holds the necessary qualifications. Although a court may occasionally agree, in most instances the applicant pool can be misleading when there are allegations of widespread discrimination because individuals may avoid applying for jobs with an employer that is known to discriminate against people in the same protected class.

Once the relevant labor market is determined, the next question is how much of a disparity must exist to create a presumption of discrimination. This concept is referred to as a "statistically significant" disparity. Very basically, statistical significance refers to disparities so large that they are unlikely to be the result of chance. Statisticians begin this analysis by establishing the variance that is expected in a given pool of employees. For example, various samples of low-skilled employees from an urban area would result in different numbers of Black and white individuals simply by chance (much like flipping a coin 100 times is likely to result in a range of outcomes, not 50 heads and 50 tails each time). The central question is how close is the racial (or other class) makeup of the employer's workforce to this expected variation. "Statistical significance" defines the point at which the number found in the employer's workforce is so different from the expected variance in the comparison pool that, barring any other explanation, discrimination is presumed. Although there is no set rule for statistical significance, statisticians usually deem a result that shows a 0%–5% chance that the employer's numbers could exist absent discrimination as statistically significant (this is referred to as a statistically significant "p-value" or showing a disparity that is two to three standard deviations from the expected outcome).

Once the plaintiff has presented evidence of a statistically significant disparity, an employer can then defend itself against the plaintiffs' statistics by challenging the data, the model, or the chosen comparator group; by providing a different statistical analysis; or by explaining the disparity in a way that is not taken into account by the plaintiffs' statistics. Statistical significance can be affected by numerous factors, such as the size of the pools being compared and level of variance in those pools. Moreover, modern statistics use a complicated model—called regression analysis—to take into account numerous nondiscriminatory factors that could influence the numbers, such as employees' education or skill level. These analyses are so complicated that attorneys usually hire statistical experts to create regression models and to help critique the other side's expert. The fact that experts are required also explains why these cases are expensive and time-consuming to litigate.

A widely cited example of these issues is *Hazelwood School District v. United States*, 433 U.S. 299 (1977), in which the Court addressed the relevant labor market for school teachers in a suburb of St. Louis. The school district had a long history of discrimination prior to its coverage under Title VII in 1972. The government later brought a pattern or practice case, arguing that the school district's practices maintained the widespread discrimination. A major issue in the case was whether the statistical evidence established a pattern or practice of discrimination.

The government pointed to the 1.4% and 1.8% of Black teachers working in the school district during 1972 and 1973, respectively. The argument was that these numbers were so low that they showed systemic discrimination, but the question was "low compared to what?" The government compared the school district's numbers to the entire St. Louis area, in which 15.4% of teachers were Black—a comparison that was well above the threshold for statistical significance. The school district objected to this comparison, however, noting that the St. Louis City district had engaged in an aggressive affirmative action plan, which included a goal of 50% Black teachers, that went beyond what Title VII required. If the city was excluded, the number of Black teachers in the area was 5.7%. This number was still a statistically significant disparity in comparison to the school district's work force in 1972 and 1973, but the district also argued that the work force numbers were not the appropriate starting point. In its decision, the Court emphasized that the proper comparison for the number of Black teachers in the school district was to the relevant labor market not, as the district court used, the number of Black students. However, it emphasized that it was not necessarily appropriate to use the 1.4% and 1.8% work force numbers because they presumably captured discrimination that occurred before the school district was covered by Title VII. Supporting that consideration was the fact that 3.7% of all teachers hired by the school district in 1972 and 1973 were Black. Using hiring, rather than the total work force, as the starting point made the determination of the relevant labor market crucial because the difference between 3.7% and 5.7% is not statistically significant, while the difference between 3.7% and 15.4% is. Thus, the Court remanded the case to determine whether the relevant labor pool should include St. Louis City and instructed the district court to consider factors such as where the employer's qualified job applicants typically came from, how past discrimination might have affected different pools of workers, how different recruitment strategies by other employers may have affected these pools, preferences of teachers in the area, and the experiences of nearby employers.

Other factors may be relevant to determining the relevant labor pool depending on the case. Take, for instance, the evidence in *EEOC v. Olson's Dairy Queens, Inc.*, 989 F.2d 185 (5th Cir. 1993), a case involving an allegation of a pattern of racial hiring. In *Olson's*, the circuit court criticized several aspects of the district court's handling of statistical evidence. First, the court held that it was inappropriate to assume that individuals would only be willing to travel a few blocks to seek work, especially given actual applications from people who lived much farther away. Second, the court held that the government's "external availability" statistics presented in the case were appropriate. That evidence compared the percentage of Black employees at the employer's restaurants to the higher percentage of Black food service workers in the relevant metropolitan area who lived within a normal commuting distance of one of the employer's restaurants. Third, the court approved the government's "applicant flow data," which compared the percentage of applications to the employer who were Black to the lower percentage of Black employees actually hired by the employer. Fourth, the court rejected the employer's evidence, which was inappropriately based on only one of the employer's restaurants and only one point in time, and improperly attempted to describe the relevant labor market based on the employer's own work force. The court stressed that this comparison was "wholly at odds with the fundamental premise of employment discrimination law. In order to test for discriminatory hiring, we evaluate an employer's work force in terms of the available labor pool, not the other way around."

b. Evidence of Intentional Discrimination

Although plaintiffs can arguably establish a presumption of systemic disparate treatment based on statistics alone, virtually all cases will supplement the statistics with evidence of various acts of intentional discrimination. This should be no surprise. Given that a systemic case must prove that discrimination is a pattern or practice throughout the business, examples of such discrimination are expected. Moreover, the expectation of this type of anecdotal evidence is tied to the statistical evidence; the lower the statistical disparity, the more alternate evidence will be needed.

The types of evidence that can be used in pattern or practice cases are the same as the types of evidence used in individual disparate treatment claims, including discriminatory comments or documents, comparator evidence, recruiting strategies, and changing explanations. In addition, examples of credible individual disparate treatment claims—such as employees of a certain race being passed over for promotions—are often featured in systemic cases. *International Brotherhood of Teamsters v. United States*, 431 U.S. 324 (1977). As the number of instances of individual discrimination increases, or the seriousness of those instances grow, the likelihood that the plaintiffs will successfully establish a pattern or practice of discrimination also increases.

B. Determining Remedies for Systemic Discrimination

If the plaintiffs establish a presumption that a pattern or practice of discrimination exists and the employer is unable to rebut that presumption, the employer is liable for systemic disparate treatment. Once the liability stage is completed (sometimes referred to as Stage 1, as described in Chapter 5's discussion on class relief), the case moves to a second, remedial phase (Stage 2). In this remedial phase, the court must determine two sets of issues. First, the court must decide whether to order certain general injunctive or equitable remedies, such as enjoining a discriminatory hiring system or implementing an affirmative action plan. Second, the court must determine the remedies appropriate for each individual plaintiff—a group that includes rejected applicants or individuals who would have applied absent the discrimination. Systemic discrimination plaintiffs may receive the same remedies as individual disparate treatment plaintiffs, such as reinstatement, backpay, compensatory and punitive damages, and seniority credit.

The question, however, is whether a given individual deserves these remedies. The starting point for determining individual remedies is that the employer has been held liable for systemic discrimination; thus, there is no dispute over motive at this phase. Instead, the question is whether an individual was actually a victim of the discrimination. The presumption is that every member of the class was a victim, and it is the employer's burden to rebut that presumption. Typically, the employer in these situations will argue that certain individuals would not have gotten a job in question because they were not qualified, they engaged in misconduct, or some other valid reason. Even if there are no disqualifications, there can also be questions about whether a given individual was interested in a certain job. This issue can be difficult to determine, especially when widespread discrimination dissuaded applications from individuals who might have been interested. However, as long as an individual can provide some evidence that they were interested in the job—such as statements of interest made at the time to family or friends—the individual will be entitled to relief. Because of the complexities involved in cases with an often large number of plaintiffs (recall the Chapter 4 discussion on class actions under Rule 23), the parties will frequently settle prior to the remedial phase.

CHECKPOINTS

- Systemic disparate treatment requires evidence that discrimination was a widespread "pattern or practice" in the employer's workplace.
- Plaintiffs generally establish systemic disparate treatment with a combination of statistical evidence and anecdotal evidence of intentional discrimination.
- Questions surrounding statistical evidence center on the appropriate comparison "relevant labor pool" and statistical techniques, like standard deviations or regression analysis.
- Evidence of intentional discrimination mirrors the evidence used in individual disparate treatment claims, but on a much broader level.
- After a systemic disparate treatment case is established, the case goes to a remedial phase to determine both employer-wide relief and remedies for individual plaintiffs.
- Individual plaintiffs are presumed to be victims of systemic disparate treatment unless the employer can rebut the presumption by showing, for example, that an individual would not have gotten a job in question absent discrimination or was not interested in the job.

CHAPTER 8

Title VII Disparate Impact Claims

ROADMAP

- Introducing disparate impact discrimination
- The history of the disparate impact analysis since *Griggs*
- *Wards Cove* and the narrowing of disparate impact
- The expansion of disparate impact under the Civil Rights Act of 1991
- *Ricci* and the future of disparate impact

A. Introduction to Disparate Impact Discrimination

The focus of a disparate treatment case is proof that the employer acted because of a protected trait. Courts often use the words *intentional discrimination* to describe disparate treatment. Title VII has another way to prove discrimination. In a "disparate impact" case, the central question turns on whether an employment action has a discriminatory *impact* or effect. If so, given certain conditions, the employer will violate Title VII even though it may not have had a discriminatory motive. The disparate impact theory of discrimination has existed for decades, but still remains controversial. Indeed, despite Congress having codified the theory in the Civil Rights Act of 1991 (CRA of 1991), in what is now § 703(c) of Title VII, at least one Supreme Court Justice has questioned whether it passes constitutional muster. *Ricci v. DeStefano*, 557 U.S. 557 (2009) (Scalia, J., concurring). The controversy over holding an employer liable for a Title VII violation despite a lack of discriminatory motive is significant, as it informs much of the development of the disparate impact theory, particularly the back-and-forth between the Supreme Court and Congress. In addition, one must be aware of the history of the disparate impact theory to understand fully the current state of the law and how it may develop in the future.

B. The History of Disparate Impact Discrimination

1. The Supreme Court Establishes the Basic Disparate Impact Analysis

The Supreme Court first recognized the disparate impact theory under Title VII in the case of *Griggs v. Duke Power Co.*, 401 U.S. 424 (1971). The facts of *Griggs* provide an excellent example of the policy behind the disparate impact theory, which the Court described as prohibiting employment policies that are "fair in form, but discriminatory in practice."

The North Carolina plant in *Griggs* was divided into five departments, with Black employees working in a single, lower-paying department as the result of years of intentional discrimination before passage of Title VII. After Title VII was enacted, the employer no longer directly barred Black employees from the other departments, but created a rule requiring a high-school diploma to transfer out of the lower-paying department. White employees without a high-school diploma who were in other departments before the rule were grandfathered and continued to perform well. Later, the employer adopted a new rule that would allow an employee to transfer to a higher-paying department if they passed two general aptitude tests. Despite the employer's history of intentional discrimination, the high-school diploma and test requirements were treated as being neutral for purposes of litigation. That is, those requirements were not considered to be motivated by discrimination. This factual premise is significant, as it defines the difference between disparate treatment and disparate impact cases. If there was evidence establishing that the employer used those requirements with the intent to discriminate, *Griggs* would have been a disparate treatment case. Absent that evidence, the requirements were viewed as facially nondiscriminatory, with the only grounds for a violation of Title VII being their discriminatory *impact*.

The plaintiffs had ample evidence of a discriminatory impact. Black individuals in Jim Crow North Carolina had a substantially lower level of schooling than whites; thus, Black employees' ability to satisfy either the high-school diploma or aptitude test requirements was much lower than their white counterparts. As a result, Black employees were still largely segregated in the lower paying department. The question for the Supreme Court was whether this de facto segregation violated Title VII.

One rejected theory for finding a Title VII violation was that the requirements perpetuated past discrimination. Although true, the district and appellate courts in *Griggs* stressed that the employer's past discrimination was legal at the time and, because the employer did not intentionally discriminate after the enactment of Title VII, there was no violation. The Court reversed, however, on another theory—that the requirements created a disparate impact on Black employees at the company.

The starting point for the disparate impact theory was getting over the hurdle that no intent to discriminate could be established. To address this, the Court looked to § 703(a)(2) of Title VII. Under § 703(a)(2), it is unlawful for an employer "to limit, segregate, or classify his employees ... in any way which would deprive or tend to deprive any individual of employment opportunities or otherwise adversely affect his status as an employee" because of the employee's protected class (similar language exists under the ADA and ADEA, as discussed in Chapters 12 and 13, respectively). The Court held that this section addressed the discriminatory consequences of employment actions, not the motivation behind them. Thus, practices that were nondiscriminatory on their face and that were not motivated by a discriminatory intent could still violate Title VII. According to the Court, the policy behind this theory of discrimination was that Title VII was intended to remove "artificial, arbitrary, and unnecessary" barriers to employment that have the effect of discriminating based on a protected status. The concept of "unnecessary" barriers fed into what the Court described as the touchstone for disparate impact cases: business necessity. Under *Griggs*, a neutral policy with a discriminatory effect would be unlawful unless the employer could show that it was necessary for its business. This requirement was limited to requirements that had a "demonstrable" or "manifest" relationship to job performance and overall business operations.

The *Griggs* employer came up short in its ability to demonstrate business and job-related reasons, as it lacked evidence to defend its practices. Notably, white employees who had been grandfathered—that is, employees who lacked a high-school diploma or did not pass the tests—were working in other departments and performing well. Thus, the employer could not argue that either requirement was needed to predict good job performance and thus was liable for violating Title VII.

Accordingly, there are two main steps to the basic *Griggs* disparate impact analysis: (1) the employee tries to demonstrate a disparate impact; and (2) if the employee is successful, the employer can try to show that the facially neutral practice with the discriminatory effect was a business necessity and had a manifest relationship to job performance. Later, an additional step was added: (3) if the employer can show business necessity and job relatedness, the employees can still win by showing that other practices would serve the employer's needs while causing less of a discriminatory impact. *Dothard v. Rawlinson*, 433 U.S. 321 (1977).

a. Establishing a Disparate Impact

The first prong of the *Griggs* disparate impact analysis is the employee's burden to establish that an employer's facially-neutral policy created a discriminatory effect. Although disparate impact cases often involve tests or other types of objective measurements, challenged policies can also involve subjective hiring criteria. *Watson v. Fort Worth Bank and Trust*, 487 U.S. 977 (1988) (plurality opinion); *but see Wal-Mart Stores, Inc. v. Dukes*, 564 U.S. 338, 356 (2011) (recognizing, in cases addressing class certification, possibility of disparate impact liability resulting from discretion to lower-level supervisors under *Watson*, but holding that such a practice in a large company makes it difficult for plaintiffs to show widespread disparate impact discrimination).

To establish a prima facie disparate impact case, employees must show the existence of a disparity that is statistically significant. As explained in Chapter 7, statistical significance is a way to capture the idea of a disparity that is larger than one would reasonably expect in the absence of discrimination actions. However, unlike with systemic discrimination claims, the statistical data in disparate impact cases are not trying to highlight an employer's discriminatory motive. Rather, the statistics in these cases are attempting to show that a seemingly neutral policy is negatively affecting one class significantly more than another.

Although parties may use the more advanced regression analysis of systemic discrimination cases, particularly at trial, a simpler measure of significance in disparate impact cases is the EEOC's four-fifths rule. Under this basic rule-of-thumb, disparate impact will be presumed if the minority's success rate under a challenged employment policy is equal to or less than four-fifths

(80%) of the majority's success rate. For example, say that 200 white applicants and 100 Black applicants took a qualification test for employment at a given business. Of the 200 white applicants, 100 scored high enough to advance to the next level of consideration (100 out of 200 equals a 50% success rate). Of the 100 Black applicants, 25 passed (25 out of 100 equals a 25% success rate). To apply the four-fifths rule in a case where the Black applicants are the plaintiffs, one takes four-fifths of the white applicants' success rate, which is 40% (the white applicants' success rate of 50% times 4/5 (or 0.80), which equals 40%). Because the Black success rate (25%) is lower than four-fifths of the white success rate (40%), the plaintiffs have met their burden to show a disparate impact under the EEOC's rule.

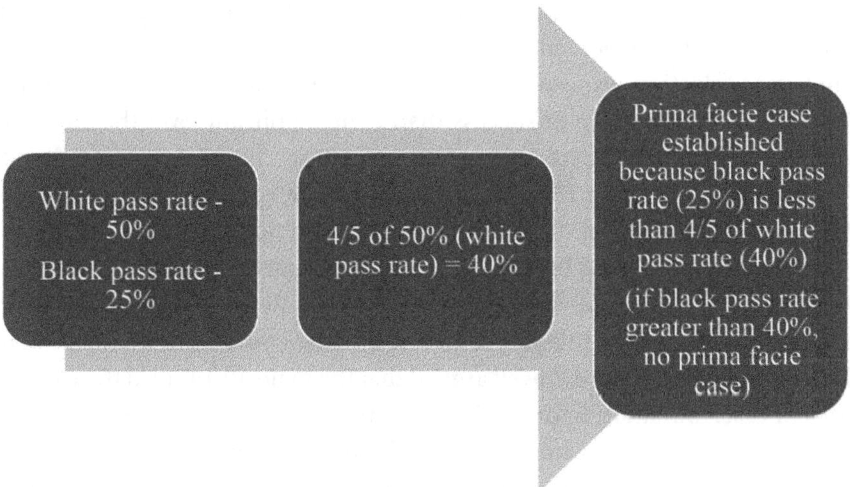

Like in systemic discrimination cases, identifying the appropriate comparator is a key issue. When a test or other requirement is applied to a large set of applicants, as in the example above, there is frequently no issue about the appropriate comparator. However, when other types of employment practices—such as recruiting strategies—are at issue, it may not be appropriate to use applicant pools as the comparator. Similarly, when a policy obviously filters out certain applicants, such as height and weight restrictions that make it nearly impossible for women to pass, applicant pools are not appropriate. *Dothard v. Rawlinson*, 433 U.S. 321 (1977). In these cases, the appropriate comparator is the "relevant labor market," which was discussed in Chapter 7 and will be addressed further in the discussion below on the *Wards Cove* case.

Yet, in certain situations, it can be quite difficult to identify an adequate comparator. For instance, in *New York Transit Authority v. Beazer*, 440 U.S. 568 (1979), the plaintiffs failed to show that the employer's drug-use prohibition caused a disparate impact because they lacked good data on the level of drug use by individuals in the relevant labor pool or the employer's applicant pool.

In a related issue, employers at times have argued that disparities caused by one stage in their selection process should not subject them to liability for disparate impact discrimination if their final or "bottom-line" numbers do not produce disparities. However, in *Connecticut v. Teal*, 457 U.S. 440 (1982), the Supreme Court rejected the bottom-line defense. In *Teal*, the employer had a two-stage application process. The first stage involved a test that disqualified a disproportionate number of Black applicants—enough to satisfy the four-fifths rule. The employer reacted to this disparity by promoting a disproportionate number of Black applicants in the final, more subjective stage. The employer's selection process in the second stage meant that Black applicants overall had a higher rate of success than white applicants, yet the employer was still liable for disparate impact discrimination. The reason, according to the Court, was that the Black applicants who were disqualified in the first stage were still victims of disparate impact discrimination, even though Black applicants as a whole did better than white applicants.

This holding also confirmed that the primary difference between disparate treatment and disparate impact claims is the existence of discriminatory intent. Dissenting in *Teal*, Justice Powell argued that the majority blurred the two theories of discrimination because disparate treatment claims should focus on individuals and disparate impact claims should focus on groups. The majority rejected that delineation, largely based on the language of § 703(a)(2), which prohibits discriminatory barriers that deprive "individuals of employment opportunities." Thus, the lack of intent—not the focus on groups—is what distinguishes disparate impact from disparate treatment cases. Ultimately, in the CRA of 1991, Congress agreed with the *Teal* majority by adding § 703(*l*) to Title VII. That section codified the underlying rationale of *Teal*, as well as limits to affirmative action goals, by prohibiting the adjustment of qualifying scores, or the use of different qualifying scores, based on a protected characteristic.

b. Establishing Business Necessity and Job Relatedness

Once the employees have established that a neutral policy has created a disparate impact, the employer has the opportunity to defend that policy as a business necessity that is related to job performance. Initially at least, this burden was a high one for employers, as it required policies that were "essential" to a job. *Dothard v. Rawlinson*, 433 U.S. 321 (1977).

How to define the level of connection to business needs or specific job duties can often be a complicated one. Lower courts have taken varying approaches on how important a policy causing a disparate impact must be to a business or job to satisfy this step. Some courts accept proof that a policy improves the overall business, such as limiting insurance benefits to heads of household because it provides benefits to the greatest number of people. *Wambheim v. J.C. Penney Co.*, 705 F.2d 1492 (9th Cir. 1983). Other courts, however, demand a more direct connection to job duties—for instance, rejecting an employer's claim that customer preference for clean-shaven pizza delivery drivers was sufficiently related to the job of making and delivering pizzas. *Bradley v. Pizzaco of Nebraska, Inc.*, 7 F.3d 795 (8th Cir. 1993). Finally, employers frequently cite the need to use professional tests as a business defense. That topic will be discussed in more detail below.

c. Establishing a Less Discriminatory Alternative

If the employer is able to establish the job relatedness and business necessity of a practice that has caused a disparate impact, the employees have one last chance to win. The third and final step of the disparate impact analysis permits employees to show that an alternative practice would serve the employer's needs without causing the same degree of discrimination.

This step traditionally required proof that another, less discriminatory, policy would "serve the employer's legitimate interest in 'efficient and trustworthy workmanship.'" *Albemarle Paper Co. v. Moody*, 422 U.S. 405 (1975). As originally conceived, such evidence was viewed in part as showing "pretext" of something resembling intentional discrimination—in particular, the employer was aware that its practice had a discriminatory impact and was also aware that an alternative practice could accomplish similar goals without such an impact, but chose not to use that less discriminatory alternative. But showing pretext or any other motive on the employer's part is not required in a disparate impact case. Thus, employees were required only to show the existence of a less discriminatory alternative that was similarly effective. That burden was not an easy one, however, as courts tended to defer to an employer's choice of practices. This difficulty was later exacerbated by the Supreme Court's substantial narrowing of disparate impact liability in *Wards Cove.*

2. The Supreme Court Narrows the Disparate Impact Theory in *Wards Cove*

In *Wards Cove Packing Co. v. Atonio*, 490 U.S. 642 (1989), the Supreme Court significantly changed the disparate impact analysis in several respects. The result was to make it much more difficult for employees to successfully bring disparate impact claims. The change was so dramatic that, in the CRA of 1991, Congress expanded disparate impact law largely back to its previous structure, while expressly disapproving of the Court's approach in *Wards Cove* (that said, the case still applies in other contexts, like the ADEA, as discussed in Chapter 13).

The plaintiffs in *Wards Cove* were employees in an Alaskan salmon cannery that was open only during the summer salmon runs. The employer hired two broad types of employees: (1) "cannery employees," who performed largely low-skilled jobs; and (2) "noncannery employees," who were either skilled employees, such as engineers and machinists, or low-skilled employees who performed work in the noncannery part of the worksite. The cannery and noncannery employees were largely segregated both at work and where they lived during the salmon runs. In addition to being physically separated at the worksite, they were also hired in very different ways. The cannery employees were hired in Alaska—many through a union hiring hall (in which a union generally selects the employees hired)—and were almost entirely Filipino or nonwhite Alaskans. Noncannery employees, however, were hired exclusively in the American Pacific Northwest and were mainly white.

The nonwhite cannery employees sued under Title VII, making both disparate treatment and disparate impact claims. The disparate impact claim was the one that reached the Supreme Court and, according to the plaintiffs, was the result of practices such as nepotism, rehire preferences, lack of objective hiring criteria, separate hiring channels, and a practice of not promoting from within. In rejecting the plaintiffs' suit, the Supreme Court transformed virtually every step of the disparate impact analysis.

a. Higher Burden for Showing Statistical Disparity

In *Wards Cove*, the Supreme Court rejected the plaintiffs' statistical proof of disparate impact, establishing a very high burden for the initial step of the analysis. The plaintiffs made two principal comparator showings. First, they compared the entire, mainly nonwhite, cannery workforce to the entire, mainly white, noncannery workforce. The Court rejected the noncannery workforce as an appropriate comparator and stressed the need to use the relevant labor pool instead. The problem, according to the Court, was that many of the noncannery jobs were much higher skilled than the cannery jobs, making comparisons between the two inapt.

Second, the plaintiffs also compared the low-skilled noncannery employees, who were mainly white, to the mainly nonwhite cannery employees in an attempt to provide a more relevant labor pool. Yet, the Court rejected that comparator as well. Although accepting that there was racial disparity between the two groups, the Court held that this disparity was not sufficient to establish disparate impact because many of the cannery employees were hired through a union hiring hall. According to the Court, because the union was mainly nonwhite, the fact that the cannery employees were also mainly nonwhite may be unrelated to any employer practice. It is unclear, however, why having a hiring hall arrangement with the union—an arrangement that the employer did not have to accept—could not be considered an employment practice subject to a disparate impact challenge.

In rejecting these two comparators, the Supreme Court emphasized that establishing statistical disparate impact depended on a comparison of the employer's workforce to the qualified population of a relevant labor pool. That requirement, on its face, is not a change from the *Griggs* analysis, but the Court's skepticism toward the plaintiffs' comparators and deference to the employer's determination of which labor market was relevant made this aspect of the disparate impact claim more difficult for plaintiffs to satisfy. The Court also appeared to impose a requirement that plaintiffs explain why a statistical disparity existed and show that factors outside of the employer's control were not responsible. This requirement will often be much harder to satisfy than the comparisons typically accepted prior to *Wards Cove*.

b. Requiring Identification of Specific Employer Practices That Caused a Disparate Impact

In addition to its approach to comparators, the Supreme Court in *Wards Cove* added another hurdle that the plaintiffs had to overcome to show that a disparate impact existed. In rejecting the plaintiffs' prima facie case of disparate impact, the Court established an explicit requirement, largely adopted from the plurality opinion in *Watson v. Fort Worth Bank and Trust*, 487 U.S. 977 (1988), that plaintiffs must identify the specific employment practice or practices responsible for causing the disparate impact. The Court stressed that this requirement was especially necessary when plaintiffs challenged both objective and subjective practices.

The Court's rationale for this requirement was that the disparate impact theory was based on challenges to particular hiring practices and that, under *Connecticut v. Teal*, 457 U.S. 440 (1982), bottom-line numbers are irrelevant. The Court was especially concerned with employers facing disparate impact liability simply because their workplace numbers looked bad, even if they did not cause the disparities.

The issue with this requirement is that it can be extremely difficult, if not impossible, to meet. Take the plaintiffs in *Wards Cove*. They complained that several practices—nepotism, rehire preferences, lack of objective hiring criteria, separate hiring channels, and a practice of not promoting from within—all contributed to the disparate impact. However, unless they could identify the exact impact caused by each of those practices, they would be unable to establish a prima facie case of disparate impact. It is unclear how plaintiffs in a case like *Wards Cove* could ever establish causation with this level of specificity. Unlike a required test or other strict requirement, it is very difficult to find evidence with enough specificity to show this level of causation. This difficulty was likely intended by the Court, which sought to ensure that employers would be held liable only when a specific practice could be definitively identified as the culprit. As discussed below, Congress was more concerned than the Court with these practical difficulties and amended this requirement in the CRA of 1991.

c. Changing Burden of Proof for Showing Business Necessity and Job Relatedness

Although the Supreme Court acknowledged that its earlier cases had stated that the employer has the burden of proof to show that a challenged practice was a business necessity and job related, it minimized that burden in *Wards*

Cove. Analogizing to the burdens in the *McDonnell Douglas* disparate treatment case, the Court held that the plaintiffs bear the burden of proof throughout a disparate impact case. Thus, the employer's burden to show business necessity and job relatedness was only one of production.

The Court's policy rationale for this low burden was to avoid courts' second-guessing employer practices. It also reflected the Court's dim view of the significance of plaintiffs' prima facie evidence in disparate impact cases and, as discussed below with regard to the recent *Ricci* case, perhaps some Justices' view on the disparate impact theory in general. However, this burden-shifting rule seemed to conflict with the emphasis that *Griggs* gave to the employer's need to show business necessity. Ultimately, as discussed below, the CRA of 1991 returned the analysis to its roots by imposing a burden of proof on the employer.

d. Redefining Business Necessity

In addition to changing the burden of showing business necessity, the Court also changed the substance of this step. Traditionally, the Court had required the employer to show that the challenged practice was "essential" to the business. In *Wards Cove*, that showing was lowered significantly to require only that the challenged practice "serves, in a significant way, the legitimate employment goals" of the employer.

The Court stressed that substantial deference is owed to employers' business autonomy; thus, the "essential" requirement was too high of a burden. The *Wards Cove* burden was quite low, however, and seemed to permit any practice that was reasonable, even if it created a disparate impact. Yet, like the change in burden, Congress also overruled *Wards Cove*'s approach to the substance of the business necessity requirement.

e. Redefining Nondiscriminatory Alternative

Finally, the Court in *Wards Cove* altered the third stage of the disparate impact analysis. Previously, plaintiffs could satisfy this stage by showing that an alternative practice would serve the employer's purposes while causing less of a disparate impact. In *Wards Cove*, the Court increased that burden, requiring instead that plaintiffs show that a less discriminatory alternative was "equally effective" as the challenged practice. The costs and benefits of the practices in question could be considered when making this determination.

In establishing this rule, the Court appeared to be using the "pretext" theory of a less discriminatory alternative. In other words, the Court seemed to be limiting this step to practices that were so similar to the one being challenged that the employer's refusal to use the alternative showed pretext for discrimination. However, as noted, the employer's intent should not matter in a disparate impact case. Preserving some degree of employer autonomy—another one of the Court's rationales on this point—is a more legitimate concern, although questions remain whether the Court gave it too much weight at the price of making the disparate impact analysis overly stringent. Once again, Congress disapproved of the Court's conclusion on this point in the CRA of 1991.

C. The Current State of Disparate Impact Discrimination under Title VII

In large measure because of *Wards Cove*, as well as other problems in Title VII law, Congress enacted the 1991 Civil Rights Act (CRA of 1991), which ushered in significant changes to Title VII. Most of these changes were to the disparate impact analysis—particularly reversing much of the Supreme Court's approach in *Wards Cove.*

One fundamental aspect of the CRA of 1991 that often gets overlooked is that Congress made clear that it approved of the disparate impact theory. Although *Griggs* relied on § 703(a)(2) to recognize disparate impact, it was not certain that the theory was part of Congress' intent in enacting the statute. The CRA of 1991 put that question to rest in what is now § 703(k) of Title VII, which explicitly states that disparate impact discrimination violates Title VII. The section also addresses many of the issues altered by *Wards Cove* and, in most cases, reversed the Supreme Court. What follows is a reformulation of the basic disparate impact analysis described above as it exists under current—post-CRA of 1991—law.

1. Establishing a Disparate Impact: Demonstrating a Statistical Disparity and Showing That It Was Caused by a Specific Employment Practice (If Possible)

The first step in the disparate impact analysis—employees' showing that a statistical disparity exists—establishes a prima facie case of unlawful disparate impact discrimination. There are two main issues in this step: the level of proof necessary to demonstrate a statistical disparity and establishing the employer practice or practices that caused that disparity. The CRA of 1991 did not substantially alter—at least on its face—the statistical proof element; thus, *Wards Cove*'s rejection of the plaintiffs' statistical comparisons is still relevant law. The statute did directly address the issue of when employees must identify specific practices, largely by splitting the difference between *Wards Cove* and the original disparate impact jurisprudence.

Under the new § 703(k)(1)(A)(i), employees will win a disparate impact claim if they "demonstrate[] that [an employer] uses a particular employment practice that causes a disparate impact on the basis of race, color, religion, sex, or national origin," and the employer "fails to demonstrate that the challenged practice is job related for the position in question and consistent with business necessity." This provision—read in isolation—appears to do little more than codify the disparate impact theory under the pre-*Wards Cove* burden-shifting analysis. However, it is plausible that Congress's general disapproval of *Wards Cove* could be applied to this first step of the disparate impact analysis. Some courts have taken this approach and permitted the type of evidence allowed in *Griggs* and other cases, such as applicant success-rate comparisons and relevant labor market determinations that are not especially deferential to the employer. Yet, other courts have continued to follow *Wards Cove*, requiring comparisons to a relevant labor pool that is either largely defined by the employer or defined so narrowly that plaintiffs are unable to establish a statistically significant disparity. It is imperative, therefore, that attorneys be aware of the approach favored in their jurisdiction. Moreover, to the extent that different types of comparator evidence are helpful to a party's case, it could be advantageous to use them even if not required.

One area in which the CRA of 1991 did implement a change is the extent to which employees must identify a specific employment practice or practices that caused the disparate impact. In contrast to the absolute requirement in *Wards Cove*, the statute took a more nuanced approach. Under the new § 703(k)(1)(B)(i), the default requirement is that employees must "demonstrate that each particular challenged employment practice causes a disparate impact." There is an exception, however, if the employees "can demonstrate to the court that the elements of [an employer's] decisionmaking process are not capable of separation for analysis," in which case, "the decisionmaking process may be analyzed as one employment practice." Accordingly, the preference is that employees establish that a particular practice or practices caused a disparate impact, as was required under *Wards Cove*. But if that type of proof is not possible—for instance, where an employer uses a complicated or haphazard set of selection mechanisms—the employees need not show causation for a specific practice or practices. The CRA of 1991 interpretative memorandum, which the statute stated was the official legislative history, explains this exception as occurring "[w]hen a decisionmaking process includes particular, functionally-integrated practices which are components of the same criterion, standard, method of administration, or test, such as the height and weight requirement" in *Dothard v. Rawlinson*, 433 U.S. 321 (1977). 37 Cong. Rec. S.15276 (daily ed. Oct. 25, 1991).

Finally, § 703(k)(1)(B)(ii) states that, if the employer "demonstrates that a specific employment practice does not cause the disparate impact, the [employer] shall not be required to demonstrate that such practice is required by business necessity." This provision suggests that an employer will have the opportunity to show that particular employment practices that make up an overall process that the plaintiffs could not separate out—but that the employer can separate—did not create a disparate impact.

One example of the integrated practices analysis occurred in *EEOC v. Joe's Stone Crab, Inc.*, 220 F.2d 1263 (11th Cir. 2000). The plaintiffs in *Joe's Stone Crab* argued for disparate impact liability based on the employer's hiring practices, which resulted in an almost all-male wait staff. The employer conducted an annual "roll call" for wait staff applicants that involved a written and oral evaluation. Some applicants were then selected by the maître d' based on several subjective factors for training, after which they were hired. The roll call was not advertised and instead attracted applicants by word-of-mouth.

The government alleged that the word-of-mouth recruiting and delegation to the maître d's subjective determinations produced the disparate impact. The court, however, rejected the government's reliance on both practices after examining their impact in isolation. First, the government could not show that the lack of advertising kept women in the dark about the roll calls, as they were widely known among area restaurant workers and no women testified that they did not apply to the employer because they had not heard about a roll call. Second, the government could not show that the employer's subjective and unregulated selection process caused a disparate impact because there was no evidence that women did not apply because of the subjective criteria or that those who did apply where disadvantaged by those criteria. Finally, the court rejected the notion that the employer's discriminatory reputation was the practice causing the disparate impact; according to the court, reputation is too amorphous an idea and could not be linked to the disparate impact. In short, the court held that the evidence showed, perhaps, that the employer had engaged in intentional discrimination, but not that the employer's facially neutral policies actually caused the dearth of female servers.

2. Establishing Business Necessity and Job Relatedness

Wards Cove altered the second step of the disparate impact analysis—the employer's showing of business necessity and job relatedness—in two ways. First, the Court in *Wards Cove* held that the employer's burden was only one of production and, second, that this showing required only that the practice effectively serves the employer's legitimate interests rather than the previous requirement that the practice be "essential." The CRA of 1991 reversed both of these changes.

First, the new §703(k)(1)(A)(i) explicitly states that the employer must "demonstrate that the challenged practice is job related for the position in question and consistent with business necessity." The use of the word "demonstrate," which is now defined in §701(m) of Title VII, clearly indicates that the employer's burden in this step is one of both production and persuasion.

Second, Congress indicated that the terms "job related" and "business necessity" in the CRA of 1991 were not consistent with the Court's interpretation of those terms in *Wards Cove*. As stated in the CRA of 1991's interpretative memorandum, the "terms 'business necessity' and 'job related' are intended to reflect the concepts enunciated by the Supreme Court in *Griggs v. Duke Power Co.*, 401 U.S. 424 (1971), and the other Supreme Court decisions prior to *Wards Cove Packing v. Atonio*, 490 U.S. 642 (1989)." Thus, despite exceptions in some occasional lower-court decisions, the *Wards Cove* "effectively serves" standard is gone, and in its stead is the previous standard that required the employer to show that a practice causing a disparate impact is job related and consistent with business necessity. An example of how this defense works is the case *Fitzpatrick v. City of Atlanta*, 2 F.3d 1112 (11th Cir. 1993), in which Black firefighters argued that their employer's ban against facial hair created a disparate impact on Black men, who are more likely to suffer from a skin disease that prevents them from shaving. The employer made a job related and business necessity defense based on safety, in particular that even a short "shadow beard" would interfere with the use of respirators. As support for this argument, the employer cited the opinion of government occupational-safety agencies that facial hair could prevent a good seal on respirators. In response, the firefighters noted that the employer had allowed shadow beards for six years without incident. The court found both types of evidence relevant, but found the agency opinions far more influential. Although not beyond reproach, such opinions serve as a trustworthy benchmark for safety claims. In contrast, the mere absence of a safety incident during the six years when shadow beards were allowed—especially when there was no attempt to study the issue at the time—did not necessarily mean that shadow beards were safe. Therefore, the employer was able to establish that banning all facial hair was a business necessity. It is also worth noting that courts are generally more willing to defer to an employer's business necessity defense when safety is a genuine issue.

In addition to—or a subset of—the job related and business necessity defense, employers have two other possibilities to rebut a disparate impact showing. These defenses, which were not addressed by either *Wards Cove* or the CRA of 1991, are the use of a professionally validated test or a bona fide seniority system under § 703(h) of Title VII. If the disparate impact at issue is the result of either of these practices, the employer will usually be immune from disparate impact attack.

a. Professionally Validated Test Defense

One issue that has resulted in a significant amount of litigation is the use of professionally prepared tests. Under § 703(h) of Title VII, an employer can give and act "upon the results of any professionally developed ability test provided that such test, its administration or action upon the results is not designed, intended or used to discriminate." The meaning of this provision has been in question since *Griggs*; indeed, the employer in that case cited Section 703(h) as a defense for its high-school diploma and aptitude test requirements. The Supreme Court, however, interpreted § 703(h) to protect only nondiscriminatory tests that were tied to job performance.

Determining when a suitable connection between a professional test and job performance exists is not always easy. Typically, that question centers on the concept of "validation." Validation refers to an attempt to show that the test is correlated to job performance, and validation studies are usually conducted by experts in the field. The EEOC has extensive regulations on validation in its Uniform Guidelines for Employee Selection Procedures, which typically receives a significant amount of deference from courts.

There are three major types of validation. The first type, "criterion validation," refers to a correlation between an individual's test score and actual job performance. For instance, in *Albemarle Paper Co. v. Moody*, 422 U.S. 405

(1975), the employer attempted to validate a couple of aptitude tests that it required for certain jobs. Its expert attempted to make a criterion validation of the tests by comparing employees' test scores with supervisory evaluations of the employees. This is often the preferred type of validation, but the effort failed in *Albemarle Paper* for several reasons. One reason was that there was a statistically significant correlation with only a few of the many jobs that used the test. Indeed, the jobs studied largely excluded the entry-level positions and entry-level applicants that were the focus of the lawsuit. Although higher-level jobs could be relevant if they are part of a normal career progression for employees, the employer did not establish that fact in the case. Moreover, there was virtually no explanation of the criteria used by the supervisors in evaluating the employees. Some subjectiveness is tolerable in validation studies, but employers must be careful to establish well-explained guidelines for evaluations and to monitor how they are being made. In *Albemarle Paper*, the evaluations were too vague to satisfy § 703(h). This failure demonstrates the relatively high standard required of validation, particularly when applied to aptitude tests that were not designed for a specific job.

A possible exception to this high standard is when a test is validated to criteria in an employer's comprehensive training. For instance, in *Washington v. Davis*, 426 U.S. 229 (1976), the employer—the District of Columbia Police Department—used a general civil service test for applicants to the police training academy, which applicants had to graduate from to become police officers. The employer could show that the test was correlated with successful completion of the academy training, but could not show the same correlation with actual job performance. The Supreme Court held that this validation was sufficient when testing for the minimum verbal and communication skills needed to complete the necessary training, even without a significant correlation with actual job performance. The relationship to public safety was also a factor, as courts generally give employers more leeway for jobs involved in law enforcement or other types of public safety.

The second type, "content validation," refers to a correlation between the skills and knowledge being tested and those needed for job performance. *United States v. State of South Carolina*, 445 F. Supp. 1094 (1977), *cert. denied sub nom. National Education Association v. South Carolina*, 434 U.S. 1026 (1978), provides an example of an acceptable content validation in combination with the training exception of *Davis*. The test in *South Carolina* was the National Teachers Exams, which had been given to teachers for decades. The district court approved its use, despite a disparate impact, because of the correlation between the knowledge tested in the exams and the knowledge required to master teacher training programs.

Finally, the third type, "construct validation," refers to a correlation between certain personal characteristics and job performance. Often, they are used to measure abstract qualities needed for a job, such as creativity, which are often difficult to measure directly. *Zamlen v. City of Cleveland*, 906 F.2d 209 (6th Cir. 1990). An example of construct validation is a general intelligence or personality test that seeks to identify certain traits needed for a job. This type of validation is acceptable, but is seen less often and is generally more difficult to satisfy. *Guardians Association v. Civil Service Commission of New York*, 630 F.2d 79 (2d Cir. 1980).

b. Bona Fide Seniority System Defense

Section 703(h) provides another defense to a disparate impact challenge: a bona fide seniority system. Pursuant to this defense, it is not unlawful under Title VII for an employer "to apply different standards of compensation, or different terms, conditions, or privileges of employment pursuant to a bona fide seniority or merit system ... provided that such differences are not the result of an intention to discriminate." Because seniority systems are a common and valued part of many workplaces—particularly unionized ones—this defense can be important.

"Seniority system" is often interpreted broadly and can encompass many different procedures that incorporate length of service. For instance, in *California Brewers Association v. Bryant*, 444 U.S. 598 (1980), the Supreme Court addressed a procedure for determining benefits and the order of hiring and layoffs, based in part on whether employees were "permanent," which was defined as working at least 45 weeks a year. Although this rule was not strictly a seniority plan, which focuses on length of employment, the Court held that because this "ancillary rule" had a nexus to seniority and was common in seniority systems, it could still enjoy protection under § 703(h). The Court contrasted the covered rule at issue with uncovered rules such as an educational requirement needed before an employee can begin accruing seniority.

The primary question involved with the seniority system defense is typically whether a system is "bona fide." This issue initially arose in challenges to seniority systems perpetuating discrimination that occurred prior to the enactment of Title VII. For instance, in *International Brotherhood of Teamsters v. United States*, 431 U.S. 324 (1977) (the same *Teamsters* case discussed in Chapter 7), the employer's seniority system had a provision under which a transfer between city and long-haul truck-driving positions would result in a loss of seniority. This was problematic because the employer had a long history of intentionally barring Black and Hispanic-surnamed drivers from higher-paying long-haul jobs prior to Title VII. Thus, the seniority system, although facially neutral, perpetuated this past discrimination. The Supreme Court held that despite this perpetuation, § 703(h) protected the seniority system. In rejecting the government's argument that perpetuating discrimination meant that the system was not "bona fide," the Court emphasized that § 703(h) represented a policy choice by Congress to protect existing, nondiscriminatory, seniority systems from the newly enacted Title VII. "Nondiscriminatory" means that the seniority system is facially nondiscriminatory and that the employer did not intend for the system to discriminate. The Court has repeatedly reaffirmed this perpetuation theory, even for systems that were implemented after Title VII's enactment or systems that caused a discriminatory effect that was not timely challenged. *American Tobacco Co. v. Patterson*, 456 U.S. 63 (1982); *United Air Lines v. Evans*, 431 U.S. 553 (1977).

As a result of these cases, § 703(h) is best understood as making bona fide seniority systems immune from disparate impact challenges. Accordingly, for a facially nondiscriminatory seniority system to violate Title VII, there must be proof that the employer intended for the system to discriminate. *Pullman-Standard v. Swint*, 456 U.S. 273 (1982). Determination of such intent is generally made pursuant to the following factors, as articulated in *James v. Stockham Valves & Fittings Co.*, 559 F.2d 310 (5th Cir. 1977) (*Stockham Valve* factors):

1. does the seniority system discourage all employees equally from transferring between seniority units;
2. are the seniority units in the same or separate bargaining units, and if not, is the structure rational and conforming to industry practice;
3. does the seniority system have its genesis in discrimination; and
4. was the seniority system negotiated and maintained free from any illegal purpose?

If employees cannot show that a seniority system is discriminatory under these factors, the system will be deemed bona fide and protected under § 703(h).

3. Establishing a Less Discriminatory Alternative

Finally, in the third step of the disparate impact analysis, if the employer has proved business necessity and job relatedness, the employees have an opportunity to show that an alternative existed that would have produced less of a disparate impact. *Wards Cove* moved away from the previous test that looked only to whether an alternative would serve an employer's business purposes to one that was "equally effective" to the challenged practice. In the CRA of 1991, Congress again rejected *Wards Cove*'s approach.

Under the new Sections 703(k)(1)(A)(ii) and 703(k)(1)(C), employees can still win after the employer shows job relatedness and business necessity if the employees demonstrate, "in accordance with the law as it existed" prior to *Wards Cove*, that an alternative employment practice exists that would cause less of a disparate impact and the employer "refuses to adopt such alternative employment practice." A lingering question is whether an employer could adopt an alternative practice during litigation and escape liability. One interpretation of the language of § 703(k)(1)(A)(ii)—employees "make the demonstration" showing an alternative practice and the employer "refuses to adopt" it—suggests this possibility, but that would render a lot of litigation moot. Another interpretation suggests that the employees should propose an alternative prior to litigation, but that may not be feasible in many instances. To date, these issues have not been resolved—in part because it is still difficult for employees to satisfy this step and, as a result, it is not litigated often.

A likely outcome is that most courts will accept the EEOC's interpretation of this step. In its Uniform Guidelines for Employee Selection Procedures, for example, the EEOC contemplates the alternative practice provision being used primarily where "two or more selection procedures are available which serve the [employer's] legitimate interest in efficient and trustworthy workmanship, and which are substantially equally valid for a given purpose." 42 C.F.R. § 1607.3(b). In this case, the EEOC expects the employer to investigate possible alternatives at the time of selection—for instance, if an employer is validating a test, it should investigate other procedures to see if they produce less of a disparate impact. If an employer does so and it chooses the less discriminatory alternative, or if it is presented with evidence that a less discriminatory alternative exists that can be validated and it uses that option, it will likely be immune from employees' attempts to show a less discriminatory alternative.

D. New Questions about Disparate Impact Discrimination Raised by the Supreme Court in *Ricci*

In 2009, the Supreme Court issued its blockbuster decision, *Ricci v. DeStefano*, 557 U.S. 557 (2009). *Ricci* involved a fire department that cancelled its promotion process after discovering that its oral and written tests had resulted in a racially disparate impact. The Supreme Court held that abandoning a promotion process where applicants had an expectation that it would be followed is disparate treatment discrimination unless the employer could show that it had a strong basis in evidence for believing that applying the tests would result in disparate impact liability. In finding that the employer could not meet that burden, the Court made some statements casting doubt on the future of various aspects of disparate impact law.

The Court acknowledged that the test resulted in a statistical disparity significant enough to establish a prima facie case of disparate impact discrimination under the EEOC's four-fifths rule. However, the Court held that a prima facie case "is far from a strong basis in evidence" that the employer would have faced disparate impact liability if it applied the results. This holding is a bit curious, as it could be read as diminishing the significance of the plaintiffs' establishing a prima facie case, which is supposed to switch the burden of persuasion to the employer. Yet it could also be read merely as an indication that the rest of the potential disparate impact claim was weak, as the Court thought the plaintiffs would clearly lose on the other two steps.

Despite the statistically significant disparity, the Court held that the plaintiffs would lose a disparate impact challenge because there was "no genuine dispute" that the tests were job related and consistent with business necessity. Despite evidence questioning the tests' appropriateness—for instance, the tests did not apply to the type of firefighting practices used by the employer—the Court cited testimony from experts concluding that the test was appropriate and could be validated. This holding appeared to place a fairly low burden on employers in showing that a test was job related and consistent with business necessity. The question is whether this is more a function of the particular circumstances of the *Ricci* case or whether it represents some degree of pushback by the Court against the CRA of 1991 and its reversal of *Wards Cove*'s refusal to place more than a burden of production on the employer.

The biggest potential change to disparate impact analysis occurred in the Court's rejection of a possible less discriminatory alternative argument. Three alternatives that might have produced a less discriminatory impact were raised: change the weights given to the oral and written tests, round the final scores, or use real-life simulation tests instead of oral and written tests. The Court rejected the simulation alternative for lack of proof of less discriminatory results and the rounding option because it would violate the prohibition against adjusting test scores under §703(*l*) of Title VII. The Court's rejection of the weighting between the oral and written tests was more significant, as the Court held that the proposed alternative weight ratio was not shown to be an "equally valid alternative." The problem with this statement is that it seems to revive the *Wards Cove* requirement that a less discriminatory alternative be "equally effective"—a standard that the CRA of 1991 rejected in favor of the previous inquiry into whether an alternative would merely serve the employer's interests. Although this "equally effective" statement seems to conflict with the CRA of 1991, it remains to be seen the extent to which other courts follow *Ricci*'s lead on this issue. *Compare Johnson v. City of Memphis*, 770 F.3d 464, 472 (6th Cir. 2014) (emphasizing plaintiffs' obligation to prove "equally effective" alternatives and not to second-guess employers), *with Erdman v. City of Madison*, 91 F.4th 465, 476 (7th Cir. 2024) ("To serve an employer's 'legitimate needs,' an alternative hiring practice need not be exactly as effective as the allegedly discriminatory practice. The issue is whether the alternative practice is 'substantially equally valid.'").

Finally, Justice Scalia's concurrence in *Ricci* raises a troubling question: is the disparate impact theory consistent with constitutional equal protection law? Justice Scalia made it clear that he thought there was a conflict when employers altered their employment practices to avoid racial disparities in their workplaces. If employers take up this question, it remains to be seen whether other members of the Court agree that disparate impact discrimination is unconstitutional. *Cf. Texas Department of Housing & Community Affairs v. Inclusive Communities Project, Inc.*, 576 U.S. 519 (2015) (holding that disparate impact claims are permissible under the Fair Housing Act, which lacks explicit statutory language permitting such claims).

CHECKPOINTS

- The basic disparate impact analysis has three steps: (1) the employees demonstrate that a facially neutral practice has created a disparate impact; (2) the employer demonstrates that the practice is job related and consistent with business necessity; and (3) the employees demonstrate that an alternative practice would create a less discriminatory effect.
- Employees have the burden of persuasion to establish a disparate impact, usually with statistics showing that minority employees or applicants succeeded at less than four-fifths the rate of majority employees, applicants, or qualified members of a relevant labor market.
- When establishing a disparate impact, employees must try to show that a particular employment practice caused the disparity, unless the employer used a multifaceted decisionmaking process that is not capable of separation.
- The employer has the burden of persuasion to show that a challenged practice or set of practices is job related and a business necessity.
- The employers can also meet its affirmative defense by showing that the disparate impact was caused by a professionally validated test or a bona fide seniority system.
- If the employer satisfies its defense, the employees can still win by showing, under a burden of persuasion, that an alternative practice exists that effectively serves the employer's business purposes and results in a less discriminatory impact.
- In *Ricci v. DeStefano*, the Supreme Court showed resistance to disparate impact claims, suggesting that it is not difficult for an employer to show job relatedness and business necessity and that an alternative practice may need to be equally effective as the challenged practice. A concurrence also questioned whether the entire disparate impact theory was constitutional.

CHAPTER 9

Harassment

ROADMAP

- Comparing harassment versus discrimination claims
- Harassment claims based on tangible versus non-tangible employment actions
- The elements of a sexual harassment claim
- Employer liability for sexual harassment by supervisors and co-workers
- Same sex harassment based on desire and animus
- Sexual orientation and gender identity discrimination and harassment
- The equal opportunity or bisexual harasser
- Third-party harassment of employees

In addition to the claims already discussed, Title VII permits harassment and hostile work environment claims brought on the basis of race, color, religion, sex, and national origin. Additionally, the ADA permits harassment and hostile work environment claims on the basis of an individual's disability, and the ADEA allows such claims on the basis of age. This chapter will explore the framework for bringing these types of harassment claims, with an emphasis on sexual harassment where many of the parameters for the framework originated.

A. Harassment Claims vs. Discrimination Claims

Harassment is a type of discrimination claim under Title VII, even though it does not necessarily lead to a tangible result like the firing of an employee. This is because the Supreme Court has held that the language of Title VII is not limited to economic or tangible discrimination. The phrase "terms, conditions, or privileges of employment" in § 703(a) evinces a congressional intent to strike at the entire spectrum of disparate treatment of men and women in employment. Consequently, harassing someone because of their sex is a type of sexual discriminatory treatment. *Meritor Savings Bank v. Vinson*, 477 U.S. 57 (1986). Moreover, the same proof scheme used for sexual harassment claims applies to all other harassment claims based on other protected classifications. *Harrison v. Metropolitan Government*, 80 F.3d 1107 (6th Cir. 1996) ("The elements and burden of proof that a Title VII plaintiff must meet are the same for racially charged harassment as for sexually charged harassment"). For instance, the supervisory vicarious liability rule in *Ellerth* and *Faragher* (discussed in more detail below) also applies to harassment by supervisors based on race, color, sex (whether or not of a sexual nature), religion, national origin, protected activity, age, or disability.

B. Tangible vs. Non-Tangible Sexual Harassment Claims

During its earlier development, sexual harassment claims were divided into quid pro quo (Latin for "this for that") and hostile work environment claims. A quid pro quo claim arises when an employer demands sexual favors in exchange for job benefits (for example, "if you don't sleep with me, you will be fired"). On the other hand, hostile environment claims involve intimidation, ridicule, or insult based on the plaintiff's sex. The U.S. Supreme Court used these terms in its first sexual harassment case, *Meritor Savings Bank v. Vinson*, 477 U.S. 57 (1986), to provide examples of the two possible types of harassment. In *Meritor*, the Court commented:

> Relevant to the charges at issue in this case, the [EEOC] Guidelines provide that such sexual misconduct constitutes prohibited "sexual harassment," whether or not it is directly linked to the grant or denial of an

economic *quid pro quo*, where "such conduct has the purpose or effect of unreasonably interfering with an individual's work performance or creating an intimidating, hostile, or offensive working environment."

More recently, the Supreme Court appears to favor a different dichotomy for dividing sexual harassment actions, at least with regard to an employer's vicarious liability for the harassment. Today, and since the *Ellerth* case, the proper dichotomy of sexual harassment claims is between tangible and non-tangible employment actions. *Burlington Industries, Inc. v. Ellerth*, 524 U.S. 742, 754 (1998) ("When we assume discrimination can be proved, however, the factors we discuss below, and not the categories *quid pro quo* and hostile work environment, will be controlling on the issue of vicarious liability.").

C. The Five Elements of a Sexual Harassment Claim

In *Meritor*, the Supreme Court established the five elements that a plaintiff bringing a sexual harassment claim must establish. For sexual harassment to be actionable under Title VII, the harassment must be severe or pervasive, unwelcome, create a hostile or abusive environment, occur because of the employee's sex, and occur either because of the employer's negligence or in circumstances under which vicarious liability (respondeat superior) may be imputed to the employer.

1. Severe or Pervasive

This first factor requires that for sexual harassment to be actionable, it must be sufficiently severe or pervasive to alter the conditions of the victim's employment and create an abusive working environment. Note that the language is severe *or* pervasive. That means if a single event of harassment is sufficiently severe (like sexual assault or rape), it may be actionable. On the other hand, less severe actions may add up to actionable harassment when they take place over a sufficient period of time. Yet, not all workplace conduct that may be described as harassment affects terms, conditions, or privileges of employment within the meaning of Title VII. The Supreme Court cautioned in later cases that Title VII does not implement a workplace civility code. So, Title VII does not prohibit all verbal or physical harassment in the workplace, like horseplay or mild flirtations. Rather, Title VII requires that the behavior be sufficiently severe or pervasive from an objective perspective to alter the terms and conditions of employment. The plaintiff must also perceive the conduct as severe or pervasive. This requirement is often seen as a sliding scale—the more severe the conduct is the less pervasive it needs to be to meet the standard, and vice versa.

The Court in later cases also made clear that a harassment victim need not suffer a psychological breakdown for the conduct to be severe or pervasive. *Harris v. Forklift Systems, Inc.*, 510 U.S. 17 (1993). Instead, the Court should consider a series of factors under a totality of circumstances test, including: (1) the frequency of the discriminatory conduct; (2) its severity; (3) whether it is physically threatening or humiliating, or a mere offensive utterance; and (4) whether it unreasonably interferes with an employee's work performance.

2. Unwelcome

"The gravamen of any sexual harassment claim is that the alleged sexual advances were 'unwelcome.'" *Meritor*, 477 U.S. at 68. In this regard, the inquiry is whether the victim of the harassment perceived the harassment to be unwelcome, not whether her actual participation in the conduct was voluntary. So, voluntariness (or consent) is not a defense to a sexual harassment complaint. It is also worth noting that the EEOC has recently provided that "Although a complainant alleging a hostile work environment must show that the harassment was unwelcome, conduct that is subjectively and objectively hostile also is necessarily unwelcome." *See* EEOC, Enforcement Guidance on Harassment in the Workplace (2024), https://www.eeoc.gov/laws/guidance/enforcement-guidance-harassment-workplace#_Toc164808023.

3. Creates a Hostile or Abusive Workplace

To establish a violation of Title VII, a plaintiff must prove that discrimination based on sex has created a hostile or abusive work environment. *Harris v. Forklift Systems., Inc.*, 510 U.S. 17 (1993). This standard has been interpreted by most courts to establish an objective "reasonable" person standard, largely because, in *Harris*, the Supreme Court made two references to a "reasonable person." *Richardson v. N.Y. State Department of Correctional Service*, 180 F.3d 426 (2d Cir. 1999) (rejecting the view of courts that look to the perspective of particular ethnic or gender groups). So, an environment that a reasonable person would not find hostile or abusive is not prohibited by Title VII. On the other hand, at least one court has found that the appropriate objective standard is that of a "reasonable woman." *Ellison v. Brady*, 924 F.2d 872 (9th Cir. 1991).

4. Because of the Victim's Sex

The actual language of Title VII makes it "an unlawful employment practice for an employer ... to discriminate against any individual with respect to his compensation, terms, conditions, or privileges of employment, *because of* such individual's race, color, religion, *sex*, or national origin'" 42 U.S.C. §2000e-2(a)(1) (§703(a)(1)).

Causation is generally not an issue in sexual harassment cases, as the "because of such individual's ... sex" is often assumed. This is because most sexual harassment actions—particularly male-on-female harassment—are based on attraction, which makes it relatively easy to draw the inference that the behavior occurred because of the employee's sex. In other words, because the harassing conduct is often explicitly sexual in nature (for example, groping, inappropriate touching, or sexually suggestive language), it is reasonable to conclude that the behavior would likely not have occurred had the victim been of the same sex as the harasser (unless, of course, as discussed below, the harasser has a sexual preference for a person of the same sex).

However, it should be noted that claims of sexual harassment are not limited to sexual conduct based on desire or attraction; as long as the conduct

Sexual Harassment Vicarious Liability

	Tangible Employment Action	**Non-Tangible Employment Action**
Supervisor	Strict vicarious liability (no affirmative defense available)	Affirmative defense to liability and damages if (a) the employer exercised reasonable care to prevent and correct promptly any sexually harassing behavior and (b) the employee unreasonably failed to take advantage of any preventive or corrective opportunities provided by the employer or to avoid harm otherwise.
Co-Worker	Not within province of co-worker to alter conditions of plaintiff's employment	Negligence standard for employer liability: negligent with respect to sexual harassment if employer knew or should have known about the conduct and failed to stop it.

occurred because of the victim's sex, the plaintiff can maintain a claim of sexual harassment. *Oncale v. Sundowner Offshore Services, Inc.*, 523 U.S. 75 (1998) ("[H]arassing conduct need not be motivated by sexual desire to support an inference of discrimination on the basis of sex"). Actual or threatened violence, without any sexual overtones (purely misogynistic), may also constitute actionable sexual harassment.

5. Respondeat Superior Liability

As to employer liability, the Court after *Meritor* developed a framework for deciding when to impute a supervisor or co-worker's sexually harassing actions to the employer (recall from Chapter 2 that individual liability does not exist under Title VII). The Supreme Court established a framework for assessing employer liability in the companion cases of *Burlington Industries, Inc. v. Ellerth*, 524 U.S. 742 (1998), and *Faragher v. City of Boca Raton*, 524 U.S. 775 (1998).

This framework first asks: was the harassment carried out by a supervisor or a co-worker? If it was a supervisor, courts look to the actual authority the harasser had over the plaintiff rather than the formal job title. In *Vance v. Ball State*, 570 U.S. 421 (2013), the Supreme Court, in a close decision, took a narrow approach as to who constitutes a supervisor. For supervisory status, the individual must typically be able to carry out a tangible employment action. After *Vance*, the Court emphasized the simplicity with which its standard can be applied, noting that "we are confident that, in every case, the approach we take today will be more easily administrable" and clearly concluding "that an employee is a 'supervisor' for purposes of vicarious liability under Title VII if he or she is empowered by the employer to take tangible employment actions against the victim." *Id.* at 450. The decision therefore provides substantial clarity in this area.

On the other hand, if the alleged harasser is a co-worker, courts apply a negligence standard, where the employer is liable if it knew or should have known of the harassing conduct and failed to take appropriate corrective action. The negligence standard always applies in co-worker cases because co-workers are not capable of taking formal actions (for example, firing, failure to promote, etc.) against the victimized co-employee.

a. Tangible Injury Caused by Supervisory Harassment

Second, with regard to supervisors, courts look to see if the harassment involved a tangible employment action or only non-tangible employment actions. If a tangible action was involved, the employer is strictly liable for the actions of the supervisor. A tangible employment action means a significant change in employment status, such as hiring, firing, failing to promote, reassignment with significantly different responsibilities, or a decision causing a significant change in benefits.

For instance, in *Pennsylvania State Police v. Suders*, 542 U.S. 129 (2004), the Supreme Court overturned the Third Circuit's holding that a constructive discharge is always a tangible employment action as a matter of law. If "the last straw" before the resignation was an official act of the employer, then the affirmative defense for non-tangible employment actions is unavailable. Absent an official act of the employer, however, the affirmative defense under *Ellerth* and *Faragher* is available. The Court defined constructive discharge in *Suders* to occur where it can be shown "that the abusive working environment became so intolerable that her resignation qualified as a fitting response." *Suders, supra*, at 133.

b. Non-Tangible Injury Caused by Supervisory Harassment

If the harassment involved non-tangible actions, the Court in *Ellerth* and *Faragher* held that the employer may have an affirmative defense to liability. First, the employer must have exercised reasonable care to prevent and promptly correct the harassing behavior. To "prevent" harassment, many courts require that the employer in most cases have an anti-harassment policy, distribute the policy to employees, and provide training on the policy to its employees. To "correct" harassment that has already occurred, employers must act promptly to investigate a sexual harassment claim and take action against the perpetrator if appropriate.

In addition to the employer acting reasonably, the employer must also show under the affirmative defense that the employee acted unreasonably by failing to take advantage of the employer's preventative or corrective opportunities, or to otherwise avoid harm. For instance, a showing that the employee failed to take advantage of the company's disseminated complaint procedure in its anti-harassment policy may suffice to satisfy the employer's burden under this second element of the affirmative defense. The burden is therefore on the employer to show *both* that it acted reasonably, and that the employee did not, with regard to the sexually harassing conduct in question.

D. Specific Types of Harassment

A number of different forms of sexual harassment arise in different contexts, including: same-sex harassment, sexual orientation and gender identity issues, and third-party harassment. These are addressed below.

1. Same-Sex Harassment

A plaintiff may bring a sexual harassment claim where the alleged harasser is of the same sex. *Oncale v. Sundowner Offshore Services, Inc.*, 523 U.S. 75 (1998). In *Oncale*, the Court held that, "nothing in Title VII necessarily bars a claim of discrimination 'because of ... sex' merely because the plaintiff and the defendant (or the person charged with acting on behalf of the defendant) are of the same sex." Instead, the "critical issue" is whether members of one sex are exposed to disadvantageous terms or conditions of employment to which members of the other sex are not exposed.

Oncale also makes clear that sexual harassment does not necessarily have to be about sexual attraction to be actionable. Although male-on-male or female-on-female, harassment could be the result of homosexual attraction, the Court in *Oncale* also noted that men and women could be harassed by members of their own sex based on animus or hatred. The *Oncale* Court noted three ways in which sexual harassment arises in the same-sex context: (1) the harasser was homosexual and sexually desired the plaintiff; (2) the harasser objected to persons of plaintiff's sex in their workplace; or (3) the harasser engaged in differential treatment at work for men and women. Although these are probably not the only means under which same-sex harassment is actionable, these illustrations probably capture the lion's share of such cases.

2. Sexual Orientation and Gender Identity Issues

Harassment because of sexual orientation and gender identity are prohibited under Title VII. *Bostock v. Clayton County, Ga.*, 590 U.S. 644 (2020).

3. Third-Party Harassment of Employees

Courts have generally adopted the approach that when a third-party, non-employee sexually harasses an employee (for example, when a third-party delivers products or services to the employer or when an employee is harassed by a customer or client), liability can attach to the employer. As the EEOC has provided recently, "Employees are further protected against unlawful harassment by non-employees, such as independent contractors; customers, including hotel guests, airline passengers, and shoppers; students; hospital patients and nursing home residents; and clients of the employer." *See* EEOC, Enforcement Guidance on Harassment in the Workplace (2024), https://www.eeoc.gov/laws/guidance/enforcement-guidance-harassment-workplace#_Toc164808023. As the agency further provides in that guidance, "An employer is liable for a hostile work environment created by non-supervisory employees or by non-employees if it was negligent because: ... it unreasonably failed to prevent the harassment; OR ... it failed to take reasonable corrective action in response to harassment about which it knew or should have known." *Id.* In short, third-party harassers are generally treated similarly to sexually harassing co-workers under a negligence standard. *Lockard v. Pizza Hut, Inc.*, 162 F.3d 1062 (10th Cir. 1998). The standards are the same because courts have reasoned that liability in these instances is direct rather than derivative (that is, direct liability is based on the employer's own conduct in correcting harassment as opposed to derivative liability, in which the harassing conduct of one of the employer's supervisors may be imputed to the employer), and it makes no difference whether the alleged harasser is an employee, an independent contractor, or a customer. *Dunn v. Washington County Hospital*, 429 F.3d 689 (7th Cir. 2005).

CHECKPOINTS

- Sexual harassment cases can be viewed as divided between tangible and non-tangible employment actions.
- Tangible and non-tangible employment actions may violate Title VII because such actions may either explicitly or constructively alter the terms or conditions of employment.
- For hostile work environment sexual harassment to be actionable, the harassment must be severe or pervasive, unwelcome, create a hostile or abusive environment, occur because of the employee's sex, and be capable of being imputed to the employer.

- Unwelcomeness is a subjective inquiry about whether the victim perceived the harassment was unwelcome, not whether her actual participation in the conduct was voluntary.
- An environment that an objectively "reasonable person" would find hostile or abusive is covered by Title VII.
- To establish liability for co-workers, the plaintiff must show that the employer knew or should have known of the harassment, and took no action.
- To satisfy the definition of a "supervisor," the worker typically must be able to carry out a tangible employment action.
- Strict liability exists for supervisory harassment involving tangible employment harm.
- If supervisory sexual harassment involves the plaintiff suffering intangible employment harm, the employer has an affirmative defense to liability if it acted reasonably and the employee failed to act reasonably.
- Sexual harassment claims can exist where the alleged harasser is of the same sex, where the harassment is based on sexual orientation and gender identity, as well as where the harasser is a non-employee.

CHAPTER 10

Retaliation

ROADMAP

- Retaliation provisions under Title VII
- Opposition clause cases
- Participation clause cases
- Establishing an adverse action
- The burden-shifting framework for retaliation claims
- Retaliation claims based on the pretext framework
- Retaliation against third parties
- Retaliation under other employment discrimination statutes

In addition to discrimination and harassment claims under Title VII, another important claim that is often brought by employment discrimination plaintiffs is the retaliation claim. Section 704(a) of Title VII prohibits discrimination against an employee because he or she has *opposed* any practice made an unlawful employment practice, or because he or she has made a charge, testified, assisted, or *participated* in any manner in an investigation, proceeding or hearing.

Retaliation claims loom large in Title VII cases. Whenever an employee files an internal complaint of discrimination with the employer or external charge of discrimination with the EEOC, any subsequent adverse employment action is likely to lead to a charge of retaliation. In fact, experience shows that even if a factfinder does not side with a plaintiff on his or her discrimination claim, it might still provide some recovery to the plaintiff by finding liability on the retaliation claim. The reason may be that factfinders—especially juries—do this with some frequency because either they want to punish an employer for bad conduct short of unlawful discrimination or because it might be easier for plaintiffs to prove retaliation than discrimination. Whatever the reason, plaintiffs have significantly more success bringing retaliation claims than any other under Title VII.

A. Title VII's Anti-Retaliation Provisions

Section 704(a) provides that "it shall be an unlawful employment practice for an employer to discriminate against any of his employees ... because he has *opposed* any practice made an unlawful employment practice by this subchapter, or because he has made a charge, testified, assisted, or *participated* in any manner in an investigation, proceeding, or hearing under this subchapter." 42 U.S.C. § 2000e-3(a). This provision creates two distinct retaliation causes of action under Title VII. Both present and former employees can bring claims for retaliation. *Robinson v. Shell Oil Co.*, 519 U.S. 337 (1997).

At the outset, it is worth noting that beyond prohibiting retaliation, the Americans with Disabilities Act makes it "unlawful to coerce, intimidate, threaten, or interfere with any individual in the exercise or enjoyment of, or on account of his or her having exercised or enjoyed, or on account of his or her having aided or encouraged any other individual in the exercise or enjoyment of, any right granted or protected by [the statute]." 42 U.S.C. § 12203(a)(b). And the PWFA contains a similar provision prohibiting such coercion or intimidation.

1. Opposition Clause

The United States Supreme Court set out what a plaintiff needs to show to prevail on an opposition clause claim in *Crawford v. Metropolitan Government of Nashville & Davidson County*, 555 U.S. 271 (2009). In *Crawford*, testimony had been given by an employee, not by her own choice, pursuant to a company investigation into alleged sexual harassment of another employee. The Court concluded that this form of internal reporting to the employer constituted protected activity under the opposition clause.

The Court observed that the meaning of "'oppose' goes beyond 'active, consistent' behavior in ordinary discourse, where we would naturally use the word to speak of someone who has taken no action at all to advance a position beyond disclosing it." Opposition exists if an employee takes a stand against an employer's discriminatory practices even if the employee does not instigate the action. For instance, if an employee refuses to follow a supervisor's order to fire a junior worker for discriminatory reasons, such an action would constitute "opposition" under § 704(a). The Court concluded that in the particular circumstance of the *Crawford* case, no reason existed to doubt that "a person can 'oppose' by responding to someone else's question just as surely as by provoking the discussion, and nothing in the statute requires a freakish rule protecting an employee who reports discrimination on her own initiative but not one who reports the same discrimination in the same words when her boss asks a question."

Justice Alito wrote a concurrence in *Crawford* that has the potential to limit its holding. He wrote separately to point out that the Court had not been asked to consider whether the opposition clause shields employees who do not communicate their views to their employers through their conduct or words (for instance, they only informally communicated their opposition to a co-worker). Because Alito believed the answer to that question is far from clear, he reserved that question for another case.

2. Participation Clause

In addition to conduct falling under the opposition clause, another form of protected conduct can arise under the participation clause. Section 704(a) provides that "it shall be an unlawful employment practice for an employer to discriminate against any of his employees ... because he has ... *participated* in any manner in an investigation, proceeding, or hearing under this subchapter." 42 U.S.C. § 2000e-3(a) (emphasis added). Conduct is typically protected under this clause where an individual engages in the formal mechanisms of the process. This can take a number of forms, but perhaps the most readily identifiable is filing a charge of discrimination with the U.S. EEOC. By submitting such a charge, an individual has participated in the formal process and is entitled to protection against retaliation for filing that charge. Beyond filing a charge, testifying in a Title VII proceeding, speaking with an EEOC investigator, or providing relevant documentation in such cases would similarly be protected. Where a claim arises under the participation clause, it is offered blanket protection under the statute, as retaliation against such conduct could imperil the very heart of Title VII as well as the legal process.

3. Establishing an Adverse Action

The primary objective of § 704(a) is to prevent conduct that might well have discouraged a reasonable employee from engaging in protected activity. Under the test set up by the Court in *Burlington Northern & Santa Fe Railway Co. v. White*, 548 U.S. 53 (2006), for retaliation to be actionable, the harm must be (1) materially adverse (2) to a reasonable employee or job applicant. In this regard, the Court stated: "In the present context that means that the employer's actions must be harmful to the point that they could well dissuade a reasonable worker from making or supporting a charge of discrimination."

Additionally, the Court held that adverse employment actions under Section 704(a) are not limited to those that occur within the workplace. To support this point, the Court pointed to *Rochon v. Gonzales*, 438 F.3d 1211 (D.C. Cir. 2006) (FBI's refusal to investigate a death threat made against an agent constituted actionable retaliation under Title VII), and *Berry v. Stevenson Chevrolet*, 74 F.3d 980 (10th Cir. 1996) (malicious criminal charge filed by the employer against a former employee constituted actionable retaliation under Title VII).

Note that the concept of adverse action in the retaliation context is different than the required harm in the discrimination context, which is a negative change in the terms, conditions, or privileges of employment. These concepts are also separate from the idea of a tangible employment action used to determine vicarious liability in the harassment context.

B. Burden Shifting Framework for Retaliation Cases

Similar to Title VII discrimination claims, retaliation claims may be analyzed under different burden-shifting frameworks depending on the type of evidence available. *Fabela v. Socorro Independent School District*, 329 F.3d 409 (5th Cir. 2003). Yet, even within the *McDonnell Douglas* pretext framework, the elements for retaliation claims differ from discrimination claims quite significantly. This is primarily the result of statutory language.

1. Plaintiff's Prima Facie Case in Pretext Action

There are three elements to the plaintiff's prima facie case under the pretext framework. First, the plaintiff must engage in a statutorily protected activity. In a participation case, the protected activity is usually filing an EEOC charge so this element is easy to meet.

Opposition clause cases, on the other hand, are a bit more complicated because there are two prongs that must be met to show a statutorily-protected activity: (1) a reasonable belief that an unlawful employment practice occurred (no violation need actually exist); and (2) a showing that the activities taken in opposition to the suspected unlawful employment action are reasonable under the circumstances. So, although the employee cannot oppose the unlawful employment practice by engaging in violence against the employer, the employee may be able to engage in a peaceful protest or boycott. *Payne v. McLemore's Wholesale & Retail Stores*, 654 F.2d 1130 (5th Cir. 1981).

The second element of the plaintiff's prima facie case is the existence of an adverse employment action. Adverse employment actions have been interpreted expansively by most appellate courts (more so than the similar concept of "tangible employment action" in the sexual harassment context). This is one of the issues explored in the *Burlington Northern* participation case. In that case, the question was whether the female railroad worker, who was retaliated against by being suspended for 37 days before being reinstated with backpay, suffered an adverse employment action. The Court said yes because the employer's actions would have been seen as a materially adverse action to a reasonable employee, even though she was eventually placed back into the position after she had been suspended. Note that this standard does not require an ultimate employment decision like firing or failure to promote. On the other hand, in a case involving the employer's transfer of employees, the Court held that the employer may proceed with previously contemplated transfers of employees upon discovering that the employee filed a charge with the EEOC. *Clark County School District v. Breeden*, 532 U.S. 268 (2001).

The third and final element of the prima facie case requires a causal link between the protected expression and the adverse action. A causal connection in a retaliation case is "frequently established by showing that there was a suspiciously short period of time between the employee's complaint and the adverse employment action." *Boumehdi v. Plastag Holdings, LLC*, 489 F.3d 781 (7th Cir. 2007).

2. The Defendant's Response and Pretext

If the plaintiff makes out a prima facie case, a rebuttable presumption of retaliation arises. The burden of production (not persuasion) shifts to the defendant to articulate a legitimate, non-retaliatory reason for its employment actions. If the defendant says nothing, then the plaintiff wins based on the presumption of retaliation established through the prima facie case. But in most cases, the defendant's reasons for its actions are sufficient to meet the burden of coming forward with evidence.

And just like the *McDonnell Douglas* discrimination framework, the burden then shifts back to the plaintiff to show that the real reason for defendant's actions was unlawful retaliation—usually by showing that the defendant's stated reason was pretextual. The plaintiff, who always has the burden of proof in pretext cases, must make this final showing by a preponderance of the evidence.

3. "But for" Cause

In *University of Texas Southwestern Medical Center v. Nassar*, 570 U.S. 338 (2013), the Supreme Court held that but-for causation is required for retaliation claims brought under Title VII. Thus, "mixed motive" cases, where there is *both* a lawful and unlawful reason motivating the retaliatory act, will now no longer be permitted to proceed unless the plaintiff can show that the unlawful reason was a "but for" cause of the outcome. According to *Nassar*, then, it is now clear that a worker must provide "proof that the unlawful retaliation would not have occurred in the absence of the alleged wrongful action or actions of the employer." *Id.*

C. Retaliation against Third Parties

Another significant issue under the retaliation provisions is whether the retaliation provisions of Title VII can provide a claim for third parties who did not personally engage in protected activity. In *Thompson v. North American Stainless, LP*, 562 U.S. 170 (2011), the Supreme Court held that such suits are possible. The Court adopted a "zone of interests" test, by which an individual can sue if he "falls within the zone of interests sought to be protected by the statutory provision whose violation forms the legal basis for his complaint." *Id.*

(citing *Lujan v. National Wildlife Federation*, 497 U.S. 871, 883 (1990) (quotation omitted)). Thus, after *Thompson*, third parties can bring suit where they fall within this zone of interest. This will often occur where the employer fires a worker who does not complain in an effort to punish an employee who has availed herself of her statutory rights. This could mean firing a spouse, relative, or even good friend of the person who complains. *See generally*, Alex B. Long, *The Troublemaker's Friend: Retaliation Against Third Parties and the Right of Association in the Workplace*, 59 Fla. L. Rev. 931 (2007).

D. Retaliation under Other Employment Discrimination Statutes

Most employment discrimination statutes have express retaliation provisions like those in Title VII, the ADA, the PWFA, and the ADEA for private-sector employees. However, there may still be retaliation protection among some of the exceptions. For instance, the Court has allowed retaliation claims under the federal employee provisions of the ADEA and § 1981 of the Civil Rights statutes.

1. Age Discrimination in Employment Act (ADEA)

Similarly, the ADEA has almost identical language to the ADA and Title VII for *private-sector employees*. Under 29 U.S.C. § 623(d): "It shall be unlawful for an employer to discriminate against any of his employees ... because such individual ... has opposed any practice made unlawful by this section, or because such individual ... has made a charge, testified, assisted, or participated in any manner in an investigation, proceeding, or litigation under this chapter."

A difference, however, exists under the ADEA's federal employee provisions. Although the ADEA provision covering federal employees (§ 633a) does not explicitly contain an anti-retaliation provision, the Supreme Court held in *Gomez-Perez v. Potter*, 553 U.S. 474 (2008), that a retaliation claim can be inferred from the language and structure of the ADEA. Relying on precedent in the Title IX education law context, *Jackson v. Birmingham Board. of Education*, 544 U.S. 167 (2005), the Court reasoned that the language concerning prohibition against age discrimination also includes a prohibition against retaliating against an employee for complaining of or opposing age discrimination.

2. Civil Rights Act of 1871 (§ 1981)

Similar to the federal provisions in the ADEA, § 1981 of the Civil Rights Act of 1871 does not contain an express retaliation provision for bringing race-discrimination claims under that statute. Nonetheless, the Supreme Court held in *CBOCS West, Inc. v. Humphries*, 553 U.S. 442 (2008), that Section 1981 does permit retaliation claims. Relying on similar precedent interpreting another Civil Rights Act (§ 1982), *Sullivan* v. *Little Hunting Park, Inc.*, 396 U.S. 229 (1969), the Court concluded "that considerations of *stare decisis* strongly support adherence to *Sullivan* and the long line of related cases where we interpret §§ 1981 and 1982 similarly," meaning that both provisions should be interpreted to permit retaliation claims. (See Chapter 14 for more on the Civil Rights Acts.)

CHECKPOINTS

- Section 704(a) of Title VII prohibits discrimination against an employee because he or she has *opposed* any practice, made an unlawful employment practice, or because he or she has *participated* in an investigation, proceeding or hearing.
- Internal reporting of discrimination in response to an employer's investigation constitutes protected activity under the opposition clause.
- Similar to Title VII discrimination claims, retaliation claims may be analyzed under a burden-shifting framework depending on the type of evidence available.
- In a pretext case under *McDonnell Douglas*, there are three elements of the plaintiff's prima facie case: existence of statutorily protected activity, an adverse employment action, and a causal connection between the protected activity and the adverse action.
- Under the test set up by the Court in *Burlington Northern*, an adverse employment action under § 704(a) must be (1) materially adverse (2) to a reasonable employee.

- Under Supreme Court case law, a plaintiff must prove "but for" cause to prevail on a Title VII retaliation claim.
- Third party retaliation claims are permissible if the individual falls in the "zone of interests."
- Most employment discrimination statutes have express retaliation provisions like Title VII, the ADA, the PWFA, and the ADEA for private employees; among the exceptions, the Court has read retaliation claims into the federal employee provisions of the ADEA and § 1981 of the Civil Rights statutes.

CHAPTER 11

Special Issues in Title VII Antidiscrimination Law

ROADMAP

- Special issues regarding race and color discrimination
- Race-plus and color-plus claims
- Special issues regarding national origin discrimination
- Citizenship discrimination and English-only rules
- Special issues regarding sex discrimination
- Pregnancy discrimination
- Sex-plus discrimination claims
- Special issues regarding religious discrimination
- Exempt religious employers under Title VII
- Meaning of religious accommodation and undue hardship

The earlier chapters of this book set forth the analyses for the basic claims under Title VII—for example, disparate treatment, systemic discrimination, and disparate impact. Those analyses apply to all of the protected classes under the statute; however, most of those classes implicate various legal issues that do not always apply to the others. This chapter will focus on these special issues.

A. Special Issues Regarding Race and Color Discrimination

1. Distinguishing Race and Color Discrimination

Title VII's protected classes included both "race" and "color." Those two characteristics are often used synonymously, but they have distinct meanings. Race refers to an employee's membership in a specific race, such as white or black. This concept often blurs into another protected class, national origin, particularly given the widespread use of the term "African American." Yet, these two concepts are not the same. For instance, an employee with African roots could be white and another employee with no African lineage could be black.

Race is not always a clear concept, as many people disagree over whether certain characteristics rise to the level of race—Latino or Hispanic being one instance, as an individual can be a black or white Latino. A good example of various classes that might be considered race, and a good benchmark for what is typically accepted as the most common races in the United States, are those listed on Census questionnaires. In 2000, six races were listed: American Indian or Alaskan Native, Asian, Black or African American, Native Hawaiian or Other Pacific Islander, White, and Some Other Race. However, this list was greatly expanded in 2010 to include what would normally be considered national origin under Title VII, such as Asian Indian, Chinese, Filipino, Japanese, Korean, Vietnamese, and other similar descriptions.

Color is a class that is not raised as frequently as race, a term with which it is often improperly merged. The protection of color as a unique class recognizes that employees of the same race may be treated differently because of their skin tone—in general, darker-skinned employees are more likely to face discrimination. There has been a growing body of research showing that color discrimination exists and can be quite significant. Thus, we may begin to see an increase in the number of claims alleging color discrimination.

2. Race-Plus or Color-Plus Claims of Discrimination

One type of alleged discrimination that can cause courts problems is the "race-plus" (or color-plus) theory. Race-plus discrimination describes an adverse employment action made because of an employee's race *and* another characteristic. For example, a black woman may allege that she was discriminated against because she was both black and a woman; if she were a white woman or black man she would not have faced such discrimination. This is referred to as race-plus (or alternatively in this example, sex-plus) discrimination. These claims are sometimes called intersectional claims. The complication is that neither race nor sex is the sole cause of the discrimination.

Some courts have focused on the "race" and the "plus" characteristics separately in a race-plus case. This approach makes it more difficult for a plaintiff to establish that the employer was motivated by race, particularly if the other characteristic is one that is not protected by Title VII, such as a claim that an employer discriminated against an employee because he was both short and black. However, the majority of courts no longer have serious problems with race-plus claims. First, even if race is not the sole cause of the discrimination, it can still be a "but-for" cause. In other words, in the example above involving a black woman, if she is correct that a white woman or black man would not have been discriminated against, then "but for" her race (and "but for" her sex), she would not have faced an adverse employment action.

Second, after the 1991 Civil Rights Act Amendments, §703(m) allows a mixed-motive theory that requires only that a protected class be a "motivating factor." As discussed in Chapter 6, the mixed-motive theory would allow the black woman to establish a violation of Title VII by showing either that race or sex were motivating factors in her adverse employment action. In essence, the race-plus claim is an argument that the employee was discriminated against because of her race, but that not every member of her race faced such discrimination. Rather, only a subset of her protected class—members of her race with the additional characteristic—faced discrimination. But as long as the employee can show that race was a motivating factor in the adverse decision, that is all that is required to establish a violation of Title VII. The difference between a "but for" cause standard and a motivating factor standard may be less important after the Supreme Court's opinion in *Bostock v. Clayton County*, 590 U.S. 644 (2020). *Bostock* described "but for" cause as a "sweeping" standard, noted that events can have multiple "but for" causes, and stated that a reason can still be a "but for" cause even if it is not the primary reason for the outcome.

3. Other Race and Color Issues

Because the focus of Title VII's enactment and much of the initial litigation exploring its structure was focused on race, there are relatively few unique issues with regard to race discrimination. There are a few special considerations, however.

A significant exception that applies to race and color discrimination is that the bona fide occupational qualification defense (BFOQ) does not apply under any circumstances. The BFOQ defense is available only for sex, national origin, and religious discrimination claims. Often students ask whether a film may only interview black applicants to play Malcolm X in a movie. The answer is that such overt discrimination cannot be defended on the basis of a BFOQ, although it is rarely challenged in such a situation.

Differences in grooming codes based on race violate federal discrimination law. Difficulties arise when an employer's policy does not contain facial distinctions, but rather the employer has a uniformly applied policy that disallows certain hairstyles or clothing more associated with a particular race or national origin. Angela Onwuachi-Willig, *Another Hair Piece: Exploring New Strands of Analysis Under Title VII*, 98 Geo. L.J. 1079 (2010); D. Wendy Greene, *Title VII: What's Hair (and Other Race-Based Characteristics) Got to Do with It?*, 79 U. Colo. L. Rev. 1355 (2008). Courts have held that it is lawful under Title VII to uniformly apply a hairstyle policy that bans the wearing of dreadlocks or cornrows. *EEOC v. Catastrophe Mgmt. Solutions*, 852 F.3d 1018 (11th Cir. 2016); *Rogers v. Am. Airlines, Inc.*, 527 F. Supp. 299, 231 (S.D.N.Y. 1981). Such outcomes are facing scrutiny because employers may be making decisions about what counts as a "professional" hairstyle based on racial norms. Some states have enacted CROWN Acts that prohibit hairstyle discrimination when the hairstyle is associated with a particular race.

However, even under Title VII, the employer would face liability if it did not evenly enforce its hairstyle policy or if it adopted it to discriminate because of race. It would also likely face liability if it banned employees from wearing hair in a natural hairstyle. EEOC guidance issued in 2024 states that racial harassment can occur when a worker is subjected to comments about a race-related hairstyle. EEOC Enforcement Guidance on Harassment in the Workplace § II.A.1. (2024).

Grooming policies can also raise racial disparate impact issues. One such issue that comes up on occasion are employer policies banning beards on male employees. Employers use a variety of reasons for such policies, from the need to present a certain look in front of customers to safety concerns for employees who have to use respirators. The problem is that black men are more likely to suffer from a skin disease that is seriously aggravated by shaving. Black employees with this disease have raised disparate impact claims to no-beard policies with mixed success. As is probably no surprise, the cases usually hinge on the employer's justifications for the policies. Thus, fire departments concerned about safety are generally protected against disparate impact challenges, while employers concerned only about a certain look for employees who deal with customers tend to lose. *Fitzpatrick v. City of Atlanta*, 2 F.3d 1112 (11th Cir. 1993) (city successful with regard to respirators for firefighters); *Bradley v. Pizzaco of Nebraska, Inc.*, 7 F.3d 795 (8th Cir. 1993) (company unsuccessful with regard to pizza delivery drivers). However, an employer citing safety as its justification must show that the policy is actually needed. For instance, in one case, a court held that the fact that a few sheriff deputies were designated as first responders in case of a terrorist attack, and some of those first responders were issued respirators, did not justify a no-beard policy for all deputies. *Simon v. Harris County Sheriff's Department*, 109 Fair Empl. Prac. Cas. (BNA) 119 (S.D. Tex. Apr. 12, 2010).

B. Special Issues Regarding National Origin Discrimination

As noted above, Title VII's national origin protected class is at times confused with race. But national origin is distinct and describes an employee's geographic or cultural ties. *Espinoza v. Farah Manufacturing Co.*, 414 U.S. 86 (1973). Typically, national origin refers to the country from where an employee or family originated. However, it can also include non-geographic classifications such as being Native American or part of an ethnic group within a country. *Dawavendewa v. Salt River Project*, 154 F.3d 1117 (9th Cir. 1998). Moreover, the EEOC broadly defines national origin as including the "physical, cultural or linguistic characteristics of a national origin group." 29 C.F.R. § 1606.1. Accordingly, some courts—although not all—have held that discriminating against an employee because of her accent could be considered unlawful national origin discrimination; although in these cases, an employer would still have the opportunity to show that speaking with less of an accent is a bona fide occupational qualification.

One limitation to this protected class was addressed in *Espinoza*, where the Supreme Court held that national origin does not include an employee's citizenship in a given country. Thus, Title VII does not prohibit an employer from making an adverse employment action because an employee is a citizen of a certain country, unless the citizenship rule has a disparate impact on, or was intended to discriminate against, employees of a given national origin. On the other hand, citizenship discrimination is covered by a related federal law, the Immigration Reform and Control Act of 1986, 8 U.S.C. § 1324b.

One issue that can be significant for national origin discrimination is an employer's policy forbidding employees from speaking certain languages. The most high-profile example of this issue is an employer's implementation of an "English-only" rule in the workplace. The EEOC has created a presumption that broad English-only rules constitute national origin discrimination because language is "often an essential national origin characteristic." 29 C.F.R. § 1606.7(a). Under the EEOC's approach, an employer can typically justify a rule, at least one that applies only to work times, by showing that it is a business necessity. Not all courts have followed the EEOC, however, and some have rejected the requirement that an employer provide a business justification for a work-time English-only rule that was not established with the intent to discriminate on the basis of national origin. *Garcia v. Gloor*, 618 F.2d 264 (5th Cir. 1980). Other courts have accepted the view that English-only policies may create a disparate impact based on national origin, thereby incorporating the "job-related" and "business necessity" elements of that analysis. *Maldonado v. City of Altus*, 433 F.3d 1294 (10th Cir. 2006), *overruled on other grounds by Burlington Northern & Santa Fe Railway Co. v. White*, 548 U.S. 53 (2006). Additionally, an English-only rule can contribute to a hostile work environment claim by employees of a given national origin. *Montes v. Vail Clinic, Inc.*, 497 F.3d 1160 (10th Cir. 2007).

C. Special Issues Regarding Sex Discrimination

The inclusion of sex as a protected class under Title VII has been an important part of an enormous shift in the American workplace, where women have become a much larger portion of the workforce and have entered jobs that few women had previously achieved. Indeed, one story about former Justice O'Connor is that, after graduating third in her class from Stanford Law School in 1952 (former Chief Justice Rehnquist was first), the only legal job she could get was as a law firm secretary. Moreover, the inclusion of sex in Title VII itself reflects some of the hostility that female workers faced. The original Title VII legislation did not include sex as a protected class—it was added by Representative Smith of Virginia potentially as a means to encourage further opposition to the bill. If this was the intent, his amendment backfired, as the bill and its protection of sex eventually passed. A by-product, however, is that there is virtually no legislative history on Title VII's protection for sex.

In addition to the normal disparate treatment and disparate impact analyses discussed in earlier chapters, several issues that take on special relevance with regard to sex are discussed elsewhere in this book, such as: sexual harassment (Chapter 9), sexual orientation or gender identity claims (Chapter 9), and the Equal Pay Act and other compensation issues (Chapter 15). What follows are some other issues particular to sex.

1. Pregnancy, Childbirth, and Related Medical Conditions

This section considers protections for pregnancy, childbirth and related medical conditions under Title VII, the Pregnant Workers Fairness Act (PWFA), and the ADA.

One of the long-vexing issues under Title VII had been whether discrimination based on an employee's pregnancy was prohibited. The argument for protection centered on the idea that pregnancy discrimination is based on the employee's sex, as only women can become pregnant. The opposing view emphasized that, despite this biological fact, pregnancy discrimination was its own, independent form of discrimination that should not be considered sex discrimination under Title VII. That opposing view won initially before the Supreme Court, but Congress ultimately overruled the Court by enacting the Pregnancy Discrimination Act of 1978 (PDA).

The Court considered whether Title VII covered pregnancy discrimination in *General Electric Co. v. Gilbert*, 429 U.S. 125 (1976). *Gilbert* involved a disability benefits plan that excluded all disabilities arising from pregnancy, which also had the effect of excluding any claimed disability for the pregnancy itself. The plaintiffs argued that this exclusion was unlawful sex discrimination under Title VII, but the Court disagreed. Although recognizing that pregnancy discrimination could be a pretext for an employer's intent to discriminate against women, absent evidence of that pretext, the Court held that discrimination against pregnancy is not discrimination based on sex. The Court characterized the disability plan as covering all employees—men and women—equally, while merely refusing to provide extra coverage for disabilities arising from pregnancy, which only women would be able to use. Using a similar argument, the Court also held that no disparate impact claim was available; because the plan gave the same amount of benefits to both men and women, the failure to cover an extra risk that only women face does not create a disparity. This final holding contrasted with a later case, *Nashville Gas Co. v. Satty*, 434 U.S. 136 (1977), in which the Court found a valid disparate impact claim based on an employer's policy that required pregnant employees to take a leave of absence, after which they lost all previously accumulated seniority. In *Satty*, the Court applied *Gilbert* in holding that the seniority policy was facially neutral. But it contrasted the two cases by holding that burdening women with an added *cost*, rather than refusing to grant them the additional *benefit* involved in *Gilbert*, created an actionable disparity.

Despite confusion over the benefit/cost distinction in *Gilbert* and *Satty*, the bottom-line holding from *Gilbert* still stood: discrimination based on pregnancy was not discrimination based on sex. It was this holding that Congress explicitly reversed in the PDA. That act amended Title VII's definition of sex by creating a new § 701(k), which states that: "[t]he terms 'because of sex' or 'on the basis of sex' include, but are not limited to, because of or on the basis of pregnancy, childbirth, or related medical conditions." Section 701(k) also directly addressed some of the benefit program disparities raised in *Gilbert* and *Satty* by mandating that "women affected by pregnancy, childbirth, or related medical conditions shall be treated the same for all employment-related purposes, including receipt of benefits under fringe benefit programs, as other persons not so affected but similar in their ability or inability to work."

However, the Court held in *AT&T Corp. v. Hulteen*, 556 U.S. 701 (2009), that § 701(k) did not make an exception to § 703(h)'s protection for bona fide seniority systems (which are discussed in Chapter 8). Thus, it was not unlawful for the employer to continue to use pension benefit credits that were accrued under a subsequently revoked seniority rule that discriminated against pregnancy leave prior to the PDA's enactment. Finally, § 701(k) states that although an employer can provide abortion benefits, the PDA does not require a health plan to cover abortion costs except where the life of the mother is threatened or there are medical complications arising from an abortion. Coverage of the Affordable Care Act is beyond the scope of this book.

Most pregnancy disparate treatment claims are analyzed the same way as other disparate treatment claims under Title VII, with the protected class being pregnancy-based "sex" as defined in the PDA.

Like other sex discrimination claims, employers may raise a BFOQ defense to pregnancy discrimination. In *UAW v. Johnson Controls, Inc.*, 499 U.S. 487 (1991), the Court read the PDA as confirming its general view that a valid BFOQ must relate to an employee's work performance. In the case of the PDA, this confirmation comes from its mandate that pregnant employees "shall be treated the same for all employment-related purposes" unless they differ "in their ability or inability to work." Thus, an employer cannot use pregnancy as a BFOQ unless the pregnancy affects an employee's ability to work. In *Johnson Controls*, this meant that workplace toxins that threatened a pregnant employee's fetus could not be a BFOQ because a pregnant employee could still do the job as well as a non-pregnant employee. Cases in which an employer successfully raised a BFOQ justification for barring pregnant employees typically involve significant safety issues, such as a rule barring airline flight attendants whose pregnancy may interfere with their ability to perform their jobs in an emergency. *Harriss v. Pan American World Airways, Inc.*, 649 F.2d 670 (9th Cir. 1980). These cases usually use pregnancy as a proxy for safety concerns, a type of BFOQ defense discussed in more detail in Chapter 6. Finally, employees can pursue disparate impact claims based on pregnancy. *Stout v. Baxter Healthcare Corp.*, 282 F.3d 856 (5th Cir. 2002).

In *Young v. United Parcel Serv., Inc.*, the Supreme Court held that a failure to accommodate pregnancy could constitute pregnancy discrimination in some instances, if the employer accommodated other conditions. 575 U.S. 206 (2015). The Court approved a modified *McDonnell Douglas* framework for evaluating these cases.

One issue that arises under the PDA involves the provision of differential health benefits to male and female employees. In *Newport News Shipbuilding & Dry Dock Co. v. EEOC*, 462 U.S. 669 (1983), the Supreme Court addressed a case in which an employer provided less health insurance coverage for the pregnancy-related hospital expenses of male employees' spouses than it did for the pregnancy expenses of female employees. The Court held that the PDA directly prohibited this disparity, which discriminated against male employees because the spouses of female employees received coverage for all hospital costs, while spouses of male employees received coverage for all hospital costs, minus those related to pregnancy. According to the Court, this is virtually identical to the disparity in *Gilbert*—a disparity that Congress intended to make unlawful in the PDA.

Another issue that has been a frequent concern following the PDA is the provision of leave. Questions arise when employers provide leave to women while they are pregnant or soon after the birth of a child. Although employers do not have to provide any benefits, if they choose to do so, do they also have to provide similar benefits for men? In *California Savings & Loan Association v. Guerra*, 479 U.S. 272 (1987), the Supreme Court addressed a Title VII challenge to a California law that required employers to provide unpaid leave and reinstatement rights to pregnant employees, but not to other temporarily disabled employees. The Court rejected the challenge, which alleged that the law unlawfully favored pregnant women over male employees who were temporarily disabled, and held that the requirement was consistent with the PDA's amendment of Title VII. First, the Court interpreted the PDA's requirement that pregnant women be treated equally under benefits programs as merely striking down the approach in *Gilbert*. Thus, the PDA created a floor below which plans cannot sink, not a ceiling that limits what plans can provide. Second, the Court noted that employers could avoid even the hint of conflict between the state law and Title VII by proving the same benefits to disabled employees as it does for pregnant ones. In essence, the Court interpreted the PDA as an attempt to expand women's ability to participate in the workforce, which the California requirement furthered.

Although the PDA does not prevent employers from providing additional benefits related to pregnancy, providing only mothers with post-birth leave to care for a child is unlawful. *Schafer v. Board of Public Education of the School District of Pittsburgh, Pa.*, 903 F.2d 243 (3d Cir. 1990). Unlike pregnancy benefits—which can only affect women—benefits related to childrearing apply to men and women. Moreover, requiring employers who provide childrearing leave to do so equally supports the PDA's goal of expanding employment options for women by ensuring that men also have the opportunity to care for children. This goal was an explicit underpinning of the Family and Medical Leave Act of 1993 (FMLA), 29 U.S.C. § 2601 *et seq.*, which requires unpaid leave for new parents, but only if they work for large employers with 50 or more employees.

The Pregnant Workers Fairness Act went into effect on June 27, 2023. 42 U.S.C. §§ 2000gg *et seq*. The EEOC issued regulations interpreting the PWFA in April of 2024, and the regulations went into effect on June 18, 2024. 29 C.F.R. § 1636.1 *et seq*. The PWFA requires covered entities to make reasonable accommodations to "known limitations related to the pregnancy, childbirth, or related medical conditions of a qualified employee" unless the entity can demonstrate that providing the accommodation is an undue hardship. 42 U.S.C. § 2000gg-1(1).

Generally, the concepts of reasonable accommodation and undue hardship should be read in tandem with the ADA. 42 U.S.C. § 2000gg(7). The PWFA also requires covered entities to engage in an interactive process related to accommodation, like that contemplated by the ADA. Unlike the ADA, the employer cannot require an employee to take leave as an accommodation, if other reasonable accommodations exist. 42 U.S.C. § 2000gg-1(4). However, leave can be acceptable under the PWFA if the employee requests or accepts it or if that is the only reasonable accommodation that does not create an undue hardship.

To receive an accommodation, a worker must be a "qualified employee." This term means that the person can, with or without reasonable accommodation, perform the essential functions of the job. 42 U.S.C. § 2000gg(6). However, a person is still qualified if the inability to meet the essential functions is temporary, the essential function could be performed in the near future, and the inability to perform the essential function can be reasonably accommodated. 42 U.S.C. § 2000gg(6).

Similar to the ADA, the limitation must be known to the employer. A limitation does not need to meet the definition of disability under the ADA to be covered by the PWFA.

In addition to the accommodation obligation, the PWFA also prohibits a covered entity from requiring a qualified employee to accept an accommodation "other than any reasonable accommodation arrived at through the interactive process." 42 U.S.C. § 2000gg-1(2). The covered entity cannot deny employment opportunities because of the need for accommodation or take an adverse action on account of the request for or use of a reasonable accommodation. 42 U.S.C. § 2000gg-1. The Act also prohibits retaliation. 42 U.S.C. § 2000gg-2(f).

In the PWFA, Congress directed the EEOC to produce regulations interpreting the statute. Those regulations are helpful in defining a number of terms under the PWFA. The regulations indicate that an unnecessary delay in providing an accommodation violates the PWFA. 29 C.F.R. § 1636.4(a)(1).

Although pregnancy is not a disability, pregnancy can lead to disability. Employers must comply with all applicable statutes related to pregnancy discrimination, including Title VII, the PWFA, and the ADA.

2. Breastfeeding at Work

Another issue is the extent to which any animus towards breastfeeding in the workplace may be covered by Title VII. In one case, the Fifth Circuit weighed in on the issue, holding that "[b]ecause discriminating against a woman who is lactating or expressing breast milk violates Title VII and the PDA, we find that the EEOC has stated a prima facie case of sex discrimination with a showing" that the worker was fired "because she was lactating and wanted to express milk at work." *EEOC v. Houston Funding, Ltd.*, 717 F.3d 425, 430 (5th Cir. 2013). It is also worth noting that the PUMP Act also requires employers to provide reasonable break time for nursing mothers, and employers should also be cognizant of possible state or local requirements as well.

3. Sex-Plus Claims of Discrimination

Like the race-plus and color-plus claims, employees can also make "sex-plus" claims. A common example of a sex-plus claim is an employee who is discriminated against because she is a mother of small children. The claim is sex-plus because the allegation is that she faced an adverse employment action because she was a woman *and* because she had small children. In other words, only a subset of women—those with small children—are alleged to have faced discrimination. This claim is actionable if there is sufficient proof to establish that her sex was a motivating factor in the adverse employment action, and the fact that women without small children were not discriminated against does not bar her claim. *Phillips v. Martin Marietta Corp.*, 400 U.S. 542 (1971); *Chadwick v. Wellpoint, Inc.*, 561 F.3d 38 (1st Cir. 2009).

4. Sex Stereotyping and Differing Dress and Grooming Standards

An issue that is not unique to sex discrimination, but occurs more frequently in that area, is stereotyping. Take, for example, a woman who was discriminated against because she was not feminine enough. The employer did not make an adverse action simply because she was a woman; rather, the action occurred because she did not meet the employer's expectations of how a woman should act. Of course, that can be equated to sex discrimination because if the employee was a man, she would not be penalized for failing to meet that stereotype.

In *Price Waterhouse v. Hopkins*, 490 U.S. 228 (1989), the Supreme Court adopted this view and held that stereotyping can constitute unlawful discrimination. In *Price Waterhouse*, an accounting firm associate was denied promotion to partner. There were some valid concerns about her work performance (hence the fact that the Court established the mixed-motive claim in *Price Waterhouse*, as discussed in Chapter 6), but there were also several comments by partners who voted on her promotion that she was too aggressive—although that trait was usually welcomed in men in her position. One partner also stated that she needed to walk, talk, and dress more femininely to have a chance at promotion in the future. The Court emphasized that the employer's attitude put the employee in a Catch-22: she could be aggressive, as required by her job, but suffer discrimination because that trait was not expected in a woman or she could be less aggressive and face negative consequences for not doing her job well. Because male employees were not placed in this Catch-22, this form of stereotyping was unlawful.

After *Price Waterhouse*, employees of any class can attempt to establish discrimination through a stereotyping theory. An important facet of such claims is that the Court treats stereotyping as evidence that sex, or another class, played a role in the adverse employment action. Thus, the mere existence of stereotyping remarks is not sufficient to establish a claim; the employee must show, as was the case in *Price Waterhouse*, that the stereotyping caused the employment decision.

An increasingly high-profile type of case that can overlap with a stereotyping claim relates to differing grooming or dress standards being applied to male and female employees. The case of *Jespersen v. Harrah's Operating Co.*, 444 F.3d 1104 (9th Cir. 2006) (en banc), highlights this issue. The female employee in *Jespersen* was a bartender in a casino bar who was fired for refusing to wear facial makeup, as required by the employer's grooming policy. That policy required all bartenders to wear black pants, white shirts, a bow tie, and black shoes. However, it also had different grooming requirements for men and women, with one of the differences being that only women had to wear facial makeup, while men were prohibited from wearing facial makeup. On its face (excusing the pun), this differing grooming standard is sex discrimination, as the employee was fired for refusing to do something that a male employee was not required to do. Yet, as the employee's loss in the *Jespersen* case illustrates, courts take into account social norms with regard to the sexes and will not automatically find different requirements unlawful.

The touchstone in evaluating different dress and grooming standards is whether the requirements are equally burdensome for both sexes. If an employee can show unequal burdens, or significantly unequal burdens in some courts, then the different standards constitute prima facie evidence of discrimination. In *Jespersen*, for example, the court held that the grooming standards were approximately equal, so the employee failed to show this type of discrimination. Different height and weight requirements for male and female employees, such as flight attendants, are typically analyzed under this equal burden rule as well. *Frank v. United Airlines, Inc.*, 216 F.3d 845 (9th Cir. 2000) (finding a violation because the female requirements met a medium-body-frame standard, while the male requirements met a large-body-frame standard).

The *Jespersen* employee, however, also alleged that the grooming standards constituted unlawful sex stereotyping. The court rejected that claim, citing the generally "unisex" nature of the required dress and concluding that the grooming standards did not force "women bartenders to conform to a commonly-accepted stereotypical image of what women should wear." The dissenting judges in *Jespersen* disagreed on this point as a factual matter, and disagreed with the unequal burdens conclusion as well, but the majority holding in *Jespersen* indicates that social norms remain quite important in these cases and an employer's policy that largely tracks such norms will usually survive a Title VII challenge. More sexually provocative requirements—such as, perhaps, the revealing outfits often required of cocktail waitresses in casinos—are in more jeopardy if the employer cannot establish a BFOQ defense for the stereotyping policy. *EEOC v. Sage Realty Corp.*, 507 F. Supp. 599 (S.D.N.Y. 1981) (sexually provocative requirement for female hotel lobby attendants).

5. Sexual Orientation and Gender Identity

Discrimination because of sexual orientation and gender identity is prohibited sex discrimination under Title VII. *Bostock v. Clayton County, Ga.*, 590 U.S. 644 (2020).

D. Special Issues Regarding Religious Discrimination

1. Defining Protected "Religious" Employees

Many of Title VII's protected classes are generally considered "immutable"—that is, a characteristic that an individual has at birth and cannot change. Prohibiting discrimination based on an employee's religion, therefore, is notable in that religious preference is something that an employee chooses and can affirmatively change.

Under § 701(j) of Title VII, "religion" is defined as including "all aspects of religious observance and practice, as well as belief, unless an employer demonstrates that he is unable to reasonably accommodate to an employee's or prospective employee's religious observance or practice without undue hardship on the conduct of the employer's business." This definition is quite broad, extending to virtually every facet of religiousness and including, as noted below, an affirmative duty on the employer to accommodate employees' religious practices.

This definition, however, does not give any precise boundaries for what is considered "religious." Courts, borrowing from a general approach in constitutional cases that seeks to avoid government entanglement with religion, typically take a very deferential view of what an individual wishes to describe as "religious." For instance, the EEOC has stated that in the rare instances when there is a question whether an employee's sincere beliefs are religious, it will define religion "to include moral or ethical beliefs as to what is right and wrong which are sincerely held with the strength of traditional religious views." 29 C.F.R. § 1605.1. This definition explicitly borrows from the Supreme Court's approach to religion in constitutional cases, as described in *United States v. Seeger*, 380 U.S. 163 (1965), and *Welsh v. United States*, 398 U.S. 333 (1970). Following an established religion is not required, but generally the belief system cannot be purely secular. However, a refusal to adopt religious beliefs—that is atheism or agnosticism—is considered "religious" and is therefore protected.

An example of the refusal to probe into an employee's claimed religious belief are several cases involving the "Church of Body Modification." The Church was established in 1999 and, as of 2004, had about 1,000 members. Members engage in practices such as piercing, tattooing, branding, cutting, and body manipulation because, according to the Church's statement of faith, "[w]e believe our bodies belong only to ourselves and are a whole and integrated entity: mind, body, and soul. We maintain we have the right to alter them for spiritual and other reasons." In *Cloutier v. Costco Wholesale Corp.*, 390 F.3d 126 (1st Cir. 2004), the EEOC concluded that an employee's membership in the Church of Body Modification constituted "religion" under Title VII. This example may be on the edge of what is considered religious and what is not; indeed, both the district and circuit courts in *Cloutier* avoided addressing the issue and instead ruled for the employer on other grounds. But the fact that the Church of Body Modification was a close case is indicative of the leeway that employees enjoy when self-identifying their religious beliefs.

2. Defining Exempted "Religious" Employers

a. Title VII's Exemption of Religious Employers

In addition to defining what qualifies as an employee's protected religion, Title VII has given special protection for the actions of certain religious employers. Courts have also held that the constitutional protection for the free expression of religion also provides some level of protection for employers. There are two similar, but distinct, provisions for religious exemption under Title VII.

Under § 702(a), Title VII provides an exemption for "a religious corporation, association, educational institution, or society with respect to the employment of individuals of a particular religion to perform work connected with the carrying on by such corporation, association, educational institution, or society of its activities." Section 703(e)(2) states that an educational institution can employ only individuals of a given religion if the institution is owned, supported, controlled, or managed in whole or in substantial part by a particular religious entity, or if the institution's curriculum "is directed toward the propagation of a particular religion." Section 703(e)(2) was originally needed because of a limitation in § 702(a) to the religious activities of religious employers; however, with the rescission of that limitation in 1972,

§ 703(e)(2) adds little, if any, additional protection for religious educational entities. Indeed, most employers will generally seek the broader protection of § 702(a) in religious exemption cases.

These exemptions can provide religious entities significant protection against Title VII religious discrimination claims. For instance, the Supreme Court has held that § 702(a) protects virtually all non-profit activities of a religious entity from discrimination claims, even a separate non-profit arm that is not itself religious. *Corporation of the Presiding Bishop of the Church of Jesus Christ of Latter-Day Saints v. Amos*, 483 U.S. 327 (1987).

There are limits to § 702(a)'s reach, however. For instance, a private, for-profit, secular employer that runs its business in accordance with strongly-held religious beliefs will not generally be exempted. *Townley Engineering & Manufacturing Co.*, 859 F.2d 610 (9th Cir. 1988). Only entities that are "primarily religious"—typically those that are part of or affiliated with a particular religious organization, rather than mere followers of a religion—will be exempted. Even an entity with an explicit affiliation with a religion is not entitled to automatic coverage. For instance, universities that have formal associations with a particular religion, including those with school officials who are also officials of a religion, may not be covered if they are not owned or controlled "in substantial part" or their institution is not "directed toward the propagation of a particular religion."

Similarly, a religious employer is exempted only from *religious* discrimination, not other types of discrimination prohibited by Title VII. Yet this line can be blurred at times. One example is a religious employer's termination of an unmarried employee who becomes pregnant. This case hinges on whether the termination was made simply because of the employee's pregnancy—in which case the employer is still liable for sex discrimination, as defined by the Pregnancy Discrimination Act—or whether the termination was made because the employee violated the employer's religious ban on premarital sex—in which case the employer is entitled to protection under § 702(a). *Cline v. Catholic Diocese of Toledo*, 206 F.3d 251 (6th Cir. 2000).

Moreover, § 702(a) exempts covered employers only "with respect to employment" of religious followers. Accordingly, some courts have held that certain employment decisions of a religious employer are not exempted by § 702(a), as the intent of the provision was merely to allow religious employers to choose employees who follow the same religion. *EEOC v. Fremont Christian School*, 781 F.2d 1362 (9th Cir. 1986) (section does not cover provision of benefits); *but see Hopkins v. Women's Div., General Bd. of Global Ministries*, 238 F. Supp. 2d 174 (D.C. 2002) (rejecting this idea).

b. Constitutional Hurdles to Applying Title VII to Religious Employers

Two aspects of Title VII's coverage of religion raise constitutional issues. First, by providing special protection for religious employers, Title VII raises the question whether it is promoting religion in violation of the First Amendment's Establishment Clause. Second, by prohibiting discrimination based on religion or other characteristics, Title VII creates potential conflicts with the First Amendment's Free Exercise Clause.

The answer to the first question is relatively settled at this point. In *Corporation of the Presiding Bishop of the Church of Jesus Christ of Latter-Day Saints v. Amos*, 483 U.S. 327 (1987), § 702(a)'s exemption of religious employers was challenged as a violation of the Establishment Clause. The Supreme Court held that the exemption was valid under the Establishment Clause.

The Free Exercise Clause issue has been more troublesome. The problem is that such cases usually involve a conflict between the requirements of Title VII and a religious organization's ability to follow its own practices. The most high-profile example is the Catholic Church's prohibition against female priests. On its face, this rule is intentional sex discrimination that violates Title VII. However, an attempt to outlaw such a rule creates serious problems with the Catholic Church's ability to follow its religious beliefs.

The solution to this conflict has been a judicially created "ministerial exemption." This exemption states that a religious choice of minister or similar clergy is solely up to that religion and should be free from the constraints of Title VII or other employment laws, including the ADA and ADEA. The ministerial exemption has been applied to more than clergy, however, as it has been extended to employees whose primary duties consist of "teaching, spreading the faith, church governance, supervision of a religious order, or supervision or participation in religious ritual and worship." *Rayburn v. General Conference of Seventh-Day Adventists*, 772 F.2d 1164, 1169 (4th Cir. 1985). For example, a Catholic university's refusal to tenure a nun—an unordained position—for a faculty position in which she taught canon law was deemed immune from Title VII challenge because the ministerial exemption "encompasses all employees of a religious institution, whether ordained or not, whose primary functions serve its spiritual and pastoral mission." *EEOC v. Catholic University of America*, 83 F.3d 455 (D.C. Cir. 1996).

The Supreme Court recognized the existence of the ministerial exception for the first time in *Hosanna-Tabor Evangelical Lutheran Church and School v. EEOC*, 565 U.S. 171 (2012). The Court held that "the members of a religious group put their faith in the hands of their ministers. Requiring a church to accept or retain an unwanted minister, or punishing a church for failing to do so ... infringes the Free Exercise Clause," as well as the Establishment Clause. *Id.* at 188. The Court, however, refused "to adopt a rigid formula for deciding when an employee qualifies as a minister." *Id.* at 190.

Factors that weighed in favor of recognizing a called teacher as a minister included the following: (1) the church held her out as a minister with duties separate from other church members; (2) the church issued her a diploma of vocation; (3) her job title was "Minister of Religion"; (4) the congregation prayed for her ministry; (5) the school evaluated her based on her ministerial activities; (5) she was required to have significant religious training, including an endorsement by the church; (6) she was required to pass an oral examination by faculty at a Lutheran college; (7) she was commissioned as a called teacher by a church congregation; (8) the teacher held herself out as a minister; (9) she took tax exemptions that applied to ministers; and (10) her job duties included conveying the church's message. Even though the teacher only performed religious duties about 45 minutes a day and otherwise taught secular subjects, the Court held that the teacher fell within the ministerial exception.

The Court further clarified the contours of the ministerial exception in *Our Lady of Guadalupe Sch. v. Morrissey-Berru*, 591 U.S. 732 (2020). In this case, a Catholic elementary school teacher alleged that her employer demoted her and did not renew her contract because of her age. The Court held the ministerial exception barred the plaintiff's ADEA claim. In so ruling, the Court evaluated four aspects of *Hosanna-Tabor*: the plaintiff had a title related to ministry, her position required religious training and a formal commissioning process, the plaintiff held herself out as a minister and received certain tax benefits, and her duties reflected a role in carrying out the church's teachings and mission.

In *Our Lady of Guadalupe*, the Court held that a person is not required to possess the formal title of minister to fall within the ministerial exception. Nor does the ministerial exception require that the position require religious training. Instead, the Court held that what a person does is the key inquiry. "And implicit in our decision in *Hosanna-Tabor* was a recognition that educating young people in their faith, inculcating it teachings, and training them to live their faith are responsibilities that lie at the very core of the mission of a private religious school." *Id.* at 753–54. Additionally, the Court rejected the idea that the plaintiff must be a practicing member of the particular religion to fall within the ministerial exception.

3. Religious Discrimination under Title VII

a. Disparate Treatment and Disparate Impact

In its most basic form, religious discrimination is analyzed the same way as other protected classes. Thus, an adverse employment action that occurs because of an employee's religion is unlawful disparate treatment that can be analyzed as a typical single or mixed-motive case, depending on the facts. But some additional issues may arise. For instance, because religion is not a characteristic that is visibly obvious to others, many courts require a plaintiff to establish as part of his or her prima facie case that the employer was aware of his or her religion. *Lubetsky v. Applied Card Systems*, 296 F.3d 1201 (11th Cir. 2001). Thus, the prima facie case often involves an employee's burden to show that (1) the employee's bona fide beliefs or practices were religious in nature; (2) the employer was aware of the employee's religious beliefs or practices; and (3) the religious beliefs or practices were the bases of the employee's discharge. *Beasley v. Health Care Service Corp.*, 940 F.2d 1085, (7th Cir. 1991).

The employee is not always required to inform the employer of their religious beliefs to prevail in a religious discrimination claim. In *EEOC v. Abercrombie & Fitch Stores, Inc.*, 575 U.S. 768 (2015), the employer argued that it could not be liable for discrimination because it did not have actual knowledge of a prospective employee's need for a religious accommodation. The applicant wore a headscarf to an interview, and the employer made the decision not to hire the applicant based on her wearing of the headscarf. The Supreme Court rejected the employer's argument. It held that the text of Title VII does not require the employer to know about the need for a religious accommodation. If the need for an accommodation is the reason the employer acts, this is enough to establish liability, even if the employer merely suspects (but does not definitely know) that the individual needed a religious accommodation.

Like other disparate treatment claims, employers facing religious discrimination allegations can raise a bona fide occupational qualification defense. This defense is not common, as most employers whose operations require employees of a specific religion are exempt under § 702(a), § 703(e)(2), or the ministerial exemption. Yet BFOQ religion cases do occur, although employers are often not successful. One exception occurred in *Kern v. Dynalectron Corp.*,

577 F. Supp. 1196 (N.D. Tex. 1983), *affirmed mem.* 746 F.2d 810 (5th Cir. 1984), where the employer was able to establish a BFOQ defense for its exclusion of a non-Muslim helicopter pilot for flights over Mecca because Saudi Arabian law threatened a penalty of death for any non-Muslim who entered the holy area.

In addition to disparate treatment, employees may also bring disparate impact religion claims. Despite earlier cases questioning the availability of religious disparate impact claims—because of a belief that such claims were subsumed by the reasonable accommodation duty—the Civil Rights Act of 1991 explicitly included religion as one of the classes covered by disparate impact. Such claims are analyzed under the general disparate impact framework described in Chapter 8. *Barrow v. Greeneville Independent School District*, 480 F.3d 377 (5th Cir. 2007). However, perhaps because of the availability of religious accommodations, religious disparate impact claims are rare.

b. Failure to Accommodate Religious Practices

Title VII's definition of "religion" creates a unique requirement on employers: the duty to accommodate employees' religious practices. Under § 701(j), "religion" is defined as including "all aspects of religious observance and practice ... unless an employer demonstrates that he is unable to reasonably accommodate to an employee's or prospective employee's religious observance or practice without undue hardship on the conduct of the employer's business." Failure to provide such accommodation violates § 703(a)(2), which incorporates this definition of religion.

Any religious accommodation cases prior to June 29, 2023, should be viewed with caution. On that day, the Supreme Court issued its opinion in *Groff v. DeJoy*, which substantially expanded the religious accommodation requirement under Title VII. 600 U.S. 447 (2023). This section discusses early Supreme Court religious accommodation cases, followed by an overview of *Groff*.

Ansonia Board of Education v. Philbrook, 479 U.S. 60 (1986), involved a public school teacher who requested a modification of the employer's leave policy, as established under a collective-bargaining agreement with the teacher's union. The agreement allowed a maximum of three days for paid mandatory religious holidays. The employee sought to use his three paid personal-leave days to cover additional religious holidays or to pay for a substitute teacher while he received his higher salary, but the employer refused both requests and instead offered the employee unpaid leave for his extra religious holidays.

As an initial matter, the Court held that the *McDonnell Douglas* analysis was not appropriate for a religious reasonable accommodation case. Instead, the Court seemed to approve the lower court's holding that an employee may be entitled to a reasonable accommodation by showing that he had a sincere religious belief that conflicted with an employment policy, the employer was aware of the employee's belief, and the employee suffered an employment action for failing to comply with the policy. Following this showing, the inquiry addressed whether the employer refused to provide a reasonable accommodation that did not impose an undue hardship, as required by § 701(j).

In *Philbrook*, the Court emphasized that the employer need only provide a reasonable accommodation, not the most reasonable accommodation or the one favored by the employee. If the employer provided any accommodation that is deemed reasonable, the case is over because the employer has satisfied Section 701(j). The Court reserved judgment on the employer's offer of unpaid leave in *Philbrook*, remanding for a more careful examination of how the collective-bargaining agreement was normally implemented. The Court stressed that unpaid leave for religious observance would generally be considered a reasonable accommodation; however, if paid leave was provided for other purposes except religious ones, it would not be a reasonable accommodation. The remand was intended to resolve a factual dispute regarding whether this type of discriminatory leave policy existed or not.

Section 701(j) offers an exception to an employer's duty to provide a reasonable accommodation if the "employer demonstrates that he is unable to reasonably accommodate to an employee's or prospective employee's religious observance or practice without undue hardship on the conduct of the employer's business." Although this is a similar structure to the ADA's reasonable accommodation/undue hardship framework (see Chapter 12), the courts originally interpreted "undue hardship" to mean something very different in the Title VII religion context.

They held that anything beyond a "de minimis" cost to the employer will constitute undue hardship and relieve the employer of its duty to provide a reasonable accommodation. The Supreme Court established this narrow interpretation of undue hardship in *Trans World Airlines, Inc. v. Hardison*, 432 U.S. 63 (1977). That case involved an employee who sought an accommodation for his need to avoid work on his religion's Saturday Sabbath. The problem was that his department operated every day of the year, 24 hours a day. The employee raised three possible accommodations, all of which the employer rejected. The Court ruled for the employer, holding that all of the possible accommodations created an undue hardship because they imposed more than de minimis costs on the employer. The first possible accommodation was to permit the employee to work a four-day work week, replacing his other shifts with another employee. The second was to find another employee who was willing to work the Saturday shift for premium overtime pay. The Court held that both of these options, which would have worked within an existing union-negotiated seniority system, created an undue hardship. The additional costs involved with less efficient operations or higher pay were more than de minimis and, therefore, constituted undue hardship. The third option was to breach the seniority system by mandating a swap in shifts. Reflecting a long-standing concern with protecting seniority systems under both Title VII and the ADA (see the *Barnett* case for this principle under the ADA in Chapter 12), the Court held that the employer did not need to breach the seniority system. It suggested that such a breach is not a reasonable accommodation or, at a minimum, was an undue hardship, especially given the protection for bona fide seniority systems under § 703(h) of Title VII. The *Hardison* Court also noted that the employer had given the employee time off for some religious holidays and authorized the union to find a volunteer to swap shifts. Requiring anything more, given the seniority system, went beyond Title VII's reasonable accommodation duty. Finally, the Court stressed that the reasonable accommodation duty did not require an employer to allocate more burdensome shifts on the basis of religion, suggesting that making nonreligious employees bear an extra burden went beyond the intent of Title VII.

In *Groff v. DeJoy*, an Evangelical Christian believed (for religious reasons) that Sundays should be devoted to worship and rest, not work. 600 U.S. 447 (2023). Groff resigned from the U.S. Postal Service after he received progressive discipline for refusing to work on Sundays. He filed suit under Title VII, alleging that the employer failed to accommodate his religious practice. The Court did not ultimately resolve Groff's claim, but instead remanded it to the lower courts for context-specific fact-finding using the new standard enunciated by the Court.

The Court held that an undue hardship means a substantial burden in the overall context of the employer's business. It rejected the de minimis language from *Hardison*. At the same time, the Court indicated that the outcome in *Hardison* was correct because the Court believed that the employer could not accommodate Hardison without violating the seniority rights of other employees.

The Court provided almost no detail about what counts as a substantial burden. The Court noted that the hardship must rise to an excessive or unjustifiable level. The inquiry is a fact-specific one that takes into account the specific accommodation at issue and the accommodation's practical effect on the specific employer given the nature, size, and operating costs of the employer. While courts can consider the impact of an accommodation on co-workers, it is not appropriate for courts to consider co-workers' dislike for expressions of religion in the workplace or their dislike of religious accommodations. Additionally, an employer cannot just consider the requested accommodation. If that accommodation causes an undue hardship, the employer must consider other options.

The Court specifically declined to further elaborate on the new standard and how it would apply in other contexts, including the case before it. Therefore, extreme care must be taken when using cases decided prior to *Groff*.

At times, a worker's expression of religious beliefs may create a hostile working environment for other workers. The employer is not required to accommodate the expression of religious beliefs in these instances. EEOC Enforcement Guidance on Harassment in the Workplace § III.C.2. (2024).

CHECKPOINTS

- Race and color are distinct classes that may involve "plus" claims and special characteristics of a given race or color, but they are the only classes under Title VII that do not have a BFOQ defense.
- Special issues involved with national origin discrimination include discrimination based on accents and English-only policies.
- Among the special issues in sex discrimination are the Pregnancy Discrimination Act (PDA), breastfeeding at work, sex-plus claims, sex stereotyping, and dress and grooming standards. The PWFA and ADA may also provide pregnancy-related claims.
- The PDA creates a floor that allows extra pregnancy benefits, but not extra leave for women to care for children.
- Stereotyping can provide evidence of sex discrimination.
- Grooming standards can be different for men and women as long as they impose substantially equal burdens on each sex.
- Religious discrimination claims are generally analyzed similar to other classes.

- Courts are reluctant to engage in a searching inquiry into an employer's claim that his or her beliefs are religious.
- Section 702(a) and § 703(e)(2) of Title VII exempt certain religious entities from religious discrimination hiring claims.
- The constitutionally based ministerial exemption (recognized by the Supreme Court) prevents the application of employment discrimination laws to the hiring of clergy or similar officials. The Supreme Court has applied the ministerial exception to teachers at religious schools.
- Under Title VII, employers have a duty to reasonably accommodate employees' religious beliefs and practices unless the accommodation would impose an undue hardship on the employer.

CHAPTER 12

Disability Discrimination under the ADA

ROADMAP

- Disability discrimination framework under the ADA
- The impact of the ADA Amendments Act of 2008
- The broad definition of discrimination under the ADA
- The new, broader definition of "disability"
- The meaning of an "otherwise qualified" individual
- Direct threat and other ADA employer defenses
- ADA retaliation and association discrimination provisions
- Medical inquiries and examinations
- Procedural and remedial issues under the ADA

Workplace disability discrimination law is a product of prior and ongoing efforts to make employment more responsive to the needs people with disabilities. The Rehabilitation Act of 1973, 29 U.S.C. § 794 *et seq.*, preceded the Americans with Disabilities Act of 1990 (ADA), 42 U.S.C. § 12101 *et seq.* The ADA Amendments Act of 2008 (ADAAA), Pub. L. 110-325 (Sept. 25, 2008), substantially expanded the definition of a "disability" under the ADA.

Nevertheless, the ADA still shares many of the same substantive and procedural characteristics of Title VII described in previous chapters. This Chapter will highlight where the two laws are similar, but also where the laws diverge in important ways.

A. The Disability Discrimination Framework under the ADA

The ADA derived from the Rehabilitation Act, which only prohibited disability discrimination in the workplace by some federal employers and by entities receiving federal grants or contracts. The ADA not only provides that none of its standards should be interpreted to provide less protection than the Rehabilitation Act, but also expands the coverage to all employers with 15 or more employees for each working day in each of 20 or more calendar weeks in the current or preceding calendar year (like Title VII). It does not apply to an Indian tribe, a bona fide private membership club, or to some federal employers. Some government agencies and those with government contracts are covered by similar provisions in the Rehabilitation Act.

Boiled down to its essence, the ADA prohibits covered entities from (1) discriminating against a (2) person with a disability who is (3) otherwise qualified for the position (4) because of that individual's disability. Each of these four elements is discussed in detail below. The ADA has five sections. Although two of the sections (Title II (state and local government) and Title III (public accommodations)) have potential application to employers, the focus of this Chapter is on Title I of the ADA, which specifically focuses on disability discrimination in employment.

1. "Discriminating Against"

Discrimination under the ADA is broader than that concept under Title VII. Although disparate treatment and disparate impact claims exist under the ADA, the statute also defines discrimination as a failure to provide a reasonable accommodation for an individual's disability that does not impose an undue hardship on the employer. Courts often use Title VII frameworks to analyze ADA claims, with some modifications.

a. Discrimination in Terms and Conditions of Employment

Congress modeled some of the ADA's language on Title VII. Thus, an employer faces liability under the ADA based on all of the theories of discrimination that apply to Title VII, such as individual disparate treatment, disparate impact, and harassment.

Congress also included additional language, more specifically articulating what counts as discrimination under the ADA. In addition to the Title

VII-like discrimination provisions, the ADA also prohibits an employer from doing the following:

- entering into an understanding with a union, temporary employment agency or other entity which would subject a covered employee to disability discrimination;
- using standards, criteria or methods of administration that either have the effect of discriminating against those with disabilities or perpetuate discrimination of others under common administrative control;
- using qualification standards that tend to screen out individuals with disabilities, unless the standard or test is shown to be job related and consistent with business necessity;
- failing to select and administer employment tests in the most effective manner to ensure that people are judged based on their skills, rather than on their disability; and
- discriminating against employees based on their association with a person with a disability.

b. Failure to Reasonably Accommodate Claims

Unlike Title VII (outside of the religious context), the ADA defines discrimination as not making reasonable accommodations to the known physical or mental limitations of an otherwise qualified individual with a disability who is either an applicant or employee. Nevertheless, an employer can avoid liability on this basis if it can demonstrate that the accommodation would impose an "undue hardship" on the operation of the business (the reasonable accommodation and undue hardship analysis are discussed in more detail below in considering the qualification prong of disability under the ADA). It is also a violation of the ADA to deny an employment opportunity to an applicant or employee who is an otherwise qualified individual with a disability where the denial is based on having to make reasonable accommodations for the physical or mental impairments of that individual.

2. "Disabled Individual"

Prior to the enactment of the ADAAA in 2008, much of the litigation under the ADA concerned who was considered disabled for purposes of the ADA. Although the overall definition is still the same, Congress made abundantly clear in the ADAAA that "the definition of disability ... shall be construed in favor of broad coverage of individuals ... to the maximum extent permitted." 42 U.S.C. § 12102(4)(A). Moreover, the ADAAA was intended "to convey that the question of whether an individual's impairment is a disability under the ADA should not demand extensive analysis." 42 U.S.C. § 12101(b)(6).

The term "disability" has three different definitions. Under the first definition, a person must have or had (1) a physical or mental impairment (2) that substantially limits (3) one or more major life activities. This first definition is sometimes referred to as the actual disability definition. A person may also qualify by having a record of such an impairment or being regarded as having such an impairment. For discrimination claims, a plaintiff may claim protection under any of these definitions. Workers may only receive an accommodation if they fall within the actual disability or record of disability definitions.

There must be an individualized evaluation of each person alleging a disability.

Some disability claims do not require the worker to be a person with a disability. For example, a person without a disability can bring an associational discrimination claim, a retaliation claim, and a claim challenging the employer's use of medical exams or inquiries.

a. Definition of Disability

The ADA covers individuals who currently have a disability, who have a record of a disability, or who are regarded as having a disability. Most of the litigation prior to the ADAAA focused on the first prong: whether the person currently has an actual disability.

The second prong, the record of disability, has historically not been used frequently. This is probably because some courts have concluded that an employer must rely on an actual tangible record indicating the existence of disability for a plaintiff to be covered under this prong.

Under the third "regarded as" prong, a person does not need to have a disability to be covered if the employer discriminated against a person for having an actual or perceived physical or mental impairment. Under the pre-ADAAA law, plaintiffs had to prove that the employer thought that the plaintiff met every element of actual disability for purposes of the ADA. The Supreme Court found this type of disability discrimination in two recurring situations: (1) where an employer mistakenly believes that an employee has a physical or mental impairment that substantially limits one or more major life activities, or (2) where an employer mistakenly believes that an actual, non-limiting impairment substantially limits one or more major life activities. *Sutton v. United Air Lines, Inc.*, 527 U.S. 471 (1999). In both cases, the

Court observed that it is necessary that the employer entertain misperceptions about the individual. The "regarded as" prong caused a lot of confusion under the pre-ADAAA law with different tests to determine whether the employer wrongly thought the employee was disabled under the ADA.

The ADAAA makes the "regarded as" prong easier to understand and prove. While pre-ADAAA cases were often litigated under the actual disability prong, post-ADAAA litigants began to rely on the regarded as prong more. The ADAAA rejects the Court's reasoning in *Sutton* and instead "reinstates the reasoning of the Supreme Court in *School Board of Nassau County v. Arline*, 480 U.S. 273 (1987)," a Rehabilitation Act case under which plaintiffs are not responsible for proving the defendant's misperception about the plaintiff's disability.

Under this new standard, a person is regarded as disabled if the individual establishes that he or she has been (1) subjected to unlawful disability discrimination (2) because of an actual or perceived physical or mental impairment, whether or not the impairment limits or is perceived to limit a major life activity.

"Regarded as" liability does not apply to impairments that are transitory—meaning an impairment with an actual or expected duration of six months or less—and minor. The ADAAA also makes clear that employers do not have the obligation to reasonably accommodate a "regarded as" disability. Nonetheless, employees with certain severe short-term or episodic impairments may be considered disabled under the ADAAA. In *Summer v. Altarum Institute Corporation*, 740 F.3d 325, 333 (4th Cir. 2014), the court held that a plaintiff with a serious, but temporary, injury could be disabled within the meaning of the ADAAA because "an impairment is not categorically excluded from being a disability simply because it is temporary."

Additionally, for coverage under the statute, it is worth consideration that the Supreme Court has held that the ADA does not provide a claim for "discrimination against *retirees* who neither hold nor desire a job whose essential tasks they can perform with reasonable accommodation." *Stanley v. City of Sanford, Florida*, 145 S.Ct. 2058 (2025) (emphasis added).

b. "Physical or Mental Impairment"

The ADA does not contain an illustrative list of physical or mental impairments. Judicial interpretations of the term have made clear that an impairment is not a mere physical characteristic, such as left-handedness or height. Nor does a relatively brief and transitory illness or injury that had no permanent or long-term effects on an individual's major life activities qualify as an impairment. Instead, as described in the EEOC's ADA regulations, a physical or mental impairment includes "[a]ny physiological disorder or condition, cosmetic disfigurement, or anatomical loss affecting one or more body systems, such as neurological, musculoskeletal, special sense organs, respiratory (including speech organs), cardiovascular, reproductive, digestive, genitourinary, immune, circulatory, hemic, lymphatic, skin, and endocrine," or "[a]ny mental or psychological disorder, such as an intellectual disability (formerly termed 'mental retardation'), organic brain syndrome, emotional or mental illness, and specific learning disabilities." 29 C.F.R. § 1630.2(h).

Sections 510 and 511 of the ADA exclude certain conditions as disabilities, including: homosexuality, bisexuality, transvestism, transexualism, current illegal drug use, pedophilia, compulsive gambling, and kleptomania. While pregnancy alone is not a disability, conditions caused by pregnancy may be impairments or fall within the definition of actual disability.

As far as drug use, current use is not protected under the ADA, but participating in a rehabilitation program, or having done so in the past, is. Questions exist about how long a person's drug-free period must be. One case says that a seven-week period is not enough time to qualify an individual as a past drug user for purposes of the statute, but there does not appear to be a bright line in this regard. *Baustian v. State of Louisiana*, 910 F. Supp. 274 (E.D. La. 1995). As discussed in the previous section, after the ADAAA, "transitory and minor" impairments are specifically excluded under the regarded as definition of disability. The ADAAA otherwise did not substantially alter the meaning of "physical or mental impairments."

c. *"Substantially Limits"*

For the actual disability definition, a person's impairment must substantially limit a major life activity. Under pre-ADAAA law, the Supreme Court read "substantially limits" to mean "prevents or severely restricts." The limitation was also evaluated with reference to any mitigating or corrective measure that the individual used to offset the effects of impairment. *Sutton v. United Air Lines, Inc.*, 527 U.S. 471 (1999). Thus, a corrective measure could make a person with a disability not covered by the ADA. So, for instance, the two female plaintiffs in *Sutton* wanted to be pilots. They were legally blind but could correct their vision with glasses. The Court said that because the glasses gave the plaintiffs 20/20 vision, they no longer had a disability within the meaning of the ADA. Similarly, in the companion case of *Murphy v. United Parcel Service, Inc.*, 527 U.S. 516 (1999), the Court found that an employee with high blood pressure was not disabled because he took medication which corrected his condition. Finally, in *Albertsons, Inc. v. Kirkinburg*, 527 U.S. 555 (1999), the Court held that an employee with the inability to see out of one eye was not disabled because his body had accommodated itself to the condition to such a degree that the limitation of seeing was no longer substantially limiting. In short, these three cases defined "limits" under pre-ADAAA law to mean a current limitation, not a potential limitation that could exist but for the mitigating measure.

Perhaps more than in any other area, the ADAAA impacts the meaning of "substantial limitation." The Amendments explicitly criticized the definitions given in *Toyota Motor Manufacturing v. Williams*, 534 U.S. 184 (2002), and in the old ADA regulations, and legislatively overruled them. Instead, the ADAAA now makes clear that "substantially" does not mean that the definition of disability needs to be interpreted "strictly to create a demanding standard for qualifying as disabled." Whether an impairment substantially limits a major life activity shall generally be made without regard to mitigating measures (largely overturning *Sutton*, *Murphy*, and *Kirkinburg* in this regard). With regard to mitigating measures, there is a special rule for eyeglasses and contact lenses in that they can still be taken into account in determining whether someone has a disability under the ADA and the court will consider whether the employer's need to have employees with 20/20 vision without glasses or contacts is job-related and consistent with business necessity. If an impairment is episodic or in remission, it is a disability if it substantially limits a major life activity when active.

d. "Major Life Activities"

Pre-ADAAA, the ADA itself did not define major life activities, but the regulations under the ADA provided a non-exhaustive list of representative activities. Under these former regulations, major life activities meant functions such as caring for oneself, performing manual tasks, walking, seeing, hearing, speaking, breathing, learning, and working. 29 CFR § 1630.2(i). In an important pre-ADAAA case, *Toyota Motor Manufacturing*, the Court limited major life activities to "those activities that are of central importance to daily life." The Court also made clear that working is not a preferred form of a major life activity, but rather a fallback if no other activity applied.

One of the central purposes of enacting the ADAAA in 2008 was to reject the standards for major life activities established in *Toyota Motor Manufacturing*. Now, the ADA has a broad definition of major life activities. The statutory language now makes clear that major life activities include, but are not limited to: "caring for oneself, performing manual tasks, seeing, hearing, eating, sleeping, walking, standing, lifting, bending, speaking, breathing, learning, reading, concentrating, thinking, communicating, and working." 42 U.S.C. § 12102(2)(A). In short, the ADAAA provides a much more expansive list than the old regulations. Additionally, the ADAAA sets out a new paragraph that includes major bodily functions as major life activities, resolving a disagreement that had existed among several lower courts. 42 U.S.C. § 12102(2)(B). They include the operation of a major bodily function like the immune system, bladder, and reproductive functions. Only one major life activity needs to be affected to be considered a disability. The term "major" does not need to be applied strictly and now includes many activities that might not make up the majority of someone's waking hours. Major, in this sense, means an *important* life activity.

3. "Otherwise Qualified"

The requirement of "qualification" creates a tension with the disability provisions because the employee is simultaneously trying to prove that he or she has a disability while trying to prove that he or she is not so disabled as to be considered unqualified.

Qualification under the ADA goes to whether the person with a disability can (1) perform the essential job functions of the job he or she holds or desires (2) with or without reasonable accommodations without (3) posing a direct threat to the health or safety of himself or herself or others in the workplace.

a. "Essential Job Functions"

The ADA states that for the purpose of determining the essential functions of a job, "consideration" will be given to the employer's judgment as to what functions of the job are essential, and a written description of the job shall be considered evidence of which functions are essential. As a result of this language, it is crucial that employers have well-thought out job descriptions for each position in their organization and that the essential and peripheral functions of those jobs are clearly defined.

Factors that demonstrate whether a function is essential include: (1) whether the function, if not present, would fundamentally alter the job; (2) whether the position exists to perform that function; (3) whether the task is one that the employee spends most of his or her time on; and (4) whether it is a skill that all employees in that position are required to have.

b. "With or Without Reasonable Accommodation"

i. The Nature of a Reasonable Accommodation

This is the second time the term "reasonable accommodation" comes up in the ADA. Recall that failure to reasonably accommodate is a type of unlawful disability discrimination. This time the term is considered in the context of whether a person with a disability is otherwise "qualified" under the ADA, and it applies to both regular discrimination claims and failure to accommodate claims. The burden is on the plaintiff to show reasonable accommodation and then on the employer to show undue hardship, which is discussed below.

"Reasonable accommodation" is given a broad definition under the ADA and includes: (1) making existing facilities readily accessible to disabled individuals; (2) job restructuring, including part-time or modified work schedules and reassignment to a vacant position; and (3) acquisition or modification of equipment, devices, examinations, training materials, and policies (for instance, by employing qualified readers or interpreters). A nexus between the requested accommodation and the essential functions of an employee's position is not needed. On the other hand, an employer does not need to make an accommodation that requires a significant difficulty or expense that is substantially disproportionate to the benefit gained by the accommodation. Also, there is no obligation for the employer to accommodate any type of request made by a person with a disability. Rather the employer must give only *an* effective accommodation for the employee that allows him or her to perform the essential functions of the job.

One area of controversy involves the accommodation language: "reassignment to a vacant position." If reassignment is a reasonable accommodation, must the employer give the vacant position to the disabled employee or must the employer just consider the employee like any other employee? The courts are divided. Some courts hold that once an employer determines that no reasonable accommodation could keep the employee in the initial job, the employer must give the alternative position to the employee if qualified. In other words, the disabled employee does not have to compete; the statute says "reassignment," not "consideration for reassignment." *Smith v. Midland Brake*, 180 F.3d 1154 (10th Cir. 1999). Likewise, an employee with the ability to perform the essential functions of a job may be able to request a transfer to a vacant position to obtain better treatment for a disability. *Sanchez v. Vilsack*, 695 F.3d 1174, 1182 (10th Cir. 2012). However, other courts hold that an employer may require the person with a disability to apply for the vacant position and be considered along with other applicants. *Elledge v. Lowe's Home Ctrs., LLC*, 979 F.3d 1004, 1014 (4th Cir, 2020). The Supreme Court has explicitly held that, in most instances, an employer would not be required to accommodate by placing a person with a disability in a vacant position, if doing so would violate a seniority system. *US Airways v. Barnett*, 535 U.S. 391 (2002).

ii. The Interactive Process

In trying to determine a reasonable accommodation, the employer must generally engage in an interactive process with the employee to determine that accommodation. In this regard, employers cannot make disability-related inquires as to whether an employee needs an accommodation. Rather, unless the disability is obvious, the employer can only start this process if requested by the employee. Once an employee requests an accommodation, the employer must work with the employee to try and find a reasonable accommodation. 29 C.F.R. § 1630.2(o)(3). If an employee refuses to participate in good faith with the employer in this interactive process, the employee can undermine the interactive process and any discrimination claim that he or she may have had. For example, if an employee summarily rejects an employer's accommodation or refuses to give an employer information about his or her abilities, the employee may be precluded from bringing a failure to accommodate claim. *Beck v. University of Wisconsin Board of Regents*, 75 F.3d 1130 (7th Cir. 1996). On the other hand, even though in most cases it is the employee's obligation to say that an accommodation is needed, the employer must then engage in the interactive process to find a reasonable accommodation. If the employer does not go through the interactive process, some courts consider this to be strong evidence of an ADA violation, unless the employer can show that no reasonable accommodation was possible. *Fjellestad v. Pizza Hut of America, Inc.*, 188 F.3d 944 (8th Cir. 1999); *see also McBride v. BIC Consumer Prods. Mfg. Co., Inc.*, 583 F.3d 92, 100–01 (2d Cir. 2009) (discussing issue).

The interactive process duty extends beyond the first attempt of accommodation. The attempt to have the employee try to perform the job through less drastic accommodations does not forfeit the right to a more substantial accommodation upon failure of the initial effort. However, some courts have been unsympathetic to employees who demand preferred accommodation when an offered accommodation suffices. *Bunn v. Khoury Enterprises, Inc.*, 753 F.3d 676 (7th Cir. 2014).

iii. Reasonable Accommodation and Seniority Systems

One of the problems that can arise with the duty to provide a reasonable accommodation is a conflict with a seniority system. The Supreme Court addressed this conflict in *US Airways v. Barnett*, 535 U.S. 391 (2002), in which an employee with a disability sought an accommodation to the normal seniority system. Factors that indicate if accommodating is reasonable include whether the accommodation is: (1) effective in providing the employee means to perform the essential functions of the job; and (2) not excessive in relation to the benefit conferred. In *Barnett*, the Court concluded that employers generally do not need to make a reasonable accommodation by modifying an employee seniority system. In such circumstances, it is usually not reasonable to require exceptions to the seniority system and to upset the expectations of other employees. That being said, plaintiffs can still overcome this presumption by showing that "special circumstances" exist that make breaching the seniority system reasonable (for example, by showing that employees do not have legitimate expectations based on the seniority system because the employer makes exceptions to the system or changes its policies frequently). Notice that if the accommodation is not considered "reasonable," courts do not even apply the undue hardship analysis.

c. *"Undue Hardship"*

The term "undue hardship" is similar but distinct from reasonable accommodation. *Vande Zande v. Wisconsin Department of Administration*, 44 F.3d 538 (7th Cir. 1995). In particular, while an accommodation's reasonableness is determined generally, in a non-employer-specific manner, "undue hardship" goes to difficulties that are particular to the employer/defendant. The determination is fact specific and there are both economic and non-economic considerations. Whether a proposed accommodation would cause an "undue hardship" is based on the following factors: (1) the nature and the cost of the accommodation; (2) the overall financial resources of the facility and the impact on the facility and other employees; (3) the overall financial resources of the company; and (4) the type of operation of the employer. 42 U.S.C. § 12111(10).

d. "Direct Threat to Self or Others"

The ADA provides employers an affirmative defense if they can show that a person poses a "direct threat" that makes him or her unqualified for the job and therefore unprotected by the statute. A direct threat means a "significant risk to the health or safety of others that cannot be eliminated by reasonable accommodation." This language has been expanded by the EEOC to include threats to oneself—an interpretation that the Supreme Court affirmed in *Chevron U.S.A., Inc. v. Echazabal*, 536 U.S. 73 (2002).

To find if there is a "significant risk," the employer must apply the "most current medical knowledge or best available objective evidence" and must focus on the person's ability to safely perform the essential functions of the job. To assess whether the risk is "significant," courts look to four factors: (1) the duration of the risk; (2) the nature and severity of the potential harm; (3) the likelihood the potential harm will occur; and (4) the imminence of the potential harm. In determining significant risk, the risk must be based on medical or other objective evidence. Good faith is not enough. *Bragdon v. Abbott*, 524 U.S. 624 (1998). As far as direct threats to oneself, the Supreme Court held that the ADA did not preclude the EEOC's regulation allowing the harm-to-self defense.

4. "Because of That Individual's Disability"

One current issue is whether the ADA allows a plaintiff to prevail by establishing that her disability was a motivating factor in a decision. The Supreme Court held that a plaintiff proceeding on an ADEA discrimination claim or a Title VII retaliation claim must prove "but for" cause, rather than the more lenient "motivating factor" standard used for Title VII discrimination claims. Courts are considering which standard to apply in ADA cases, and the Supreme Court has not resolved this issue. It should be noted that the ADA discrimination provisions do not fully mimic the language of either Title VII or the ADEA, and the ADA uses the words "based on" rather than "because of." The ADA incorporates by reference the Title VII remedies provision, including its reference to 42 U.S.C. § 2000e-5(g). However, Congress did not amend the ADA to include the motivating factor language that it added to Title VII.

B. Association Discrimination Claims

One form of discrimination provided in the text of the ADA is associational discrimination. The ADA explicitly provides that denying a job or benefit to an individual because of the known disability of another individual with whom the first individual has a relationship or association, is unlawful disability discrimination. Common examples of associational discrimination include (1) "expense," where an employer believes (rightly or wrongly) that employee's association with a disabled person will generate insurance costs; (2) "disability by association," where an employer believes that the employee may contract or is genetically predisposed to develop the disability of the associated person; and (3) "distraction," where an employer believes the employee will be inattentive at work due to the care required for the disabled person. *Graziadio v. Culinary Institute of America*, 817 F.3d 415, 432 (2d Cir. 2016) (citing *Larimer v. IBM Corp.*, 370 F.3d 698 (7th Cir. 2004)). So, for instance, decisions to discharge an employee because that employee decides to do volunteer work with AIDS patients or refusing to hire an employee with a disabled spouse or child because of increased insurance costs and time away from work, could potentially be covered under the association discrimination provisions. The ADA regulations provide that cases of association discrimination do not need to be reasonably accommodated.

C. Retaliation under the ADA

Generally speaking, at least one part of the retaliation provisions under the ADA is almost identical to those in Title VII (see Chapter 10 for more discussion of retaliation claims). Under 42 U.S.C. § 12203(a): "No person shall discriminate against any individual because such individual has opposed any act or practice made unlawful by this chapter or because such individual made a charge, testified, assisted, or participated in any manner in an investigation, proceeding, or hearing under this chapter." So, there is both a participation and opposition clause for retaliation claims in the disability discrimination context.

One important difference, however, is that the ADA also makes it unlawful to "coerce, intimidate, threaten, or interfere with any individuals in the exercise or enjoyment of" any right granted or protected by the ADA. This clause is similar to § 8(a)(1) of the National Labor Relations Act, and therefore, also protects individuals from interference with their ADA rights, regardless whether an employer or another person intended to retaliate or discriminate on that basis. In that sense, the ADA provides greater protection for individuals from retaliation than Title VII.

D. Medical Exams and Inquiries

Because disclosures of physical abilities or mental conditions can be used to discriminate against people with disabilities, the ADA created rules regarding testing and documentation. The ability to make medical inquiries or request medical exams varies depending on timing. Pre-employment questions about the ability of the applicant to perform job-related functions are permitted, but medical exams are generally precluded. In any event, employers are not permitted to ask disability-specific questions: that is, those questions likely to elicit information about disability (for instance, have you ever been treated for AIDS?). Drug tests are not "medical exams" and are specifically excluded from ADA coverage.

As far as post-offer, pre-employment inquiries, an employer can make a request for a medical examination after an offer of employment and may condition employment on the results of the exam. To be able to do this, all employees in this job category must take this exam, results of that exam must be kept confidential, and the exam may be as broad as the employer wishes. If the employee fails the exam, the employer must show that the standard is job related to the position and is consistent with business necessity.

With regard to existing employee medical inquiries, such inquiries must be job related and consistent with business necessity. This means that the employer must have a reasonable belief, based on objective evidence, that a medical condition will impair an employee's ability to perform essential job functions or cause the employee to pose a direct threat.

Lastly, under the ADA, medical information about employees must be kept separately from other personnel files.

E. Procedural and Remedial Issues under the ADA

Generally speaking, the procedural and remedial issues relevant to Title VII also apply to the ADA, with some limited exceptions.

As far as remedies, employers under the Civil Rights Act of 1991 have an affirmative defense to failure to accommodate claims. In these types of claims, if the employer demonstrates good-faith efforts, in consultation with the disabled employee, to identify and make reasonable accommodations that would provide an equally effective opportunity and would not cause an undue hardship on the business, compensatory and punitive damages may not be awarded. More generally, and similar to Title VII, compensatory and punitive damages are available only for intentional discrimination claims.

There are also Eleventh Amendment sovereign immunity issues under the ADA. For a further discussion on that topic, see Chapter 1; but suffice it to say that state employees cannot sue their state employers for monetary damages under the ADA. *University of Alabama v. Garrett*, 531 U.S. 356 (2001).

CHECKPOINTS

- The ADA prohibits employers from (1) discriminating against (2) a person with a disability who is (3) otherwise qualified for the position (4) because of that individual's disability.
- The ADA Amendments Act of 2008 (ADAAA) has substantially expanded the meaning of a person with a disability for purposes of the ADA.
- Discrimination under the ADA is broader than under Title VII and also includes a cause of action for failure to accommodate.
- The definition of a person with a disability is someone who has or had (1) a physical or mental impairment (2) that substantially limits (3) one or more major life activities. A person may also meet the definition of disability if there is a record of impairment or the employer regards the person as having an impairment.
- Under the ADAAA, the plaintiff is no longer responsible for proving the defendant's misperception about the plaintiff's disability under the "regarded as" prong.

- Whether an impairment substantially limits activity generally shall be made without regard to mitigating measures.
- "Qualification" is based on whether the disabled individual can (1) perform the essential job functions of the job he or she holds or desires (2) with or without reasonable accommodations without (3) posing to the employee or others a direct threat.
- Employers need not make any reasonable accommodation that requires an undue hardship, meaning a significant difficulty or expense for the employer.
- Employers have a number of defenses under the ADA including direct threat and undue hardship.
- One form of discrimination present in the ADA is associational discrimination.
- Unlike Title VII, the ADA retaliation provisions also prohibit interference with any individual in the exercise of any right granted or protected by the ADA.
- Medical examinations and inquiries are permitted to different degrees based on whether they take place pre-employment, after a conditional offer, or for existing employees.
- Procedural and remedial issues under the ADA are for the most part handled the same way as they are under Title VII, with a few exceptions.

CHAPTER 13

Age Discrimination in Employment Act

ROADMAP

- Introducing the ADEA
- Coverage and remedies under the ADEA
- Disparate treatment claims under the ADEA
- Single-motive *McDonnell Douglas* cases vs. mixed-motive cases
- Disparate impact claims under the ADEA
- Employer defenses under the ADEA
- Valid waivers of ADEA rights under the OWBPA

A. Introduction to the ADEA

When Congress debated the Civil Rights Act of 1964, it considered including age as one of Title VII's protected classes. However, recognizing differences between age and protected classes such as race and sex, Congress decided to leave age out of Title VII and instead order the Secretary of Labor to investigate whether age discrimination legislation was justified. What is now referred to as the Wirtz Report, named after then-Secretary of Labor Willard Wirtz, ultimately concluded that such a law was needed because of possible prejudice against older workers; employer attempts to avoid generally higher compensation for older workers; and, most significantly, stereotypes about older workers' value. Congress agreed and, in 1967, enacted the Age Discrimination in Employment Act (ADEA), 29 U.S.C. § 621 *et seq*.

B. Coverage and Remedies

In addition to the coverage issues discussed in Chapter 2, the ADEA has some special rules that warrant attention. These issues involve the identification of both covered employees and employers.

First, the ADEA covers only employees who are 40 years old or older. Even among those employees, some individuals are excluded from coverage in certain instances. For instance, public firefighters and law enforcement officers can be subject to maximum hiring ages and mandatory retirement ages, although other protections of the ADEA will apply. Some executives and high-ranking policymakers may also face mandatory retirement under special circumstances. Tenured professors used to lack protection against mandatory retirements once they turned 70 years old, but that exception ended in 1993.

Second, the ADEA covers many of the same employers as Title VII. Thus, most private and public employers, unions with more than 25 members or unions that run a hiring hall, and employment agencies, are all generally covered by the ADEA. The ADEA, like Title VII and the ADA, also has a small-employer exception. However, the ADEA's small-employer exception requires only that private employers have 20 or more employees to be covered—a slightly higher threshold than the 15-employee exception under Title VII and the ADA. Unlike Title VII and the ADA, whose small-employer exceptions apply to both private and public employers, the ADEA lacks a small-employer exception for public employers. *See Mount Lemmon Fire District v. Guido*, 586 U.S. 1 (2018).

Remedies for a successful ADEA plaintiff are similar to those of a Title VII plaintiff, although because the ADEA's remedies (like the Equal Pay Act, as discussed in Chapter 15) are based on the Fair Labor Standards Act (FLSA), there are differences. Under both the ADEA and Title VII, possible remedies include injunctive relief, backpay, reinstatement, frontpay, attorney's fees, and costs. One difference is that compensatory and punitive damages are not available under the ADEA, but unlike in Title VII, the ADEA permits liquidated damages, which can be an additional award in an amount equal to the actual damages. The threshold for liquidated damages is similar to punitive damages under Title VII, as both require willful violations, meaning a knowing or reckless violation of the statute. *Trans World Airlines, Inc. v. Thurston*, 469 U.S. 111 (1985).

The statute of limitations for the ADEA, like the FLSA, used to be two or three years, depending on the willfulness of the employer's actions. However, the Civil Rights Act of 1991 (CRA of 1991) changed that rule by bringing the ADEA under the EEOC's enforcement process. Thus, the ADEA has the same 180-day or 300-day statute of limitations period as Title VII (as discussed in Chapter 3).

C. Disparate Treatment Age Discrimination

The central provision of the ADEA is its prohibition against intentional age discrimination—the ADEA disparate treatment claim. Under § 4(a)(1) of the ADEA, it is unlawful for an employer "to fail or refuse to hire or to discharge any individual or otherwise discriminate against any individual with respect to his compensation, terms, conditions, or privileges of employment, because of such individual's age." The key issue in many disparate treatment cases is the meaning of "because of age." The starting point for the ADEA disparate treatment analysis is Title VII, as there are many similarities between the ADEA and Title VII disparate treatment claims. However, there are many differences as well. Some of those differences are the result of the non-applicability of the CRA of 1991, while others derive from fundamental differences between age discrimination and the types of discrimination proscribed by Title VII.

1. Single-Motive Disparate Treatment

As explained below, most single-employee disparate treatment claims under the ADEA are analyzed under the Title VII *McDonnell Douglas* analysis. Even if multiple motives are in play, the plaintiffs in an ADEA disparate treatment action must prove that age was a "but for" cause of an adverse employment action. *McDonnell Douglas*, described in more detail in Chapter 6, has three steps when applied to the ADEA: (1) the employee has the burden of persuasion to establish a prima facie case of age discrimination; (2) the employer has the burden of production to provide a legitimate nondiscriminatory reason for the employment action; and (3) the employee has the burden of persuasion to establish that the true motivation was age discrimination, such as by showing that the employer's nondiscriminatory reason was pretext and the real reason was discrimination or by showing other evidence to establish the causal link. The ADEA also permits employers various affirmative defenses if the employee successfully meets their *McDonnell Douglas* burden.

Application of the *McDonnell Douglas* analysis is generally the same under both Title VII and the ADEA, and most of the issues discussed in Chapter 6 regarding that analysis are applicable here. One difference, however, occurs in the prima facie case. That difference is largely the result of the unique type of discrimination involved in ADEA cases.

a. The Employee's Prima Facie Case

Title VII involves class discrimination: individuals are discriminated against because they are a member of a protected class or not. Age discrimination is somewhat different. Instead of a strict class-based analysis, age discrimination is more relative. In particular, plaintiffs typically make out a case of age discrimination by showing that they faced an adverse employment action because they were *older* than other employees or applicants. This point was driven home in *O'Connor v. Consolidated Coin Caterers Corp.*, 517 U.S. 308 (1996), in which the Supreme Court addressed whether a plaintiff could argue that the employer discriminated against him in favor of a younger employee who was over 40 years old and therefore also covered by the ADEA. In holding that such a comparison was allowed, the Court emphasized that the 40-year-old rule was simply a threshold indicating which workers could pursue claims under the statute. Once that requirement is satisfied, the central question in an ADEA disparate treatment case is whether the employer acted because of the plaintiff's age, and if the favored employee is younger—even if over 40 years old—the plaintiff can still use that comparison as evidence of discrimination. Indeed, the Court noted that comparison evidence of a 40-year-old employee being replaced by a 39-year-old creates less of an inference of discrimination than a 56-year-old being replaced by a 40-year-old. Thus, an ADEA plaintiff is not required to establish that the comparator is outside the ADEA's coverage.

As a result of the *O'Connor* decision, the ADEA prima facie case looks a bit different than Title VII. Under the ADEA, the prima facie case requires these elements: (1) the plaintiff is in the protected class—that is, at least 40 years old; (2) the plaintiff faced a negative employment action; (3) the employee was minimally qualified; and (4) the favored employee or applicant was younger than the plaintiff. Prong four can also be established with other evidence suggesting discrimination because of age. Some courts, including the appellate court in *O'Connor*, had required in this last step that the favored employee be outside of the protected class—that is, under 40 years old—which is more similar to the Title VII analysis. But, as the Supreme Court made clear in *O'Connor*, the focus in the ADEA analysis is whether the favored employee was younger than the plaintiff. Moreover, to win an ADEA claim by showing that discrimination was the cause of the employment action—or, for some courts, to satisfy the fourth step of the prima facie case—plaintiffs will typically have to show that there was a significant age difference between the plaintiff and the favored employee or employees. Finally, the ADEA does not prohibit discrimination that favors older employees; in other words, it does not permit a reverse discrimination claim. *General Dynamics Land Systems v. Cline*, 540 U.S. 581 (2004).

b. The Employer's Legitimate, Nondiscriminatory Reason

Under the *McDonnell Douglas* analysis, once the employee makes out their prima facie case, the employer then has the burden of production to articulate a legitimate, nondiscriminatory reason for the adverse employment action. As noted in Chapter 6, "legitimate" simply means that the motivation was not barred under the statute at issue. So, for an ADEA claim, the employer need only show that it acted for some reason other than age.

This interpretation of the term "legitimate" as meaning merely something "lawful" under the ADEA was underscored by the Supreme Court's decision in *Hazen Paper Co. v. Biggins*, 507 U.S. 604 (1993). The employer in *Hazen Paper* fired an employee just before his pension was going to vest. Although a pretty clear violation of the Employee Retirement Income Security Act (ERISA), the Court held that this reason could still be "legitimate" for purpose of the employee's ADEA claim because the motivation was not age. The conclusion that the employer's motivation in *Hazen Paper* was not based on age also illustrates the strictness of that requirement. The employee in the case argued that because pension vesting was generally tied to an employee's age—a worker must work for a certain number of years to reach the vesting threshold—the employer's motive should be considered age-based. The Court disagreed and held that although there is often a correlation between age and vesting, that correlation is not always present. Thus, the employer's motivation was to avoid paying out pension benefits, not to discriminate on the basis of age. According to the Court, the fact that attempting to avoid paying pension benefits will disproportionately affect older employees raises a disparate impact issue—which was not alleged in *Hazen Paper*—rather than a disparate treatment issue.

c. The Employee Ultimately Establishes That Discrimination Was the Employer's Motive

If the employer meets its burden of producing a legitimate, nondiscriminatory reason, the *McDonnell Douglas* analysis moves to the third and final step: the employee's burden of persuasion to show that age discrimination motivated the employment action. The step is applied virtually identically in both ADEA and Title VII cases, as discussed in detail in Chapter 6. Under both statutes, the central focus is proof that the employee has been a victim of intentional discrimination. *Texas Department of Community Affairs v. Burdine*, 450 U.S. 248 (1981). One of the more common ways of establishing discrimination is by showing that the employer's legitimate, nondiscriminatory reason is pretext; such a showing by itself can, but does not always, establish a discriminatory motive. *Reeves v. Sanderson Plumbing Products, Inc.*, 530 U.S. 133 (2000); *St. Mary's Honor Center v. Hicks*, 509 U.S. 502 (1993). Therefore, plaintiffs often supplement pretext evidence with other evidence of discrimination—or, if not making a pretext argument, simply use such evidence—including comparators, the employer's past practices, the employee's qualifications in relation to more favorably treated individuals, comments that suggest discrimination, changing explanations by the employer, the time between the employment action and some type of protected activity, and statistics on the employer's workforce.

2. Mixed-Motive Disparate Treatment

In addition to the straightforward single-motive scenario, discrimination cases often involve several motives that contribute to an adverse employment action. A mixed-motive case—one in which multiple motives, some age-based and others not—can still exist under the ADEA, but there will be no liability in such cases if age is not a "but for" cause of the outcome. In other words, if age is taken out of the scenario and the same outcome would occur, then age is not a "but for" cause. It is only when age is one of the "but for" reasons that there will be liability.

Following the Supreme Court's decision in *Price Waterhouse v. Hopkins*, 490 U.S. 228 (1989), most courts used the same mixed-motive analysis for ADEA claims as they did for Title VII claims. As described in Chapter 6, this analysis applied Justice O'Connor's concurrence in *Price Waterhouse*. Her analysis gave the plaintiff the burden of persuasion to show, by direct evidence, that unlawful discrimination was a substantial factor in an adverse employment action. If the plaintiff makes this showing, the employer then has the burden of persuasion to show that it would have made the same decision absent the discrimination. An employer who makes such a showing would escape all liability.

Matters got more complicated after the CRA of 1991. In codifying the mixed-motive claim, the CRA of 1991 altered the plaintiff's burden to show—by direct or circumstantial evidence according to the Supreme Court—that discrimination was a motivating factor; if the plaintiff is successful, the employer can limit damages, but not escape liability, by showing that it would have made the same decision absent the discrimination. However, the CRA of 1991 only explicitly applied to Title VII. Thus, courts struggled to determine how to treat ADEA mixed-motive claims. Some courts emphasized the exclusion of the ADEA from the CRA of 1991 and continued using Justice O'Connor's *Price Waterhouse* analysis. Other courts stressed that because the ADEA was explicitly modeled after Title VII and generally read the same way, they would apply the CRA of 1991 to the ADEA. Finally, in 2009, the Supreme Court settled the issue, choosing a third approach.

In *Gross v. FBS Financial Services, Inc.*, 557 U.S. 167 (2009), the plaintiff argued that he was demoted because of his age, while the employer claimed that the plaintiff was merely reassigned due to business restructuring. The Court granted certiorari in *Gross* initially just to answer whether direct evidence was required in an ADEA mixed-motive case—essentially whether the Court's decision in the Title VII case, *Desert Palace, Inc. v. Costa*, 539 U.S. 90 (2003), applied to the ADEA. Yet, the Court went much further, holding instead that there is no unique mixed-motive claim at all under the ADEA.

The Court's decision in *Gross* heavily stressed the ADEA's absence from the CRA of 1991. This was not a surprise, as the Court had made a similar holding when addressing disparate impact claims under the ADEA, as explained below. But the Court did not stop at simply saying that the CRA of 1991 did not apply. Most courts that took the same view had then turned to Justice O'Connor's *Price Waterhouse* analysis. In *Gross*, however, the Court essentially overturned both the plurality and concurring opinions in *Price Waterhouse*—at least as applied to the ADEA (and, most likely, the ADA). Indeed, the Court in *Gross* explicitly stated that the current Court likely would have decided *Price Waterhouse* differently, as it viewed the default meaning of "because of" as requiring but-for causation. The *Gross* decision follows this reasoning by holding that ADEA disparate treatment claims must always show but-for causation. "Motivating" or "substantial" factors are not enough to establish liability.

Although the history of mixed-motive claims under the ADEA is complicated, the current rule for such claims is not. Under *Gross*, all ADEA disparate treatment claims—even those involving multiple motives—must show that unlawful age discrimination was a but-for cause of the adverse employment action. This almost certainly means that *McDonnell Douglas* will be the analysis for most ADEA individual disparate treatment cases. Technically, as noted in *Gross*, the Court has not expressly held that the *McDonnell Douglas* analysis is appropriate for ADEA cases. But practically, until the Court takes the unexpected step of barring use of that analysis beyond Title VII, courts will use the *McDonnell Douglas* analysis for ADEA disparate treatment claims based on circumstantial evidence, whether involving a single-motive or mixed-motives. Accordingly, in a mixed-motive ADEA case, the plaintiff will now have to convince the factfinder that, although other nondiscriminatory factors were at work, age discrimination was a but-for cause of the adverse employment action.

The difference between a "but for" cause standard and a motivating factor standard may be less important after the Supreme Court's opinion in *Bostock v. Clayton County*, 590 U.S. 644 (2020). *Bostock* described "but for" cause as a "sweeping" standard, noted that events can have multiple "but for" causes, and stated that a reason can still be a "but for" cause even if it is not the primary reason for the outcome. Pre-*Bostock*, some courts misapplied "but for" cause, requiring the plaintiff to establish that their protected activity was "the" cause of an outcome, rather than a "but for" cause.

In *Babb v. Wilkie*, 589 U.S. 399 (2020), the Supreme Court held the ADEA's federal sector provision, 29 U.S.C. § 633a(a), does not require the plaintiff to establish "but for" cause. The Court held that, in ADEA federal sector cases, the entire process (not just the outcome) must be "free from any discrimination based on age." However, a plaintiff is required to establish "but for" cause to obtain certain kinds of remedies.

3. Systemic Disparate Treatment

The ADEA does not contain an explicit "pattern or practice" action, as exists under Title VII. However, courts recognize ADEA systemic disparate treatment claims and analyze them in the same manner as Title VII systemic disparate treatment cases, which are discussed in Chapter 7. Under both statutes, the key issue is the plaintiffs' use of statistics and other evidence showing that discrimination is widespread throughout the workplace. Regression analysis, which is typically used to analyze statistical evidence under both statutes, is especially important under the ADEA. Because age discrimination is relative—the issue is whether plaintiffs are "older" than others and by how much, rather than whether the plaintiffs are "old" or not—simple rules of thumb like the EEOC's four-fifths rule are less useful. Regression analysis can take into account a variable like age that can have many different outcomes and show whether it has a statistically significant impact on hiring, pay, or whatever employment action is at issue.

D. Disparate Impact Age Discrimination

In addition to disparate treatment, employees may also argue that an employer violated the ADEA under the disparate impact theory. In contrast to disparate treatment's focus on the employer's motivation, disparate impact claims argue that an otherwise nondiscriminatory employment practice has a disparate impact. Under the ADEA, this means that, despite a lack of intent on the employer's part to treat someone different because of their age, a neutral employment practice has a disproportionately negative effect on older employees, as compared to younger employees.

Whether disparate impact claims were available in any form under the ADEA was the source of much disagreement among courts. This question was further complicated by the CRA of 1991, which codified the disparate impact claim under Title VII, but made no mention of the ADEA. Courts then fell into multiple camps. Some held that there was no disparate impact claim under the ADEA. Others held that there was such a claim, but it was analyzed under the Court's analysis in *Wards Cove Packing Co. v. Atonio*, 490 U.S. 642 (1989), which Congress largely overturned in the CRA of 1991. Still others recognized the claim, but used the CRA of 1991 analysis. In 2005, the Court finally settled the issue—holding that there was an ADEA disparate impact claim, with its own, unique analysis.

Smith v. City of Jackson, 544 U.S. 228 (2005), involved a police department that restructured its pay scale to give less-senior officers higher percentage raises in order to make the department more competitive for entry-level hires.

Older officers argued that the plan violated the ADEA under both disparate treatment and disparate impact theories. Looking just at the disparate impact issue, the Supreme Court held that such claims were available under the ADEA. The Court in *Smith* stressed that the language of § 4(a)(2) of the ADEA—prohibiting actions that "limit, segregate, or classify ... employees in any way which would deprive or tend to deprive any individual of employment opportunities or otherwise adversely affect his status as an employee, because of such individual's age"—was virtually identical to Title VII's § 703(a)(2), which the Court in *Griggs* held to encompass the disparate impact theory. According to a majority of Justices in *Smith*, this showed either that the ADEA's text, on its face, permitted disparate impact claims or showed that the EEOC's interpretation of that text to permit disparate impact claims was reasonable.

Further support for this conclusion was based on one significant difference between disparate impact claims under Title VII and the ADEA, which is the latter's "reasonable factor other than age" defense. Under § 4(f)(1) of the ADEA, it is not unlawful for an employer "to take any action otherwise prohibited under [the ADEA] ... where the differentiation is based on reasonable factors other than age." The existence of the RFOA defense was cited by the Court as further evidence of the existence of the disparate impact theory under the ADEA, as the defense is not needed in disparate treatment cases; if an adverse employment action was based on a factor other than age—any non-age factor, even one that is not reasonable—there is no disparate treatment that needs to be defended. According to the Court in *Smith*, the RFOA defense is useful when a factor other than age creates an outcome that would otherwise be unlawful and such an outcome exists where there is a practice causing a disparate impact. The RFOA defense, while supporting the Court's conclusion that the ADEA recognizes disparate impact claims, also significantly altered the analysis of such claims. That defense, in addition to the CRA of 1991's failure to mention the ADEA, represents a substantial difference between the ADEA and Title VII disparate impact analyses. Those differences are described in the following, post-*Smith*, ADEA disparate impact analysis.

Under the ADEA, a plaintiff still must show that an employment practice has caused a disparate impact. However, the Court in *Smith* stressed that, because of the exclusion of the ADEA from the CRA of 1991, this stage of the case is analyzed under the pre-1991 Title VII analysis of *Wards Cove Packing Co. v. Atonio*, 490 U.S. 642 (1989), discussed in Chapter 8. Thus, plaintiffs must establish a statistical disparity, typically showing significance under the EEOC's four-fifths rule. In showing that statistical disparity, however, plaintiffs must also identify the specific employment practice causing the disparity, which the plaintiffs in *Smith* failed to do.

If the plaintiffs make out their prima facie case of disparate impact, the burden of persuasion then shifts to the employer. *Meachem v. Knolls Atomic Power Agency*, 554 U.S. 84 (2008). In contrast to Title VII's job related and business necessity defense, under *Smith* the employer's burden at this step in an ADEA case is tied to the RFOA language. In particular, the employer need only show that the challenged employment practice was a "reasonable factor other than age." For instance, in *Smith*, the Court noted that had the plaintiffs established their prima facie case, the employer could defend its decision to give junior officers proportionally larger raises because it was a reasonable strategy to make their salaries similar to nearby communities and, therefore, make their hiring more competitive. The reasonableness defense also changes another aspect of the disparate impact test. Under Title VII, if the employer satisfies its burden, the plaintiffs can still win by showing that an alternative practice would result in a less discriminatory impact. However, in *Smith*, the Court held that this alternative practice step is not available under the ADEA. Because the RFOA defense states that any reasonable factor other than age does not violate the ADEA, there is no burden on the employer to use a less discriminatory practice as long as the one it used was reasonable. Accordingly, even if the plaintiffs in *Smith* could have shown a less discriminatory practice that was as effective, or even more effective, at satisfying the employer's recruitment goals, the employer would not have been liable under the ADEA because the practice it used was reasonable.

E. Employer Defenses

Section 4(f) of the ADEA lists several defenses to actions "otherwise prohibited" under the statute. If the employer meets its burden of persuasion in establishing one of these defenses, it escapes liability. *Meachem v. Knolls Atomic Power Agency*, 554 U.S. 84 (2008). One less common defense occurs when an American employee works for an American employer in a foreign country and compliance with the ADEA would violate the foreign country's laws. The ADEA also permits an employer to fire or discipline an employee for "good cause," although that defense seems redundant given that good cause is already a defense under the disparate treatment analysis. Beyond these relatively minor defenses, there are others with a more substantial impact in the workplace, which could be described as the "bona fide defenses," as they apply to bona fide occupational qualifications, bona fide seniority systems, and bona fide employee benefit plans.

1. Bona Fide Occupational Qualification

As is the case under Title VII, an employer that discriminates can escape liability by making out a "bona fide occupational qualification" (BFOQ) defense. Under § 4(f)(1) of the ADEA, a BFOQ defense requires that age be "reasonably necessary to the normal operation of a particular business." This mirrors the language of Title VII; therefore, the BFOQ under both statutes has been analyzed the same way. As described in more detail in Chapter 6, the BFOQ defense is a narrow one and requires proof that the occupational qualification at issue is essential to the core business of the employer.

One frequent issue in ADEA cases is an attempt by employers to use age as a proxy, especially for safety concerns. Because most individuals' health and physical capabilities decline as they age, many employers attempt to limit older employees' ability to serve in certain high-risk jobs. In *Western Airlines v. Criswell*, 472 U.S. 400 (1985), the Supreme Court approved two different approaches to allow this proxy defense, although they are fairly limited.

Criswell involved an airline's mandatory retirement age of 60 years for flight engineers, who are responsible for the plane if the pilots are incapacitated. Although some older flight engineers no doubt could have suffered physical or mental impairments that interfered with their ability to fly a plane in an emergency, others were perfectly capable of performing that task. The rule, therefore, was using age as a proxy for an increased risk of a debilitating health problem. In *Criswell*, the Court held that when significant safety risks were at issue, an employer could use age as a proxy for this risk under two conditions: (1) the employer can show that it had reasonable cause to believe, and that there is a factual basis for believing, that all or substantially all older employees would be unable to perform safely and efficiently the necessary job duties; or (2) the employer can show that it is "impossible or highly impractical" to make individual assessments of older employees' ability to satisfy a safety-related qualification. Although courts take threats to public safety seriously, these proxy defenses are not easy to satisfy. In *Criswell*, for instance, the employer lost because it could not justify why it chose the specific age of 60 years old and because it could not show that flight engineers needed the same retirement age rules as pilots, especially because many other airlines did not use the same age for both their flight engineers and pilots.

2. Bona Fide Seniority Systems

Another similarity between Title VII and the ADEA is the safe haven given for bona fide seniority systems. Under § 4(f)(2)(A) of the ADEA, it is lawful to apply a "bona fide seniority system that is not intended to evade the purposes" of the statute, even if that system discriminates against older workers. One exception to this defense is that provisions in seniority plans that require or permit involuntary retirements because of age are not protected.

Although the bona fide seniority system defense can be important to employers, it is not a frequent issue under the ADEA. The reason is that the vast majority of provisions in seniority systems favor older employees, as they place a premium on the number of years on a job.

3. Bona Fide Seniority Employee Benefit Plans

The ADEA—following its amendment under the 1990 Older Workers Benefit Protection Act (OWBPA)—also protects certain aspects of bona fide employee benefit plans (such as employer-provided health plans) that discriminate on the basis of age. Under § 4(f)(2)(B) of the ADEA, it is lawful for an employer "to observe the terms of a bona fide employee benefit plan" under two conditions: (1) "where, for each benefit or benefit package, the actual amount of payment made or cost incurred on behalf of an older worker is no less than that made or incurred on behalf of a younger worker"; or (2) that the plan is a voluntary early retirement incentive plan that complies with the OWBPA's waiver requirements, which are discussed below.

The first condition gives employers a safe harbor when faced with different cost structures for younger versus older employees. For instance, life insurance will generally be more expensive the older an individual becomes. Under § 4(f)(2)(B), an employer will not violate the ADEA for buying less life insurance coverage for older employees as long as the employer spends the same amount in premiums for those employees as it does for its younger employees. This is referred to as the "same cost" defense.

F. Older Workers Benefit Protection Act Waivers

One of the aims of Congress in enacting the OWBPA was to clarify the standard that would apply to older employees' waiver of their right to sue under the ADEA. The courts had been sharply split on the issue, requiring varying tests to determine whether a waiver was valid. That split was increasingly problematic for the ADEA, because waivers are a frequent component of early retirement offers or other plans that disproportionately affect older employees. The OWBPA establishes a minimum legal standard for such waivers and implements several procedural rules that employers must follow to obtain a valid waiver from an ADEA-covered employee.

As a general matter, the OWBPA—codified under § 7(f) of the ADEA—requires that all valid waivers of future claims under the ADEA be "knowing and voluntary." To be considered knowing and voluntary, a waiver must comply with the following:

- the waiver is part of an agreement between the parties that is written in a way that can be understood by the employee or by the average employee eligible to participate in the offer;
- the waiver specifically refers to rights or claims arising under the ADEA;
- the employee does not waive rights or claims that may arise after the agreement is executed;
- the employee waives rights or claims only in exchange for consideration that does not include anything that the employee is already entitled to;
- the employer advised the employee in writing to consult with an attorney prior to signing the agreement;
- the employee is given at least 21 days to consider the agreement, or if a waiver is part of an exit incentive or other employment termination program offered to a group of employees, the employee is given at least 45 days to consider the agreement;
- the agreement provides a period of at least 7 days after its execution during which the employee may revoke the agreement and during which the agreement is not effective or enforceable; and

- if a waiver is part of an exit incentive or other employment termination program offered to a group of employees, the employer informs each employee in writing (in a way that can be understood by the employee or by the average employee eligible to participate in the offer) of any class, unit, or group of individuals covered by the program, any eligibility factors for the program, and any time limits applicable to the program—as well as the job titles and ages of all employees eligible or selected for the program and the same information for employees not selected.

Settlements of claims already filed under the ADEA have special rules under §7 as well. In particular, such settlements must comply with the first five of the above requirements and provide employees a "reasonable time" to consider the settlement. The party seeking to enforce either a waiver or settlement has the burden to show that the employee's waiver was knowing and voluntary under these rules. Moreover, even if an employee has accepted payment for a waiver and later sues under the ADEA, claiming that the waiver was not valid, the employee need not return the payment to maintain the action. *Oubre v. Energy Operations, Inc.*, 522 U.S. 422 (1998).

CHECKPOINTS

- The ADEA covers most employees who are 40 years old and older.
- The ADEA covers most private employers with 20 or more employees, unions with 25 or more members or hiring halls, employment agencies, and public employers of any size.
- Successful ADEA plaintiffs can be awarded injunctive relief, backpay, reinstatement, frontpay, attorney's fees, costs, and liquidated damages; compensatory and punitive damages are not available.
- Most ADEA single-plaintiff disparate treatment claims are analyzed under the Title VII *McDonnell Douglas* analysis. The steps under that analysis are (1) the employee establishes a prima facie case; (2) the employer articulates a legitimate nondiscriminatory reason; and (3) the employee establishes that age was a but-for cause of the adverse employment action, often by showing that the employer's stated reason was pretext.

- ADEA systemic disparate treatment claims are analyzed similarly to Title VII pattern or practice systemic claims, which require the plaintiffs to establish through statistical and other evidence that discrimination was widespread throughout the workplace.
- Disparate impact claims are permissible under the ADEA and are analyzed under two steps: the employees establish that a particular employment practice caused a statistically significant disparity based on age and, if the employees meet their burden, the employer can escape liability by showing that the challenged practice was a reasonable factor other than age.
- Defenses to actions that would otherwise be unlawful under the ADEA include a bona fide occupational qualification (BFOQ) that relates to the core of the employer's business, a bona fide seniority system, a bona fide employee retirement plan, foreign law under certain circumstances, and good cause.
- An employer can use age as a proxy for a serious safety concern under the bona fide occupation qualification defense if it can show reasonable cause to believe that all or substantially all older employees would be unable to perform safely and efficiently the necessary job duties or that that it is impossible or highly impractical to make individual assessments of older employees' ability to satisfy a safety-related qualification.
- Under the Older Workers Benefit Protection Act, valid waivers of ADEA claims must be knowing and voluntary—which exists only when the waiver is part of an agreement that meets the OWBPA's set of procedural safeguards.

CHAPTER 14

Other Civil Rights Protection Against Employment Discrimination

ROADMAP

- Introducing the post-Civil War enactments
- Equal protection challenges against discriminatory governmental action
- The constitutional affirmative action defense
- Section 1981 and the prohibition against race discrimination in employment
- Section 1983 and the prohibition against state deprivation of employees' federal rights

A. Introduction to the Post-Civil War Enactments

After the end of the Civil War, Congress passed several pieces of legislation intended to guarantee black citizens' newly-won right to freedom. The key piece of legislation for employment discrimination purposes was the Fourteenth Amendment, which guaranteed all individuals the right to due process and equal protection from state actors. Soon thereafter, Congress exercised its new powers to enforce the Fourteenth Amendment against the states by enacting several civil rights statutes. Several of these provisions apply in the employment context.

B. Equal Protection under the Constitution

Following the end of the Civil War, Congress passed and the states ratified the three Civil War Amendments. The Thirteenth Amendment abolished slavery and the Fifteenth Amendment guaranteed the right to vote without respect to race, color, or "previous condition of servitude." More relevant for employment discrimination purposes was the Fourteenth Amendment, which among things, guaranteed individuals the right to equal protection from the states. This equal protection right applies to public employment, which has given covered employees an additional avenue to challenge workplace discrimination. However, this option is limited to class-based discrimination claims, as the Supreme Court has held that "class-of-one" equal protection claims do not exist for public employees. *Engquist v. Oregon Department of Agriculture*, 553 U.S. 591 (2008).

Moreover, equal protection only permits disparate treatment claims in which a plaintiff can prove the government employer's intent to discriminate, as the Supreme Court has held that disparate impact claims are not available under the Constitution. *Washington v. Davis*, 426 U.S. 229 (1976). This holding reflects an unwillingness by the Court to allow challenges to government action simply because it produces an unintentional discriminatory impact. Indeed, the Court has been stringent about the intent requirement, holding that mere knowledge that a policy will result in a disparate impact is not enough; there must be proof of intent to cause that action. *Personnel Administrator of Massachusetts v. Feeney*, 422 U.S. 256 (1979).

The Fourteenth Amendment's Equal Protection Clause (§ 1 of the Amendment) mandates that: "No State shall . . . deny to any person within its jurisdiction the Equal Protection of the laws." By its terms, the Fourteenth Amendment applies only to state, and by judicial extension, local action. However, the Supreme Court has imported an equal protection guarantee into the Fifth Amendment's Due Process Clause, which applies to federal action. *Bolling v. Sharpe*, 347 U.S. 497 (1954). The analysis under both clauses is identical, despite their different sources of law. *Adarand Constructors, Inc. v. Pena*, 515

U.S. 200 (1995). Finally, as is the case for virtually all constitutional amendments (the Thirteenth Amendment is a rare exception), the equal protection guarantees of the Fifth and Fourteenth Amendments apply only to government actors; purely private actions are not covered.

1. Traditional Disparate Treatment Discrimination under the Constitution

The starting point for any equal protection claim is to identify the class allegedly facing discrimination. The reason for this first step is that the equal protection analysis evaluates governmental discrimination based on its justification. Judicial deference to that justification, in turn, differs significantly depending on the protected class involved.

a. Race, Color, National Origin, and State Alienage Discrimination

Race and color discrimination, which were the primary focus of the equal protection guarantee, receive the most searching review: "strict scrutiny." *Adarand Constructors, Inc. v. Pena*, 515 U.S. 200 (1995). National origin discrimination, which is often considered the same as race discrimination, is also considered a "suspect" class that is entitled to the same level of review. *Korematsu v. United States*, 323 U.S. 214 (1944). Alienage discrimination by the states is usually analyzed under the strict scrutiny standard as well, but because the federal government has substantial powers over immigration matters, federal alienage discrimination is entitled to far more deference.

Under the strict scrutiny analysis, courts will presume that any governmental race, color, national origin, or state alienage discrimination is unconstitutional unless the government action can demonstrate a "compelling governmental purpose." Even if such a purpose is established, the government actor must also show that the discrimination at issue was "narrowly tailored" to further that interest. *Adarand Constructors, Inc. v. Pena*, 515 U.S. 200 (1995). This test is very difficult for the government to meet—so difficult that Justice Marshall once characterized it as "strict in theory, fatal in fact." *Fullilove v. Klutznick*, 448 U.S. 448 (1980) (Marshall, J., concurring) (quoting Gerald Gunther, *The Supreme Court, 1971 Term—Foreword: In Search of Evolving Doctrine on a Changing Court: A Model for a Newer Equal Protection*, 86 Harv. L. Rev. 1 (1972)). Thus, virtually any time a government is found to have intentionally discriminated against an employee because of their membership in a minority racial group, color, national origin, or alienage group, the employee will win his or her equal protection claim. As discussed below, public employers have a less difficult task—although certainly not an easy one—in justifying intentional discrimination to aid minority employees pursuant to an affirmative action plan.

b. Sex Discrimination

Sex discrimination—which is viewed by the Court as a serious problem, albeit less so than discrimination based on race and the other suspect classes—is reviewed under a more deferential standard. Under the "intermediate scrutiny" analysis, a government actor must justify sex discrimination by showing an "important government objective." *J.E.B. v. Alabama ex rel. T.B.*, 511 U.S. 127 (1994). The Court has stressed that this is still a "heightened" standard of review that requires an "exceedingly persuasive justification." *United States v. Virginia*, 518 U.S. 515 (1996). The discrimination being challenged must also have a "substantial relationship to the important government objective."

Despite the lower standard of scrutiny, the rare cases in which there are findings that a government employer intentionally discriminated against women have resulted in an equal protection violation. However, government policies that advantage women tend to fare better, at least where the policies address disadvantages that women faced in the workforce. *Schlesinger v. Ballard*, 419 U.S. 498 (1975).

c. Discrimination Based on Other Classifications

Discrimination against most of the remaining classes—which include age, disability, and state residence—are reviewed under the most deferential standard. Under this "rational basis" analysis, governmental discrimination against one of these classes must be justified by a mere "legitimate" governmental interest, and there must be a rational basis for using the challenged discrimination to further that interest. *City of Cleburne v. Cleburne Living Center*, 473 U.S. 432 (1985) (disability); *Massachusetts Board of Retirement v. Murgia*, 427 U.S. 307 (1976) (age). There are many instances of governmental employment discrimination that have satisfied rational basis review. A common example is a mandatory retirement policy for certain public employees, such as police officers. *Massachusetts Board of Retirement v. Murgia*, 427 U.S. 307 (1976). In another case, a public radio and television station successfully defended the transfer of an older female television personality to a radio show because the move furthered the goal of maximizing viewership of the station. *Izquierdo Prieto v. Mercado Rosa*, 894 F.2d 467 (1st Cir. 1990). Finally, requirements that employees reside in the city for which they work have also been upheld under rational basis review, although residency requirements can also be challenged under the Fourteenth Amendment's Privileges and Immunities Clause. *Hicklin v. Orbeck*, 437 U.S. 518 (1978) (privileges and immunities); *McCarthy v. Philadelphia Civil Service Commission*, 424 U.S. 645 (1976) (equal protection). Not all plaintiffs lose under rational basis review, however. Indeed, in the non-employment case establishing rational basis review for disabled individuals, *City of Cleburne v. Cleburne Living Center*, 473 U.S. 432 (1985), the Supreme Court held that the disability discrimination at issue could not be justified under this low standard.

Separately, it is also worth noting that when pursuing religious discrimination claims, it can be helpful to keep in mind that many of these actions are brought under Title VII (*see* Chapter 6, *supra*). *See generally Employment Division, Department of Human Resources of Oregon v. Smith*, 494 U.S. 872 (1990).

d. Sexual Orientation Discrimination

The appropriate level of review for equal protection claims alleging discrimination based on employees' sexual orientation is currently an open question. In *Romer v. Evans*, 517 U.S. 620 (1996), the Supreme Court held that a non-employment law classifying individuals on the basis of sexual orientation failed the rational basis test—a rare example of the government losing under that standard. Because of this holding, however, the Court did not address whether sexual orientation is deserving of more heightened scrutiny. To date most courts have been unwilling to go farther than *Romer* and, therefore, use a rational basis review for sexual orientation claims. The rationale for using the rational basis review often emphasizes that homosexuality, unlike race or other suspect classes, is not an immutable characteristic and that homosexuals are not a politically powerless group. *High Tech Gays v. Defense Industrial Security Clearance Office*, 895 F.2d 563 (9th Cir. 1990). These conclusions can be questioned as a factual matter, and homosexuals have clearly faced a history of severe discrimination, but as of yet, arguments for a more heightened standard of review have been largely unsuccessful. *Price-Cornelison v. Brooks*, 524 F.3d 1103 (10th Cir. 2008) (citing cases). Despite this scrutiny issue, sexual orientation claims have fared relatively well under rational basis review. Claims by members of the armed forces generally fail because of deference to the military, but in the normal public employment context, sexual orientation claims frequently succeed. *Glover v. Williamsburg Local School District Board of Education*, 20 F. Supp. 2d 1160 (S.D. Ohio 1998).

Finally, *Lawrence v. Texas*, 539 U.S. 558 (2003), in which the Court held a Texas anti-sodomy law to be unconstitutional, suggests that there might be additional protection for public employees' sexual privacy under the substantive component of the Due Process Clause of the Fourteenth Amendment. Paul M. Secunda, *The (Neglected) Importance of Being Lawrence: The Constitutionalization of Public Employee Rights to Decisional Non-Interference in Private Affairs*, 40 U.C. Davis L. Rev. 85 (2006). One court has even found the firing of a sheriff's department dispatcher for failure to marry her live-in boyfriend unconstitutional in light of *Lawrence*. It is also important to look to the Supreme Court's decision in *Bostock v. Clayton County*, discussed in earlier chapters, for additional guidance on this issue.

2. The Affirmative Action Defense under the Constitution

One of the more common, and most controversial, uses of equal protection in employment discrimination cases is to challenge a public employer's affirmative action plan. It is difficult to get a firm grip on the affirmative action analysis because judicial views on such plans are often diametrically opposed and very strongly held. As a result, the Supreme Court's approach to these cases has shifted significantly depending on its membership. Additionally, recent affirmative action cases have been in the educational context, and it is not clear whether these cases apply in the employment context.

There are several different circumstances under which an affirmative action plan could be challenged. One circumstance involves judicially created affirmative action plans that address widespread and repeated discrimination by an employer. *Local 28, Sheet Metal Workers v. EEOC*, 478 U.S. 421 (1986). Similarly, parties to a discrimination suit may, as part of a settlement, agree to a court-approved affirmative action plan. *Local No. 93, International Association of Firefighters v. Cleveland*, 467 U.S. 561 (1984).

The federal government has also mandated certain affirmative action requirements with regard to contractors on federal projects. Executive Order 11246; *Adarand Constructors, Inc. v. Pena*, 515 U.S. 200 (1995). President Trump rescinded some executive orders related to affirmative action. Finally, a government employer may decide to implement an affirmative action plan to further some type of antidiscrimination, diversity, or other type of workplace goal. Judicial review of affirmative action plans may differ slightly depending on the circumstance, but the basic analysis for all such plans is essentially the same. Note as well that this discussion is limited to constitutional challenges to affirmative action plans; Title VII also applies to government employers, and the affirmative action analysis under that statute is discussed in Chapter 6. And recent Supreme Court cases that express skepticism or disapproval of affirmative action in the education context have reiterated that affirmative action as a remedy to proven discrimination is permissible.

In *Wygant v. Jackson Board of Education*, 476 U.S. 267 (1986), the Supreme Court set forth the basic constitutional affirmative action analysis, which requires two steps. First, there must be a justification for some sort of affirmative action plan—one that reflects a "compelling government interest." Second, if the government employer can show a compelling reason for "why" it implemented a plan, it must still defend "what" that plan does. In particular, a valid affirmative action plan must be "narrowly tailored" to achieve the compelling government interest.

Whether there is a compelling government interest for some form of affirmative action plan is highly dependent on the facts. The Court has made clear that it does not matter whether the affirmative action plan was created by a state or federal actor, or that the plan was seeking to help minorities rather than hurt them; all government discrimination, for whatever purpose, requires the same showing of a compelling government interest. *Adarand Constructors, Inc. v. Pena*, 515 U.S. 200 (1995). That said, the level of scrutiny is still dependent on the class of employees affected by the plan. Thus, an affirmative action plan targeting racial problems will have a more difficult time surviving an equal protection challenge than one targeting sex. *Califano v. Webster*, 430 U.S. 313 (1977).

What then is likely to serve as a compelling government interest? For those who do not reject affirmative action in all instances, one of the least controversial justifications is past discrimination by the government employer. A discriminatory past—typically defined as widespread discrimination that would violate the Equal Protection Clause under the appropriate level of scrutiny for the class involved—is generally regarded as warranting some type of affirmative action plan. *Richmond v. J.A. Croson Co.*, 488 U.S. 469 (1989); *Wygant v. Jackson Board of Education*, 476 U.S. 267 (1986). A far more controversial justification is societal discrimination that cannot be traced directly to the government employer. The Court in *Wygant* rejected societal discrimination as a compelling government interest and, given the current Court's general hostility to affirmative action plans, there is no reason to believe that it will rethink that view in the near future. *Parents Involved in Community Schools v. Seattle School District No. 1*, 551 U.S. 701 (2007). The open question at this date is whether diversity can ever serve as a compelling government interest. The Court has accepted the diversity justification with regard to admissions to higher education institutions. *Grutter v. Bollinger*, 539 U.S. 306 (2003); *Regents of California v. Bakke*, 438 U.S. 265 (1978) (Powell, J., concurring). But in a decision involving elementary and secondary schools, a plurality of the Court firmly rejected the diversity justification, while Justice Kennedy's concurrence stated that diversity might serve as a compelling government interest in very limited circumstances. *Parents Involved in Community Schools v. Seattle School District No. 1*, 551 U.S. 701 (2007). What these education cases say about a future employment affirmative action case is anybody's guess.

If a compelling government interest is established, there must be a demonstration that the affirmative action plan was narrowly tailored to achieve that goal. Because of the potential harm to majority employees, this step seeks to ensure that the plan does no more than necessary. The severity of the compelling government interest plays the biggest role in this step, as that provides the target for the plan's details. More generally, the Court has warned against the use of plans that seek to "maintain" affirmative action goals rather than merely "attain" them. As a result, valid plans are typically temporary; build in flexibility to adapt to changing conditions or the realization that a specific goal is not achievable; address hiring rather than layoffs; avoid strict quotas; and usually use race, sex, or another protected class only as part of a larger selection process. *Grutter v. Bollinger*, 539 U.S. 306 (2003); *Local 28, Sheet Metal Workers v. EEOC*, 478 U.S. 421 (1986); *Wygant v. Jackson Board of Education*, 476 U.S. 267 (1986).

In *Students for Fair Admissions, Inc. v. President & Fellows of Harvard Coll.*, the Supreme Court indicated that race-based decisions were allowable under the Equal Protection Clause of the Constitution, but only "within the confines of narrow restrictions." 600 U.S. 181 (2023). The Court held the admissions plans of Harvard and the University of North Carolina did not meet the requirements of strict scrutiny.

The Court articulated strict scrutiny as requiring that the use of race both furthers a compelling government interest and is narrowly tailored to achieve that interest. The Court noted that its precedents had identified two compelling government interests: (1) remedying past proven instances of race discrimination that violate the Constitution or statutes, and (2) avoiding serious and immediate risks to human safety in prison. The Court noted that it has rarely accepted race-based reasons for government action.

The Court addressed Justice Powell's ruling in *Bakke* that diversity is a compelling government interest; however, the Court then noted that no other member of the Court joined that opinion. The majority opinion then described how later opinions had accepted the diversity rationale as meeting the requirements of strict scrutiny, at least in the educational context.

The Court then articulated what it considered to be three core ideas relevant to evaluating the admissions criteria related to race: (1) they must comply with strict scrutiny, (2) they may not use race as a positive or a negative stereotype, and (3) they must end at some point in time.

The Court found that the reasons articulated by the universities were not "sufficiently coherent" for strict scrutiny because courts could not measure the goals. The Court characterized the articulated reasons given by Harvard as "(1) training future leaders in the public and private sectors"; (2) preparing graduates to "adapt to an increasingly pluralistic society"; (3) "better educating its students through diversity"; and (4) "producing new knowledge stemming from diverse outlooks." The Court articulated UNC's reasons for its plan as "(1) promoting the robust exchange of ideas; (2) broadening and refining understanding; (3) fostering innovation and problem-solving; (4) preparing engaged and productive citizens and leaders; [and] (5) enhancing appreciation, respect, and empathy, cross-racial understanding, and breaking down stereotypes." The Court noted that it could not evaluate when these goals had been reached, and the plans did not have a logical endpoint. It also noted that it could not determine the connection between the articulated plans and their expressed goals.

The Court opined that the admissions programs rested on stereotypes in that the universities assumed that certain students would bring something different to the university based on that person's race. The Court also rejected the end point offered by the universities, that the plans would end when there is meaningful diversity and representation on the college campuses.

The Court did indicate that universities could consider applicants' discussions of how race impacted their lives.

It is not clear how this analysis intersects with affirmative action in the employment context because the latter cases have traditionally not relied on diversity as the underlying interest.

C. Prohibiting Discrimination under the Post-Civil War Civil Rights Acts

In addition to its substantive provisions, § 5 of the Fourteenth Amendment provides Congress the "power to enforce, by appropriate legislation, the provisions of" the Amendment. This was a radical shift in federal-state relations, as it gave Congress explicit authority to regulate directly many facets of state conduct. Soon after the Fourteenth Amendment was ratified, Congress took advantage of this new power—in addition to its traditional power to regulate commerce—by enacting several of the earliest Civil Rights Acts. These statutes included § 1985(3), which prohibits conspiracies to deprive individuals of their right to equal protection, and § 1986, which imposes liability on an individual who could have prevented such a conspiracy, but refused to do so. 42 U.S.C. §§ 1985(3), 1986. Although these provisions can be used in the employment context, they are rarely invoked. § 1988, which permits the award of attorney's fees to a prevailing party, also applies to employment discrimination actions and is discussed in Chapter 5. More substantively, two other provisions provide causes of action that are frequently used in employment discrimination cases: § 1981 of the Civil Rights Act of 1866 and § 1983 of the Civil Rights Act of 1871.

1. Prohibiting Race Discrimination under § 1981

In the Civil Rights Act of 1866, the first of the post-Civil War civil rights statutes, Congress enacted § 1981, which states that: "All persons within the jurisdiction of the United States shall have the same right in every State and Territory to make and enforce contracts ... as is enjoyed by white citizens. ..." 42 U.S.C. § 1981. Employment contracts, including those that are at will, are included in the reference to "make and enforce contracts." *Walker v. Abbott Laboratories*, 340 F.3d 471 (7th Cir. 2003). Moreover, the Civil Rights Act of 1991 (CRA of 1991) added § 1981(b), which defines "make and enforce contracts" as including "making, performance, modification, and termination of contracts, and the enjoyment of all benefits, privileges, terms, and conditions of the contractual relationship." This amendment overruled *Patterson v. McLean Credit Union*, 491 U.S. 164 (1989), which had held that the original § 1981 extended only to the formation of contracts, but not subsequent actions made during the life of the contract. Thus, the current Section 1981 prohibits not only discrimination in the formation of employment contracts—that is, hiring—but also other types of discrimination that can occur during the employment relationship, such as discriminatory harassment, failure to promote, and termination. Moreover, the Supreme Court held in *CBOCS West, Inc. v. Humphries*, 553 U.S. 442 (2008), that § 1981 also permitted retaliation claims.

Section 1981 prohibits intentional race discrimination, including reverse discrimination—despite its statement that all persons shall have the same rights as "white citizens." *McDonald v. Santa Fe Train Transportation Co.*, 427 U.S. 273 (1976). The "white citizens" language has had a larger effect in limiting § 1981 to race discrimination; discrimination against other classes, such as sex or age, is not covered. *Saint Francis College v. Al-Khazraji*, 481 U.S. 604 (1987). However, the Court has classified both ancestry or ethnicity as race under Section 1981. *Id.*; *Shaare Tefila Congregation v. Cobb*, 481 U.S. 615 (1987) (Jewish plaintiff covered). Similarly, alienage discrimination can be claimed against state and local employers, but claims against private employers have received mixed success in the lower courts. *Takahashi v. Fish & Game Commission*, 334 U.S. 410 (1948) (state alienage discrimination is covered); *compare Sagana v. Tenorio*, 384 F.3d 731 (9th Cir. 2004) (private alienage discrimination is covered) *with Bhandari v. First National Bank of Commerce*, 887 F.2d 609 (5th Cir. 1989) (en banc) (private alienage discrimination is not covered). This expansive interpretation is the result of courts' construing the scope of § 1981 based on the definition of "race" when the law was initially enacted. The broader meaning of "race" in the nineteenth century also explains why § 1981 may apply to certain types of Title VII national origin claims.

Employees can pursue § 1981 claims against private employers, a rule that the Supreme Court had inferred from the statute for some time and that Congress ultimately made explicit in § 1981(c), a provision of the CRA of 1991 that applied § 1981 to "nongovernmental discrimination." *Runyan v. McCrary*, 427 U.S. 160 (1976). Traditionally, state and local employers could be held liable under § 1981, but only through a § 1983 claim and the limits on liability and remedies that apply to such actions. *Jett v. Dallas Independent School District*, 491 U.S. 701 (1989). However, § 1981 claims are not allowed against the federal government because Title VII is the exclusive remedy for federal employment discrimination claims. *Brown v. General Services Administration*, 425 U.S. 820 (1976).

The enforcement of § 1981 differs significantly from Title VII. For instance, unlike Title VII, § 1981 has no administrative exhaustion requirement, no small-employer exception, no cap on punitive and compensatory damages, and no exclusion of independent contractors. Individual supervisors or perpetrators of discrimination may face liability under § 1981. Moreover, § 1981 prohibits only intentional discrimination; thus, disparate impact claims are not permissible. *General Building Contractors Association v. Pennsylvania*, 458 U.S. 375 (1982).

The Supreme Court clarified a disagreement with respect to causation rules under Section 1981. *See Comcast Corporation v. National Association of African American-Owned Media*, 589 U.S. 327 (2020). According to the Court, to show causation for § 1981 claims, "a plaintiff must first plead and then prove that the injury would not have occurred 'but for' the defendant's unlawful conduct." *Id.* at 329–30. Thus, the Court in *Comcast* was clear in requiring but-for causation to establish allegations brought under this statutory provision.

2. Prohibiting the Deprivation of Federal Rights by State Actors under § 1983

Section 1983, enacted under the Civil Rights Act of 1871, provides a private right of action by which an individual can sue a state or local government, or state or local officials, for a violation of his or her constitutional rights. The section states that:

> Every person who, under color of any statute, ordinance, regulation, custom, or usage, of any State or Territory or the District of Columbia, subjects, or causes to be subjected, any citizen of the United States or other person within the jurisdiction thereof to the deprivation of any rights, privileges, or immunities secured by the Constitution and laws, shall be liable to the party injured in an action at law, suit in equity, or other proper proceeding for redress....

42 U.S.C. § 1983. "Under color of law" is generally interpreted broadly to include any actions of state or local officials that appear to be under the authority of state law. *Monroe v. Pape*, 365 U.S. 167 (1961). Federal officials and the federal government are not covered by § 1983. *Wheeldin v. Wheeler*, 373 U.S. 647 (1963).

Section 1983 provides a remedy for a violation of rights granted by federal constitutional and statutory law. However, there are significant exceptions. In particular, the federal employment discrimination statutes by themselves do not support a § 1983 claim, otherwise a plaintiff could bypass the comprehensive enforcement schemes of those statutes—including their administrative exhaustion requirements—by suing under § 1983. *Jackson v. City of Atlanta*, 73 F.3d 60 (5th Cir. 1996). But employer actions that violate the Constitution (for instance, the Fourteenth Amendment's Equal Protection Clause) can be challenged under § 1983, even if those actions also give rise to a claim under one of the federal employment discrimination statutes. Because the damages available under § 1983 can be broader than Title VII, the ADA, and the ADEA, it is not unusual to see suits alleging violations of both § 1983 and one or more of these statutes.

Available remedies for § 1983 violations include monetary and injunctive relief. Actual damages are available, as are compensatory and punitive damages and attorney's fees, and there is no cap on these damages. However, there are many special remedial limitations. For instance, although punitive damages are available against individual officials, they are unavailable against governments. *City of Newport v. Fact Concerts, Inc.*, 453 U.S. 247 (1981). Moreover, state sovereign immunity, often referred to as "Eleventh Amendment immunity" (discussed in various chapters in relation to Title VII, the ADA, and ADEA) prevents § 1983 actions against nonconsenting state governments. *Edelman v. Jordan*, 415 U.S. 651 (1974). There is an exception to this immunity that often allows injunctive relief against a state by suing state officials in their official capacities. *Ex parte Young*, 209 U.S. 123 (1908).

Officials who violate § 1983 are personally liable, although several immunities are available. For instance, judges, legislators, and prosecutors are fully immune if acting in their official capacity. *Id.* More generally, officials may have "qualified" immunity if they did not violate a clearly established right. *Harlow v. Fitzgerald*, 457 U.S. 800 (1982). Also, although local officials have been covered since the 1978 case of *Monell v. Department of Social Services*, 436 U.S. 658 (1978), a local government cannot be held liable for the actions of its officials under the respondeat superior doctrine. That is, the government must have ordered or sanctioned the action to be held liable. *Pembaur v. Cincinnati*, 475 U.S. 469 (1986).

CHECKPOINTS

- The Fourteenth and Fifth Amendments guarantee individuals the right to equal protection against state and federal governmental action, respectively.
- Equal protection prohibits only disparate treatment discrimination, not disparate impact.
- Race, color, national origin, and state alienage equal protection challenges are reviewed under "strict scrutiny."
- Sex discrimination equal protection challenges are reviewed under "intermediate scrutiny."
- Age, disability, state residency, and usually sexual orientation equal protection challenges are reviewed under a "rational basis review."
- A constitutional affirmative action plan must have a compelling government interest and must be narrowly tailored to that interest.
- Section 1981 prohibits intentional race, ancestry, ethnicity, and state alienage discrimination in employment relationships. The provision applies to private employment, but not federal. Under § 1981, there is no administrative exhaustion requirement, no small-employer exception, no cap on punitive and compensatory damages, and no exclusion of independent contractors.
- Section 1983 provides a private right of action for state violations of employees' federal constitutional or statutory rights, and plaintiffs can bring claims under both § 1983 and one or more of the federal employment statutes in certain instances.

CHAPTER 15

Equal Pay Act and Other Compensation Issues

ROADMAP

- Introducing the Equal Pay Act
- Relationship between the EPA and sex discrimination under Title VII
- Burden-shifting framework for EPA claims
- The Bennett Amendment to Title VII
- Lilly Ledbetter Fair Pay Act
- Other compensation issues

Passed in 1963 (the year before Title VII), the Equal Pay Act (EPA), 29 U.S.C. § 206(d), prohibits sex-based discrimination in wages. Its regulations are codified at 29 C.F.R. § 1620. Among its interesting features are that it was passed under the Fair Labor Standards Act of 1938 (FLSA), it protects both men and women from wage discrimination, and it has significant overlap with sex discrimination claims under Title VII.

A. An Introduction to the EPA

The major reason for the enactment of the EPA is the perception that women's work was, and is still, being undervalued. According to the U.S. Bureau of Labor Statistics, in 2023, women were paid only 83.6 cents for every dollar a man is paid. Other experts estimate the wage gap costs the average fulltime American woman worker between $700,000 and $2 million over the course of her work life. And these figures are even worse for women of color.

The EPA seeks to guarantee that women will not be paid less for the same and similar jobs just because they are women. It is therefore not surprising that the EPA was enacted with the part of the FLSA which deals with minimum wages and overtime premiums.

The EPA does not legislatively implement the concept of "comparable worth." *Brennan v. Prince William Hospital Corp.*, 503 F.2d 282 (4th Cir. 1974). The comparable worth theory of discrimination posits that jobs being held mostly by women pay less than comparable jobs held mostly by men, even when jobs provide comparable value to the employer. If an employer pays the market rate of compensation for a certain job and that rate reflects broad-based discrimination, should the individual employer be liable under Title VII? Proponents of the comparable worth theory argue that the risk of liability would prompt employers to fix the problem. However, this theory has not succeeded, as courts have generally rejected the idea that an individual employer was discriminating by paying market wages, even if the employer is aware that those wages may be undervaluing the worth of the job at issue. In short, as stated in the Ninth Circuit case, *AFSCME v. State of Washington*, 770 F.2d 1401 (9th Cir. 1985), "Title VII does not obligate [an employer] to eliminate an economic inequality that it did not create."

The EPA uses the same scheme as the FLSA for determining covered employers and employees. An employer "includes any person acting directly or indirectly in the interest of an employer in relation to an employee and includes a public agency, but does not include any labor organization (other than when acting as an employer) or anyone acting in the capacity of officer or agent of such labor organization." 29 U.S.C. § 203(d). Somewhat unhelpfully, an employee means "any individual employed by an employer." 29 U.S.C. § 203(e)(1). Courts will apply the economic realities test from the FLSA to determine if a worker is an employee or independent contractor.

B. The Relationship between EPA and Title VII

As an initial matter, the EPA is much narrower in scope than the sex discrimination provisions under Title VII. The vast majority of EPA violations also constitute violations of Title VII, 29 C.F.R. § 1620.27(a) ("[A]ny violation of the Equal Pay Act is also a violation of Title VII"), but the opposite is not necessarily true, *Fallon v. Illinois*, 882 F.2d 1206, 1213 (7th Cir. 1989). While the EPA focuses on wage discrimination, Title VII covers wage discrimination and other kinds of discrimination because of sex.

The two statutes are not mutually exclusive, and thus a claim can be brought under both statutes. Yet, there are purposeful similarities. Consider that the Bennett Amendment to Title VII, which added a sentence to § 703(h) of Title VII requiring that whatever statutory defenses the employer has under the EPA, they also have under Title VII. 42 U.S.C. § 2000e-2(h). These four affirmative defenses (discussed in more detail below) available in an EPA case thus are also available to prevent a finding of wage discrimination under Title VII.

Why might a plaintiff want to bring a claim under both statutes? One reason is that although the EPA is enforced by the EEOC, there is no requirement to exhaust administrative remedies like there is for Title VII claims. This is because the EPA is contained within the FLSA and therefore, the enforcement and remedial schemes of the FLSA govern the EPA. Similarly, the EPA does not include any administrative requirements—like the right to sue letter requirement under Title VII—prior to filing a civil action. *County of Washington v. Gunther*, 452 U.S. 161 (1981).

As for remedies, instead of compensatory and punitive damages available for intentional discrimination claims under Title VII, the remedy under the EPA is for lost wages and liquidated (double) damages in willful situations. The liquidated damages are not subject to the caps found in Title VII. 29 U.S.C. § 216(b). However, the liquidated damages are limited in the sense that they can only be an additional amount that is equal to the other damages awarded. For example, if a worker proves an EPA violation and receives $10,000 in damages, the worker may receive an additional $10,000 in liquidated damages. Liquidated damages are subject to the defense that the employer acted subjectively in good faith and objectively had reasonable grounds for believing that its conduct did not violate the EPA.

Finally, the limitations period under the EPA is two years for non-willful claims and three years for willful claims, rather than the 180/300-day statute of limitations for Title VII claims. So, while an employee may be time-barred from bringing a Title VII claim, an EPA claim can be brought directly to federal or state court for up to three years after the wage violation took place.

C. The Allocation of Proof in EPA Claims

The allocation of proof in EPA claims is much different from the schemes familiar to Title VII law. Plaintiffs can establish a prima facie violation of the EPA by showing that the employer, on the basis of sex, paid lower wages "to employees of the opposite sex in the same establishment for equal work on jobs requiring equal skill, effort, responsibility, and which are performed under similar working condition." 29 U.S.C. § 206(d)(1). In short, the plaintiff in an EPA case must show that she has received unequal pay for equal work in the same establishment because of sex. The defendant employer can defend against the EPA prima facie case with affirmative defenses based on seniority of the employee, the merit of the employee, the fact that earnings were calculated based on quality or quantity, or that a factor other than sex accounted for the unequal pay. If the defendant meets its burden of proof on one of these defenses, then the plaintiff may still prevail if he or she shows the defendant's reasons are pretextual. There is currently a circuit split regarding whether this third step is part of the EPA analysis.

1. The Plaintiff's Prima Facie Case

A word about each of the required elements for the plaintiff's prima facie case: As for unequal pay, although the statute uses the term "wages," courts have found that differentials in employee benefits are also covered.

Much of the analysis under the EPA involves the second element of "equal work" and that analysis is very fact-intensive. Although minor differences between jobs are not enough to defeat an EPA claim, the jobs must be "substantially equal." Job descriptions and titles are not decisive in making this comparison; a fact-finder needs to look at the actual work performed by the employees being compared. In particular, the plaintiff must prove that the jobs in question: (1) required equal skill; (2) required equal effort; (3) required equal responsibility; and (4) took place in similar working conditions. As to the fourth element, "similar working conditions" is a term of art which encompasses a worker's surroundings and workplace hazards. In turn, surroundings measure the elements regularly encountered by the worker, their intensity, and their frequency. Hazards, on the other hand, consider the physical hazards regularly encountered on the job. So, for example, night shift work and day shift work are considered to be performed under similar working conditions within the meaning of the EPA. *Corning Glass Works v. Brennan*, 417 U.S. 188 (1974). Shift differentials are not irrelevant, but are considered as part of the defendant's affirmative defense under factors other than sex.

An employer may claim that men got higher pay because they performed extra work or extra duties; however, higher pay for men is impermissible when one of the following factors is present: (1) some male employees received higher pay without doing extra work; (2) female employees also performed extra duties of equal skill, effort, and responsibility; (3) qualified female employees were not given the opportunity to do the extra work; (4) the supposed extra duties did not in fact exist; (5) the extra task consumed a minimal amount of time and was of peripheral importance; or (6) third persons who did the extra task as their primary job are paid less than the male employees in question.

As to the third element of the EPA prima facie case, the plaintiff must show that the male and female workers being compared worked within the "same establishment." In this regard, consider a male professor at one campus and a female professor at another campus, who work for the same university. One would need to determine whether the two campuses make up a single establishment where a central authority controls the important personnel decisions for all campus locations. Notice that a separate location does not go to "similar working conditions" under the second element, because that is a term of art dealing with surroundings and hazards. Even if there are different costs of living at the two campuses, that fact would not go to the same establishment element, but would rather be considered under the employer's fourth statutory defense involving factors other than sex.

Finally, the alleged wage discrimination has to be based on sex. In this regard, the plaintiff needs only to show that different wages were paid to persons of the opposite sex for equal work. This is an easy burden to meet because all one needs to do is to point to one person of the opposite sex performing equal work for unequal pay to meet this element.

2. The Defendant's Statutory Defenses

Once a plaintiff establishes a prima facie case of an EPA violation, the burden of proof (not just the burden of production as in Title VII *McDonnell Douglas* cases) switches to the defendant to prove one of four statutory affirmative defenses.

The first three employer defenses—seniority, merit, and a system measuring earnings by quantity or quality (piecework)—already exist under Section 703(h) of Title VII and generally are given the same meaning in the EPA. In fact, as discussed above, the Bennett Amendment to Title VII makes clear that the four affirmative defenses available in an EPA case are also available to prevent a finding of wage discrimination under Title VII. Consequently, if a pay practice is immune from EPA liability, it is also immune from Title VII liability.

However, if a pay practice is valid under the EPA, a Title VII violation can still be found. *County of Washington v. Gunther*, 452 U.S. 161 (1981) (holding that affirmative defenses under the EPA are also available under Title VII and that the Bennett amendment did not limit Title VII sex-based wage-discrimination claims to those actionable under the EPA). Under *Gunther*, for instance, plaintiffs are permitted to bring claims under Title VII that are not actionable under the EPA because the plaintiff cannot satisfy the "equal work" standard (where the employer does not employ a member of the opposite sex in an equivalent job). Consider an employer who intentionally discriminates against a woman by lowering her compensation because she told the employer that she plans to start a family and have children. Although that scenario clearly can establish a sex discrimination claim for Title VII purposes, it may not meet the required elements of the EPA prima facie case if there is not a man who does "equal work" in the "same establishment."

Most EPA litigation has historically dealt with the fourth affirmative defense—does the woman receive unequal pay for equal work because of another "factor other than sex"? In other words, the employer is arguing that the differential pay is based on a legitimate business consideration. Although the contours of this defense are unclear, this much is known: First, the defense does not encompass a factor that is sex-based. For example, an actuarial distinction, such as life expectancy, that is sex-based would not qualify for the defense. Second, factors that frequently influence salary decisions such as educational background or work experience probably satisfy this defense.

The complications inherent in the "other than sex" affirmative defense are illustrated where an employer pays employees differently based on prior salary history. The Ninth Circuit has held that relying on past salary is not a sufficient affirmative defense, because salary structures often reflect historic patterns of pay discrimination because of sex. *Rizo v. Yovino*, 950 F.3d 1217 (9th Cir. 2020). There is currently a circuit split on this issue with some circuits allowing prior salary history to serve as an affirmative defense. *Boyer v. United States*, 97 F.4th 834, 841 (Fed. Cir. 2024) (discussing split).

3. Plaintiff Showing of Pretext

If the defendant meets its burden by demonstrating an affirmative defense, the plaintiff may still prevail on her EPA claim if she demonstrates that the affirmative defense is a pretext for sex discrimination. *Belfi v. Prendergast*, 191 F.3d 129 (2d Cir. 1999); *but see Baker v. Upson Regional Medical Ctr.*, 94 F.4th 1312 (11th Cir. 2024) (holding there is no third step); *Rizo v. Yovino*, 950 F.3d 1217 (9th Cir. 2020) (same). Following proof of an affirmative defense by the employer, the plaintiff may counter the employer's showing by producing evidence that the defendant did not actually rely on the reasons it gave for the wage discrimination and those reasons are, therefore, actually a pretext for sex discrimination.

D. Lilly Ledbetter Fair Pay Act

The Lilly Ledbetter Fair Pay Act of 2009, P.L. 111-2, was the first piece of legislation signed into law by President Obama. The Ledbetter Act amended Title VII and overturned the case of *Ledbetter v. Goodyear Tire & Rubber Co.*, 550 U.S. 618 (2007). That case had held that the issuance of each discriminatory paycheck must be treated as a single discrete employment action, not as part of a continuing violation. The Ledbetter Act now treats paycheck discrimination similar to sexual harassment actions and requires only one discriminatory paycheck in the statutory limitations period (see Chapter 3 for a more complete discussion of this topic). Further, the filing period in a paycheck discrimination case does not commence until (1) a discriminatory compensation decision or other practice is adopted; (2) an individual becomes subject to the decision or practice; or (3) an individual is affected by an application of a discriminatory compensation decision or practice (including each time wages, benefits, or other compensation are paid). 42 U.S.C. § 2000e-(5)(e)(3)(A).

E. Other Compensation Issues

Some types of compensation discrimination do not fit well under either the EPA or the Title VII framework. One area of particular concern has been pensions. Sex discrimination is often an issue with pensions because women tend to live longer than men. Many employers have attempted to account for this longevity difference in their pension plans, which in turn has led women to challenge those plans on sex discrimination grounds.

The Supreme Court's first foray into this area was *Los Angeles Department of Water & Power v. Manhart*, 435 U.S. 702 (1978). The employer in *Manhart* took into account women's greater longevity by requiring female employees to make larger contributions to its pension plan, which provided monthly benefits for retirees that did not differ based on sex. By requiring women to contribute more, the expected payout for men and women remained the same because women tended to live longer and therefore receive more monthly benefits checks. Despite this overall equality, the Court held that the requirement was unlawful sex discrimination. This holding hinged on an important feature of most disparate treatment cases: the focus is on individual employees, not on the class of women as a whole. Accordingly, although women live longer in general, many women will die as soon as or earlier than men. By lumping these women in with the more general trend—even though the employer cannot identify life expectancy ahead of time—the employer engaged in an unlawful stereotype of its female employees.

The follow-up case to *Manhart* was *Arizona Governing Committee v. Norris*, 463 U.S. 1073 (1983). In *Norris*, the employer adjusted for women's longevity at the opposite end from *Manhart*: women paid in the same amount, but under a plan that gave monthly payments for the rest of a retiree's life, they received a lower benefit. Like in *Manhart*, the effect was to equalize the benefits that men and women received in general. Also like in *Manhart*, the Court held that the plan unlawfully discriminated against women because it improperly looked at them as a class rather than as individuals who may, or may not, live longer than their male counterparts. In short, under *Manhart* and *Norris*, an employer cannot treat sex as a proxy for longevity (or virtually anything else, unless the proxy falls under the limited safety exception discussed in Chapter 6).

CHECKPOINTS

- The Equal Pay Act (EPA), enacted in 1963, prohibits wage discrimination between men and women.
- The EPA does not legislatively implement the concept of comparable worth.
- Under the Bennett Amendment to Title VII, whatever statutory defenses the employer has under the EPA, it also has under Title VII.
- The vast majority of EPA violations also constitute violations of Title VII, but the opposite is not necessarily true.
- There is no requirement to exhaust administrative remedies for EPA claims like there is for Title VII, ADA, and ADEA claims.
- The enforcement and remedial schemes of the FLSA govern the EPA.
- Remedies under the EPA include lost wages and liquidated (double) damages in willful situations.
- Plaintiffs can establish a prima facie violation of the EPA by showing that the employer, on the basis of sex, pays lower wages to employees of the opposite sex in the same establishment for equal work on a job requiring equal skill, effort, and responsibility, and which are performed under similar working conditions.
- If the plaintiff establishes a prima facie case, the defendant then carries the burden of proof to show that one of four affirmative defenses applies, with "reasonable factor other than sex" being the one most litigated.
- Under *Manhart* and *Norris*, an employer cannot treat sex as a proxy for longevity in pension plans.

Mastering Employment Discrimination Law Master Checklist

Chapter 1 • Introduction to Employment Discrimination Law

- ☐ The scope of employment discrimination law
- ☐ Classification of employment discrimination cases
- ☐ Jurisdiction over employment discrimination law claims

Chapter 2 • Coverage

- ☐ Employers covered by employment discrimination laws
- ☐ Employees covered by employment discrimination laws
- ☐ Employment decisions covered by employment discrimination laws

Chapter 3 • Administrative Procedural Issues

- ☐ EEOC charge of discrimination
- ☐ The different statutory time limits
- ☐ The relationship between federal and state antidiscrimination agencies

Chapter 4 • Procedural Issues in Employment Discrimination Litigation

- ☐ The relationship between the EEOC charge and the lawsuit
- ☐ Compulsory arbitration provisions
- ☐ EEOC and private class actions

Chapter 5 • Employment Discrimination Remedies, Settlement, and Tax Issues

- ☐ Equitable and injunctive relief under Title VII
- ☐ Damages under the Civil Rights Act of 1991
- ☐ Prevailing attorney's fees

Chapter 6 • Title VII Individual Disparate Treatment Claims

- ☐ Single-motive disparate treatment claims and the *McDonnell Douglas* analysis
- ☐ Mixed-motive disparate treatment claims and the Civil Rights Act of 1991
- ☐ Employer defenses to disparate treatment claims

Chapter 7 • Title VII Systemic Disparate Treatment Claims

- ☐ Systemic disparate treatment cases
- ☐ "Pattern or practice," disparate treatment framework
- ☐ Determining remedies for pattern or practice cases

Chapter 8 • Title VII Disparate Impact Claims

- ☐ Disparate impact framework
- ☐ Expansion of disparate impact under the Civil Rights Act of 1991
- ☐ *Ricci* and the future of disparate impact

Chapter 9 • Sexual and Other Forms of Harassment

- ☐ Harassment claims based on tangible vs. non-tangible employment actions
- ☐ The elements of a sexual harassment claims
- ☐ Employer liability for harassment
- ☐ Sexual orientation and gender identity discrimination and harassment

Chapter 10 • Retaliation

- ☐ Retaliation provisions under Title VII
- ☐ The burden-shifting framework for retaliation claims
- ☐ Retaliation claims under other employment discrimination laws

Chapter 11 • Special Issues in Title VII Antidiscrimination Law

- ☐ Special issues regarding race, color, and national origin discrimination
- ☐ Special issues regarding sex discrimination
- ☐ Special issues regarding religious discrimination and exempt religious institutions

Chapter 12 • Disability Discrimination under the ADA

- ☐ Disability discrimination framework under the ADA
- ☐ The impact of the ADA Amendments Act of 2008
- ☐ Other procedural and substantive issues under the ADA

Chapter 13 • Age Discrimination in Employment Act

- ☐ Coverage and remedies under the ADEA
- ☐ Disparate treatment claims under the ADEA
- ☐ Other procedural and substantive issues under the ADEA

Chapter 14 • Other Civil Rights Protection against Employment Discrimination

- ☐ Equal protection challenges against discriminatory governmental action
- ☐ Section 1981 and the prohibition against race discrimination in employment
- ☐ Section 1983 and the prohibition against state deprivation of employees' federal rights

Chapter 15 • Equal Pay Act and Other Compensation Issues

- ☐ Relationship between EPA and sex discrimination under Title VII
- ☐ Burden-shifting framework for EPA claims
- ☐ Paycheck Fairness Act of 2009 and other compensation issues

INDEX

D

L

M

N

Q

R

T